OXFORD READINGS IN PHILOSOPHY

ENVIRONMENTAL ETHICS

Published in this series

Other volumes are in preparation

ENVIRONMENTAL ETHICS

edited by

ROBERT ELLIOT

OXFORD UNIVERSITY PRESS

Oxford University Press, Great Clarendon Street, Oxford OX2 6DP

Oxford New York

Athens Auckland Bangkok Bogota Buenos Aires Calcutta
Cape Town Chennai Dar es Salaam Delhi Florence Hong Kong Istanbul
Karachi Kuala Lumpur Madrid Melbourne Mexico City Mumbai
Nairobi Paris São Paolo Singapore Taipei Tokyo Toronto Warsaw

and associated companies in
Berlin Ibadan

Oxford is a registered trade mark of Oxford University Press

Published in the United States by
Oxford University Press Inc., New York

© Introduction and selection Oxford University Press 1995

First published 1995
Reprinted in hardback 1996
Reprinted in paperback 1995, 1996, 1998

British Library Cataloguing in Publication Data
Data available

Library of Congress Cataloging in Publication Data
Data available
ISBN 0-19-875143-5
ISBN 0-1-875144-3 (Pbk)

Printed in Great Britain
on acid-free paper by
Biddles Ltd., Guildford and King's Lynn

CONTENTS

CONTENTS

INTRODUCTION

ROBERT ELLIOT

HUMAN-CENTRED ENVIRONMENTAL ETHICS

Human activity has caused extensive modifications to the natural environment and continues to do so. Many of these modifications, such as the build-up of greenhouse gases, the depletion of the ozone layer, deforestation, land degradation, the elimination of species, and the pollution of the atmosphere and of rivers and oceans, threaten the well-being of both presently existing and future humans. Such modifications are claimed by some even to render continuing human civilization tenuous if not improbable.[1] Others, although not envisaging such catastrophic outcomes, nevertheless warn of adverse impacts on human well-being and lament the destruction of natural resources which have important economic, scientific, medical, recreational, and aesthetic uses. It is also sometimes urged that human well-being is more subtly dependent on the integrity of the natural environment than is suggested by such a list of instrumental values. Thus some have argued that human nature is such that humans can genuinely and fully flourish only if there is frequent contact by humans with wild nature.[2]

Consequently, prudence and a concern for other humans, including future humans, is sufficient to motivate unease about such modifications and to motivate the advocacy of policies which will significantly reduce the pace of such modifications. The prominence of environmental issues in political debate, particularly in the Western democracies, testifies to this. Self-interest and morality, evidenced in beliefs about the rights of, and duties and obligations towards, other humans, combine to persuade many

---

[1] Richard Sylvan, *Universal Purpose, Terrestrial Greenhouse and Biological Evolution* (Canberra: Division of Philosophy and Law, Research School of Social Sciences, Australian National University, 1990).

[2] Janna L. Thompson, 'Preservation of Wilderness and the Good Life', in Robert Elliot and Arran Gare, eds., *Environmental Philosophy: A Collection of Readings* (St. Lucia: University of Queensland Press, 1983).

people that modifications of the natural environment should at the very least be scaled down.

Much human-centred concern about the integrity of the natural environment has a welfarist orientation, focusing exclusively on how things will be for humans, how their interests will be advanced or retarded. This orientation is often linked to concerns about distribution, such as the concern to ensure that future people, whoever they turn out to be, are not worse off than present people. Patterns of distribution may be among the, perhaps many, consequences of policies which an ethical system requires us to take into account.[3] And while there is scope for debate about what the effects of environmental modifications will actually be and about exactly what environmental modifications mooted policies will cause or prevent, the claim that the well-being of humans, especially as it is affected by our actions and by the policies of the institutions in which we participate, is something we are morally required to take seriously is not wildly controversial. Even those who resist environmentalist policies are unlikely to publicly disclaim the core principles of a welfarist human-centred ethic.[4] They are more likely to challenge predictions of the effects of modifications of nature, to suggest that means of ameliorating or compensating for such effects will be developed, or to urge that the alternatives to business as usual will produce even worse consequences.

These are factual claims about what motivates environmentalism as a political movement and about what prompts individuals to worry about our present treatment of the natural environment. They are not claims about what justifies or rationally underpins environmentalist concerns. On reflection we might conclude that some such concerns are to an extent misplaced or ill-founded because we believe them to be insufficiently justified or lacking rational foundation. For instance, concern about harm to future generations is apparently salient among the bases of many people's environmental concern but it turns out to be controversial, to say the least, whether this particular concern will bear the justificatory weight placed on it. The relevant point is that future humans are distinctive in that the policies which we adopt now determine the identity of those humans who will exist in the future. In other words the policy choices we make now will determine which of the multitude of possible people become actual. The point supposes that a person's identity, that is who they are, is determined by, among other things, their genetic constitution, which itself

3 On this see Herman B. Leonard and Richard J. Zeckhauser, 'Cost-Benefit Analysis Defended', in Donald Van DeVeer and Christine Pierce, eds., *The Environmental Ethics and Policy Book: Philosophy, Ecology, Economics* (Belmont, Calif.: Wadsworth, 1994).

4 Julian Simon, *The Ultimate Resource* (Princeton: Princeton University Press, 1981).

is determined by the timing of their parents' procreative act. Since, as biology implies, even a minute difference in timing virtually guarantees a difference in genotype, it is easy to see how policy choices could sufficiently impact on people's lives so as to affect exactly which possible people become actual.

So, for example, a resource-conserving policy will not make some set of future humans better off than they otherwise would be, it will instead make one set of possible humans actual as opposed to making some other set of humans actual. Likewise a couple's decision to delay conception, until the mother recovers from an illness, in order to avoid some foetal impairment, does not make some particular infant better off than it would have been were there no delay but results instead in a different infant coming into existence. These points cast doubt on the coherence of any strong defence of environmentalist policies on the basis of the rights of future people, since rights seem to have to be understood as pertaining to particular individuals. And it is by no means obvious that, by rejecting the conserving policy and bringing into existence people who are, generally speaking, less well-off than those who would have instead come into existence had the conserving policy been adopted, any future person's rights are violated.[5]

There are, of course, approaches to the question of our obligations to future generations which seem untouched by the problems which have their roots in the indeterminacy issue. These approaches eschew ethical categories that make essential reference to how things are for particular individuals and exhibit, instead, an impersonal orientation. An example is utilitarianism, which recommends that happiness be maximized in the long run. So, utilitarianism takes no account of which particular individuals might or might not exist in the future, focusing instead on the amount of happiness the future contains irrespective of the identity of those who experience it. Other things being equal, we should, according to the utilitarian, bring about that future in which there is the greatest net surplus of happiness over unhappiness. Williams, in her contribution to this volume, discusses the implications of utilitarianism for our actions and

---

[5] While this issue is of considerable importance to environmental ethics, especially those which are primarily human-centred, it is not taken up by any of the papers in this anthology. Interested readers might pursue it elsewhere. The issue of the present indeterminacy of future people is discussed in, for example, Robert Elliot, 'The Rights of Future People', *Journal of Applied Philosophy*, 6 (1989), 159–70; Derek Parfit, *Reasons and Persons* (Oxford: Clarendon Press, 1984); Robert Schwarz, 'Obligations to Posterity', in Brian Barry and R. I. Sikora, eds., *Obligations to Future Generations* (Philadelphia: Temple University Press, 1978). The broader issue of obligations to future people is covered by many of the essays in, for example, Barry and Sikora, *Obligations to Future Generations*; Peter Laslett and James Fishkin, eds., *Philosophy, Politics and Society* (New Haven: Yale University Press, 1979); and Ernest Partridge, ed., *Responsibilities to Future Generations* (Buffalo: Prometheus Books, 1981).

policies concerning the future. She reminds us that utilitarianism cannot discount future happiness with respect to present happiness. Utilitarianism is indifferent to the temporal distribution of happiness, attributing, for example, as much value to the happiness of a future person as to the similar happiness of a contemporary. In deciding how to act and which policies to endorse, the utilitarian will adopt the principle of maximizing expected benefit. A utilitarian may urge a policy with a high chance of a small benefit and condemn a policy with a very small chance of a substantial benefit. So, utilitarianism may discount for the uncertainty of how things will turn out in the future, since, generally at least, we can be much more certain of the short-term effects of our actions and policies than of their very long-term effects. The greater the uncertainty, the greater the permissible discounting. One such discounting response is to treat presently competing actions and policies as having negligibly different consequences in the distant future. This response, says Williams, is completely inappropriate for evaluating resource use policies. Instead, she argues, utilitarianism combined with certain relevant facts of biology entails that choice between competing resource use policies should be guided by the principle of *maximum sustainable yield.*

There are also human-centred environmental ethics which do not emphasize welfare, although they may be conjoined with welfarist ethics. There are, for example, perfectionist ethics which concern themselves not so much with how things are for particular humans but rather with human accomplishments in general, such as the development of knowledge, the refinement of culture and the creation of new forms of aesthetic expression.[6] While such accomplishments may contribute to the well-being of humans and so be instrumentally valued, they may also be valued intrinsically, or in their own right, as well. The relevant accomplishments may depend on the preservation of nature and the maintenance of biospheric health, for example as a source of inspiration, as an object of enquiry, or as a precondition for civilized life.

Virtue ethics may also provide a framework for condemning those human actions which degrade, spoil, or destroy the natural environment.[7] The underlying idea is that certain kinds of action, in so far as they manifest particular traits of character, are ethically dubious. The dubiousness of such actions does not reduce to their intrinsic value and that of their consequences. Nor does it reduce to the intrinsic wrongness of the actions

---

[6] Jan Narveson, 'On the Survival of Humankind', in Elliot and Gare, *Environmental Philosophy.*

[7] Thomas Hill Jr., 'Ideals of Human Excellence and Preserving Natural Environments', *Environmental Ethics,* 5 (1983), 211–24.

themselves, as a deontological ethic might suggest. Rather the actions are dubious allegedly because they are indicative of an inappropriate, less than virtuous character. For example, vandalism and destructiveness, manifested in the despoliation and degradation of wild nature, are seen by some as detracting from virtue and as involving actions, dispositions, and traits that a virtuous person should strive to avoid, to resist, and to eliminate. Passmore, in his contribution to this volume, speculates about this virtue approach to environmental ethics.

Some variants of ecofeminism, that is environmentalism which is theoretically informed by feminism, can be understood as virtue ethics. These variants urge that despoliation of the natural environment reveals a stymied capacity for caring, a stunted aesthetic sensitivity, a limited affective capacity, and a disposition to dominate. The thought seems to be that environmental despoliation is evidence of some weakness or defect of character and that the weakness characterizes male modes of being and relating. These ideas are touched upon in Plumwood's contribution to this volume, where it is urged that the view, strongly represented in Western traditions, that nature is 'sharply discontinuous from the human sphere' has functioned to encourage a devaluing of nature.[8] Plumwood says that the human–nature dualism is one of a set of interrelated dualisms and suggests that nature is often associated with the feminine. Given this, it is no surprise that the domination of nature is partly fuelled by the same ideology as the domination of women by men. Of course particular perfectionist avowals and accounts of virtuous character will be contested. Some, for instance, have thought that the taming of wild nature is a valuable human accomplishment and that participation in it exemplifies virtue.[9] And some have urged that that rational, self-interested action, which might well involve despoliation of the natural environment, is supremely virtuous.[10]

There is a related idea, with perfectionist overtones, which should be mentioned. Some urge the preservation of parts of the natural environment as both an exemplification and celebration of human ideals. For

---

[8] See also Susan Griffin, *Women and Nature: The Roaring Inside Her* (New York: Harper and Row, 1978); Carolyn Merchant, *The Death of Nature* (New York: Harper and Row, 1980); Rosemary Radford Ruether, *New Woman, New Earth* (New York: Seabury Press, 1975); Karen Warren, 'The Power and Promise of Ecological Feminism', *Environmental Ethics*, 12 (1990), 121–46.

[9] Clarence Glacken, *Traces on the Rhodian Shore* (Berkeley: University of California Press, 1967); Merchant, *The Death of Nature*; Roderick Nash, *Wilderness and the American Mind* (New Haven: Yale University Press, 1982); and John Passmore, *Man's Responsibility for Nature* (London: Duckworth, 1974).

[10] Ayn Rand, *The Virtue of Selfishness* (New York: New American Library, 1965); and Julian Simon, *The Ultimate Resource* (Princeton: Princeton University Press, 1981).

example, allowing a wild river to run free and unimpeded is to allow an exemplification in nature of an ideal of human action, such as autonomy or self-realization, and thereby to celebrate and endorse that ideal. Sagoff, in his contribution to this volume, urges a view of this kind, linking respect for the autonomy of natural items with an affirmation, even consolidation, of liberal democratic principles.[11]

Perhaps ironically, some so-called deep ecological perspectives can be seen as, if not human-centred, then at least self-centred, although with an unusual notion of self. The thought is that our ordinary sense of the boundaries of the self involves a fundamental misunderstanding of the metaphysics of the universe. Selves, in the ordinary sense, are claimed to be metaphysically dependent on the existence of other things, including other selves: selves are said to be constituted out of relations with other things and cannot exist apart from them. Comprehending that our existence is metaphysically, not merely causally, dependent on our relations with other things, is supposed psychologically to move us to identify with the ecosystems and biosphere which contain us, indeed to identify with the universe as a whole.[12] Odd though it might at first seem, concern for self telescopes into concern for everything and self-realization expands into the development of the universe according to its *telos*. Moreover, it might be claimed, the identification of our lesser selves with the great self that is the universe renders our lives meaningful. So, this variant of deep ecology employs the device of identification to transform an ethic of self-interest into an ethic of holistic environmental concern. The papers by Mathews and Plumwood in this volume bear on these issues. The former, drawing on recent theories in physics as well as more speculative metaphysics, offers some support for the identification of self with nature. The latter is more critical of the suggestion.

It is appropriate to conclude this overview of human-centred environmental ethics by highlighting certain connections with issues in political philosophy. Some have argued that environmentalism, as a political movement, is inconsistent with political liberalism, even that it exemplifies elements of fascism.[13] The idea is that environmentalism reflects one set, among a plurality of coherent sets, of value judgements. Political liberalism

---

[11] See also Tom Regan, 'The Nature and Possibility of an Environmental Ethic', *Environmental Ethics*, 3 (1981), 19–34.

[12] Warwick Fox, *Towards a Transpersonal Psychology* (Boston: Shambala, 1990). See also, Richard Sylvan, *A Critique of Deep Ecology* (Canberra: Research School of Social Sciences, Australian National University, 1984).

[13] See, for some relevant historical material, Susan Bramwell, *Ecology in the Twentieth Century* (New Haven: Yale University Press, 1989).

requires that no one such set be privileged by the state, that no one such set be permitted to dictate policy. Not to require this would be to unjustifiably impose the ideals or values of some citizens on all citizens and so to violate rights which embody the liberal ideal of equal respect for all citizens. Moreover, so the argument might continue, views contrary to environmentalism do not even derive from mistaken beliefs, misunderstandings, cognitive error, or the like, thus implying that the imposition of environmentalist policies cannot be justified paternalistically. Of course, one response to this apparent conflict is to modify significantly or even to jettison political liberalism. This would be a radical step and, given the assumption that political liberalism is in many ways attractive, it is worth asking whether there is scope for reconciliation.

There are several ways of reconciling environmentalism with liberalism. First, it might be argued that environmentalist policies protect the rights of humans, including, perhaps, future humans. Most straightforwardly, such policies might work to prevent the impermissible imposition of harms on others, for instance through pollution of the atmosphere. Or they might work to restore to some citizens control of natural resources which has been impermissibly wrested from them by others. So, it might be urged that natural resources are the property of all citizens and that this fact is not mirrored in the degree of control that environmentalists have in determining their use; one use, so to speak, being to leave them as they are.

Second, there are indirect liberal defences of environmentalism. For example, it could be argued that the preservation of wild nature contributes to the maintenance of liberal structures. Central to the framework of political liberalism is a citizenry which is free and autonomous. The ideals of freedom and autonomy might find symbolic representation in nature; for example, in the natural and unfettered flow of a wild river. Preserving the river in its natural state might be defensible as an affirmation of liberal political structures. And it might, in addition, be urged that citizens have a right of access to such natural symbolism. Sagoff, as noted above, argues for such a position in his contribution to this volume. Conversely, the destruction, exploitation, or domination of nature by humans might be thought to encourage or model politically objectionable forms of domination, such as the domination of women by men or of blacks by whites. More generally, it might be argued that political liberalism will flourish only if certain material conditions obtain, which conditions are threatened by the destruction of wild nature. It might be argued that failure to protect the natural environment will create, and according to some has created, a scarcity of resources which destabilizes liberal political institutions.[14]

A third pattern of reconciliation is the extension of the liberal political framework to include non-humans. So, it might be argued that non-human animals, living things, and even inanimate natural entities are worthy of respect and, furthermore, that they are worthy of respect because they are, in a relevant sense, autonomous.[15] But this takes us beyond the boundaries of human-centred ethics and well and truly into the domain of ethics which are not human-centred, although they may take some cognizance of human interests and concerns. Indeed it is the ethics which fall within this domain which are distinctively environmental, which involve significantly more than the straightforward, mechanical application of more traditional human-centred ethics to environmental issues.[16] Ethics which are not human-centred are among the theoretical results, sometimes interestingly novel, of philosophical thinking about the natural environment and the human impact on it. It is from this domain of ethical inquiry that most of the papers in this anthology are drawn.

ENVIRONMENTAL ETHICS WHICH ARE NOT HUMAN-CENTRED

A human-centred appraisal of environmental policies may well underwrite support for environmentalism and the adoption of green policies. But not all who advocate environmentalist policies are moved by human-centred reasons alone and some indeed might regard them as comparatively insignificant. They claim that to be limited to human-centred ethical principles is to exhibit partial moral blindness and shallowness, to display an unjustifiable human chauvinism. Indeed the further environmental ethics move from the standard human-centred position the more philosophically interesting, as well as normatively controversial, they become. For example, they generate foundational discussions in meta-ethics and metaphysics, force reappraisals of notions such as *self* and *individual*, demand reappraisals of the place of non-humans in ethical theories, invite consider-

---

[14] See Garrett Hardin, *Exploring New Ethics for Survival* (New York: Viking Press, 1978); and William Ophuls, *Economics and the Politics of Scarcity: A Prologue to a Political Theory of the Steady State* (San Francisco: Freeman, 1977).

[15] See Andrew Brennan, 'The Moral Standing of Natural Objects', *Environmental Ethics*, 6 (1984), 35–56; and Paul Taylor, *Respect for Nature: A Theory of Environmental Ethics* (Princeton: Princeton University Press, 1986).

[16] See Arne Naess, 'The Shallow and the Deep, Long-Range Ecology Movements: A Summary', *Inquiry*, 16 (1973), 95–100, for a classic statement of the distinction.

ations of the relationship between ecology and ethics, invite reflection on the relationship between humans and nature, and add new dimensions to thinking about appropriate political arrangements.

A first step in moving away from such allegedly unjustifiable human chauvinism in environmental ethics is to extend moral concern to the well-being of non-human animals, at least those with the neurophysiological capacity for experiencing well-being and its opposite. The case for extending welfarist moral concern to non-human animals has been compellingly made in various recent writings, both from consequentialist and deontological perspectives.[17] After all, it is not only human well-being that may be adversely affected by environmental modifications. Pollution of habitats through oil spills, destruction of habitats through clear-felling and dam building, and other more subtle disruptions of ecosystems has a devastating impact on the well-being of non-human animals.

There are two general points to make about the extension of moral concern to all animals capable of experiencing well-being or its opposite. First, the extension proceeds by representing species membership as a morally irrelevant difference between individuals. It suggests that the properties which generally underpin at least some aspects of the moral standing of humans are to be found in members of other species and indeed are absent in some humans such as anencephalic neonates. It claims that the natural limit of moral concern is the point on the phylogenetic scale at which the capacity for experience with positive or negative affect disappears. Second, the extension need not involve all the bases for moral concern with which we are familiar. For example, many might agree that the duty to avoid causing suffering extends to animals with the capacity for experience with positive or negative affect. They might deny, however, that the scope of the right to life is similarly broad. They might think that the right to life is possessed only by organisms capable of forming preferences about their own future states, thus excluding from its scope most non-human animals and some humans.[18] While some normative ethics, such as hedonistic utilitarianism, will yield a complete extension, more plausible consequentialisms and most deontological ethics will not.

While a partial or complete extension of moral consideration of the kind just described does challenge human chauvinism, many environmental

---

[17] Stephen R. L. Clark, *The Moral Status of Animals* (Oxford: Clarendon Press, 1977); Andrew Lindzey, *Animal Rights* (London: SCM Press, 1976); Tom Regan, *The Case for Animal Rights* (Berkeley: University of California Press, 1983). Bernard E. Rollin, *Animal Rights and Human Morality*, rev. edn. (Buffalo: Prometheus Press, 1992); and Peter Singer, *Animal Liberation* (New York: Basic Books, 1975).

[18] Michael Tooley, *Abortion and Infanticide* (Oxford: Clarendon Press, 1983).

ethicists believe that it constitutes yet another unjustifiable chauvinism and that further extensions are required. Thus it has been claimed that all living things are morally considerable, independently of their psychological capacities.[19] On this view, the moral significance of felling a tree is not exhausted by the relationship of the act to humans and other animals capable of positive or negative affect. The thought is that the tree itself has a claim to moral consideration and that the death of the tree is a feature of the act relevant to its moral evaluation. So, one response to extending moral concern to animals is to argue that it is an incomplete extension, which fails to take proper account of what it is to harm something or to act contrary to something's interests. Limiting the extension to sentient creatures assumes that harm and interests presuppose a capacity for experience, which assumption, it is argued, is false. All that is required, so the argument continues, in order to speak coherently of harms or interests is some set of loosely specifiable biological goals in terms of which a being might be characterized as flourishing to some degree. For example, to harm, or to act contrary to the interests of, a plant is to act so as to impede its flourishing or to frustrate its biologically determined goals. Elements of such a view are defended by Rolston in his contribution to this volume. Indeed Rolston develops them to support the conclusion that species as such, that is independently of the individuals which constitute their membership, have value which generates, on our part, certain duties of preservation.

Again the extension may be either partial or complete. It is difficult to think of even vaguely plausible normative systems which would yield a complete extension. Perhaps an example would be an ethic derived solely from a principle of respect for the biologically goal-directed activity of natural entities. Such an ethic would take biological organization, including biologically-based tendencies and dispositions to behave or act in certain ways, as the defining characteristic of living things. It would urge that these tendencies and dispositions, which define what it is for a living thing to flourish according to its kind, are to be respected equally in every living thing.

An apparent problem for this ethic is that the flourishing of many living things is at the expense of the flourishing of others. There would seem to be multitudinous cases of conflicting interests which it is impossible to adjudicate unless there has been only a partial extension of other categories of moral consideration. This problem would seem to render the

---

[19] Robin Attfield, 'The Good of Trees', *Journal of Value Inquiry*, 15 (1981), 35–54; Kenneth Goodpaster, 'On Being Morally Considerable', *Journal of Philosophy*, 78 (1978), 308–25; and Taylor, *Respect for Nature*.

ethic vacuous. There is another possibility worth mentioning though. It might be argued that there are two senses in which an extension could be complete. According to the first, an extension would be complete across the class of living things if every category of moral consideration applying to any member of the class applies to all. The second sense involves the additional claim that the categories apply to the same degree or with the same intensity in every instance. So, a human and a crab might each have the right to flourish but, it might be said, the former has the stronger right.[20] This suggestion combats the threat of vacuousness but generates its own problem. We are left wondering about the basis for the possession of rights of varying strength. Locating the basis in some property possessed by, for example, humans but not crabs would seem to imply that the extension is only partial after all. But this is not to say that it is unjustifiably chauvinist.

There is an extension even beyond living things which some have suggested and which must be considered. According to this suggestion, all natural entities are morally considerable, irrespective of whether or not they are living things. On this view, represented in this volume in the paper by Elliot, moral considerability is extended to such things as rocks, fossils, mountains, rivers, waterfalls, stalactites, patterns of weathering on cliffs, glaciers, dunes, and lifeless planets. Some of these entities are hosts to living things but this extension gives them independent moral standing. The chief basis of this extension is the very fact of the naturalness of these items. Moral extensionism which includes not only living things but all natural entities in the class of the morally considerable would seem to provide the basis for a powerful environmental ethic which promises to justify strong environmentalist, or deep green, positions.

Some environmental ethicists who are sympathetic to such positions are, however, critical of moral extensionism, claiming that it is hopelessly atomistic and individualistic, that it fails to recognize, and is in tension with, the compelling claims of a holistic environmental ethic, and, even, that it exemplifies the morally dubious domination of nature by humans. The underlying thought seems to be that human chauvinisms cannot be repaired simply by extending the range of kinds of individual to which moral standing or moral consideration is accorded, for example by including within the scope of the right to life non-human animals and even plants and microbes. What is supposedly required instead is a more general alteration in the form of ethical theories which reflects the moral worth or value of wholes, such as the biosphere itself and ecosystems. Moral

---

[20] Donald Van DeVeer, 'Interspecific Justice', *Inquiry*, 22 (1979), 55–79; and Mary Anne Warren, 'The Rights of the Nonhuman World', in Elliot and Gare, *Environmental Philosophy*.

extensionism allegedly distorts our view of nature, inclining us to see it as an aggregation of individuals as opposed to an integrated, dynamic whole. A critique of extensionism is to be found in the contribution to this volume by Callicott. Moreover, Callicott brings out a tension, some might say inconsistency, between holistic environmental ethics and the ethics proposed by, loosely speaking, animal liberationists.

Some who offer this line of criticism take the view that the value of individuals is purely instrumental and that intrinsic value is exemplified only by certain systemic properties such as the integrity of, and diversity within, ecosystems. It is possible, however, to combine the holistic view with more individualistic consideration, taking each into account in evaluating environmental policy. Indeed there is a sense in which holism is a variant of individualism, treating, as it does, the biosphere and ecosystems as complex items worthy of moral consideration in their own right. Thought of this way, the move to holism can be counted as a further extensionist step, falling outside the extensionist model only where the individuals recognized by the earlier steps are denied moral considerability altogether. Indeed Callicott, as his Preface to his contribution to this volume clearly indicates, now advocates combining or supplementing the holistic principle with principles which generate extensive obligations to human beings and to individual, non-human animals, including domestic animals.

METHODS, META-ETHICS AND METAPHYSICS

There are, is indicated above, numerous competing environmental ethics, which ethics will often, although not always, suggest quite different environmental policies. Their various proponents argue for them and against their competitors and there is some indication above of how such arguments might go. It is useful, though, to discuss the nature of such arguments more explicitly. This is helped by the use of two slightly technical terms: 'moral considerability', which has in fact already been encountered, and 'moral significance'. So, first of all, something is morally considerable if it has a claim to be directly taken account of in our moral evaluations and judgements. There is no suggestion here, by the way, that only those things we tend normally to think of as individuals can be morally considerable; whole states of affairs, such as ecosystems, the biosphere, or even the universe itself might be morally considerable.

One thing that is interesting and compelling about environmental ethics is its attempt to say exactly which kinds of things are morally considerable and why. But even where there is agreement about which kinds of things are morally considerable, there is almost certain to be disagreement about their degree of moral significance. Moral considerability does not entail equal moral significance. So, moral significance is, if you like, a measure of degree of considerability. And environmental ethics seeks also to map and to justify patterns of moral significance.

Meta-ethical considerations are sometimes adduced to settle questions as to moral considerability. For instance, it has been argued that only entities which have interests can be morally considerable and that entities can only have interests if they have desires.[21] Here a conceptual connection is claimed to hold between having desires and being morally considerable, which limits our choice of ethics to human or animal-centred ethics. This assumes of course that only animals are conscious but an attack on this assumption would not be an attack on the normative basis of animal-centred ethics; rather it would be like accepting that persons have the right to life and then establishing that dolphins, as well as humans, are persons because they are, in morally relevant respects, like them.

Now one tactic adopted by those who favour a biocentric ethic is to accept the alleged conceptual connection between having interests and being morally considerable but to deny that having interests presupposes a capacity for desires. So something might be said to have interests if it has a good which can be advanced or harmed, and organisms which are not conscious arguably have, in this sense, a good of their own. We can judge that a plant is flourishing according to its own kind, according to its biologically programmed ends of growth and reproduction. A plant may be treated in a way such that its capacity for growth and reproduction is reduced or destroyed and this, so the claim would run, is contrary to its interests.

If we grant this, there is some temptation to allow that plants are morally considerable. And even though in allowing this we have allowed only that it is possible that plants are morally considerable it is also difficult to resist the move from the admission of this conceptual or meta-ethical point to the normative conclusion that they are in fact considerable. This latter move might be assisted by striving to show that what really motivates our attribution of moral considerability to humans and to other conscious animals is the recognition that they each have a good of their own, and so interests. Talk of desires drops out.

---

[21] See the classic statement of this position in Joel Feinberg, 'The Rights of Humans and Unborn Generations', in William T. Blackstone, ed., *Philosophy and Environmental Crisis* (Athens, Ga.: University of Georgia Press, 1974). Note, too, that the connection may be more narrowly expressed, claiming only that some particular species of moral considerability, for instance considerability based on rights, presupposes a capacity for desire. This leaves it open as to whether some other species of considerability, for instance that based on intrinsic value, likewise presupposes a capacity for desire.

So what has gone on here? We started with an account of moral considerability in terms of interests and an account of interests in terms of desires. The former was accepted but, divorced from the latter, was shown to have surprising implications. A biocentric ethic was shown to be possible. And furthermore it was claimed that what really underpinned our attribution of intrinsic value in the case of animals with consciousness is the recognition that they have a teleologically defined good of their own and hence interests. This, of course, is the normative claim into which the earlier meta-ethical claim is supposed to ease us. Indeed some have suggested that the apparent interests, such as an interest in being free from pain which the capacity for consciousness makes possible, are not particularly normatively significant.[22] The general strategy is to extend the circle of moral considerability by establishing similarities between kinds of thing which are acknowledged to be morally considerable and others which are not generally thus regarded. And there is also the additional and crucial move of redefining, or at least modifying, the basis for moral considerability in the former category. In the case just considered this is the move of redefining interests in terms of a thing's having a good of its own where this is not itself defined in terms of the thing's desires.

The circle of moral considerability might be further extended, using a similar strategy. It might, for instance, be extended to include natural items, other than living things, which exhibit organization or structure. Consider a stalactite, an organized collection of mineral compounds created by natural processes over time. It is not completely implausible to suggest that the stalactite is a natural item with a good of its own defined in terms of its organization. To smash it would be to act contrary to that good. Admittedly its organization is not biological but why, it might be asked, must an item's good be defined in terms of biological organization? To insist on this is, according to some, to display sheer bio-chauvinism! And, it might be added, in the case of the stalactite we are not considering an inert item, rather we are considering an item in the process of developing according to its kind. It might be that biological organization is initially more obvious and impressive but, so the suggestion might run, it is the basic fact of organization that counts.[23]

[22] Robin Attfield, 'The Good of Trees'; Kenneth Goodpaster, 'On Being Morally Considerable'; Tom Regan, 'Feinberg on What Sorts of Beings Can Have Rights', *Southern Journal of Philosophy*, 14 (1976), 485–98; and Taylor, *Respect for Nature*. But see also Robert Elliot, 'Regan on the Sorts of Beings that Can Have Rights', *Southern Journal of Philosophy*, 16 (1978), 701–5.

[23] See Holmes Rolston III, *Environmental Ethics: Duties to and Values in the Natural World* (Philadelphia: Temple University Press, 1988); and T. L. S. Sprigge, 'Some Recent Positions in Environmental Ethics Examined', *Inquiry*, 34 (1991), 107–28.

There is another way in which the circle of moral considerability might be extended. The extensions so far considered are individualistic, focusing concern on particular items, whether they be persons, animals, living things, or natural items. This new extension, and some would object to thus categorizing it, introduces a holistic element. It is urged that whole ecosystems, the biosphere, and even the universe as a whole are morally considerable and that the particular individuals which constitute them are themselves only insignificantly, if at all, considerable. The move here rests on a metaphysical claim, or at least gains strength from it if it succeeds, to the effect that these large systems exhibit sufficient organization and integration to count as alive, as having a good of their own or, less controversially, as possessing intrinsic value. The view is represented in this volume in the papers by Callicott and Mathews and it is criticized in the paper by Brennan. It is possible of course to combine the holism with more straightforwardly individualistic principles, as the Preface to Callicott's contribution suggests. And, as where principles of any kind are combined, there is then the problem of establishing priorities and trade-offs.[24]

Talk of moral considerability may be given an axiological, deontological, or even Kantian twist. On the latter two construals, attributions of moral considerability function not unlike attributions of rights. The idea is that morally considerable items are to be treated as ends in themselves, and that consequently it is at least prima facie impermissible to destroy them. For example, it has been claimed that all living things, including plants, have inherent value and are worthy of respect.[25] In particular, it is claimed that the inherent value in question is distinct from intrinsic (axiological) value, usually on the basis of the claim that living things are goal directed and so have ends of their own. So, the destruction of a plant cannot be justified simply by the value of the consequences of its destruction; nor can the wrongness of destroying a plant be put right simply by replacing it with another plant of the same kind and quality.

It is possible for something to be morally considerable even though it possesses neither rights nor inherent value. Instead, intrinsic value may be the basis for moral considerability and may even provide for the idea of items being worthy of respect. It would not be, of course, that the item itself is worthy of respect but rather something along the lines of the idea that the value the item manifests must be respected. Further, the value is respected by not interfering with the item exemplifying it. For example,

---

[24] See Taylor, *Respect for Nature*.
[25] See Tom Regan, 'Does Environmental Ethics Rest on a Mistake?', *Monist*, 75 (1992), 161–82; and Taylor, *Respect for Nature*.

plants might be thought intrinsically valuable because, for example, of the positive aesthetic properties they exhibit or because of their biological organization and complexity. And it might be urged that the values *aesthetic worth* or *biological complexity* demand respect. Thus it would be at least prima facie wrong to destroy or disrupt the plant which exemplifies these values.

Similarly, non-living things such as rock-formations, dunes, stalactites, and crystals might be thought intrinsically valuable, because of their aesthetic properties, because they exhibit non-biological organization, or because they are the outcomes of natural processes. Collections of individuals, such as ecosystems or geographic aggregations, might be judged intrinsically valuable, particularly on account of their aesthetic properties: intrinsic value does not seem to require genuine individuals as its basis. This is important, since some, like Brennan in his contribution to this volume, have questioned the metaphysical assumptions of those who think ecosystems or the biosphere are proper objects of moral concern on the grounds that they are not, as wholes, living or indeed genuinely unified individuals of any kind at all. They argue instead that such wholes are not, in any less than a fanciful sense, alive or more devastatingly, as in Brennan's case, that such wholes are not individuals in their own right but mere aggregations of individuals. This same style of argument also threatens the claim that non-living natural items are morally considerable, since they also may be regarded as mere aggregations, lacking that integrated organization distinctive of genuine individuals.

In discussions of moral considerability, meta-ethical and normative issues tend to be intertwined but there are other instances in which discussion of the credentials of environmental ethics are much more straightforwardly meta-ethical. For example, it has been argued that core claims in environmental ethics entail a false meta-ethical theory. Many environmentalists claim that nature would have intrinsic value even were there no valuers such as ourselves. And this claim has been thought to require acceptance of an objectivist theory of value, specifically objective non-naturalism, which is at best dubious.[26] This challenge to environmentalism is met by showing, as Routley and Routley do in their contribution to this volume, that its core normative claims do not presuppose the complete

---

[26] Don Mannison, 'A Critique of a Proposal for an Environmental Ethic: Just Why Is It Bad to Live in a Concrete Jungle?', in Don Mannison, Michael McRobbie and Richard Routley, eds., *Environmental Philosophy* (Canberra: Research School of Social Sciences, Australian National University, 1980); H. J. McCloskey, *Ecological Ethics and Politics* (Totowa, NJ: Rowman and Littlefield, 1983); and Ernest Partridge, 'Values in Nature: Is Anybody There?', *Philosophical Inquiry*, 7 (1986), 96–110.

detachment of values from valuers and that these claims can be made within a meta-ethic which is, in effect, subjectivist.[27]

Meta-ethical challenges to environmentalism may be less direct, deriving from assumed, as opposed to critically justified, features of moral discourse. So it might be assumed that enforceable morality has a largely contractual basis, involving, at least notionally, agreements between agents to abide by certain constraints. This impression of morality as contractual is helped by the political significance, perhaps dominance, of the language of rights. There is arguably a resulting tendency to exclude from the scope of moral considerability entities not easily fitted into the contractualist model. While non-human animals with consciousness may be brought within the contractualist model, it is doubtful that other mooted candidates for moral considerability can be.[28] So effective critiques of contractualist morality, particularly of the claim that duties derive only from rights, which in turn derive from agreements, notional or real, between agents, are important justifications of the deep environmentalist position. Such a critique is provided by Routley and Routley, and by Midgley in their contributions to this volume.

Justifying an environmental ethic is also likely to require some consideration of metaphysical issues. As Passmore, Mathews, and, to some extent, Brennan, and Plumwood, indicate in their contributions to this volume, beliefs about the metaphysics of the natural world have been closely intertwined with, and have helped to shape, ethical views concerning it. For instance, some, like Mathews, argue that opposition to deep environmentalist positions, in particular to ecological holism, is fuelled partly by the conceptual influence of a false atomistic metaphysics deriving from Descartes and Newton. The thought is that such a metaphysics encourages, although it does not entail, a conception of the self as isolated from others, as not at all constituted by others, and that it consequently encourages a contractualist conception of morality. Uncovering such patterns of conceptual influence, thereby assisting critical self-evaluation of one's moral beliefs, is an important element in justifying a deep environmentalist position. And some think that the articulation of a sounder metaphysical position, for example one which encourages a conception of the self consonant with deep ecology or of the universe as a unified

[27] See also Robert Elliot, 'Meta-Ethics and Environmental Ethics', *Metaphilosophy*, 16 (1985), 103–17; Robert Elliot, 'Intrinsic Value, Environmental Obligation and Naturalness', *Monist*, 75 (1992), 138–60; Val Plumwood, 'Ethics and Instrumentalism: A Reply to Janna Thompson', *Environmental Ethics*, 12 (1991), 139–49.

[28] Although see Robert Elliot, 'Rawlsian Justice and Nonhuman Animals', *Journal of Applied Philosophy*, 1 (1984), 95–106.

whole in which all so-called individuals are interconnected, is likewise important.

These metaphysical considerations have a cosmological orientation and draw heavily on the physical sciences. And it is important to note that more unambiguously scientific, in particular ecological, considerations are relevant to the justification of environmental ethics. As already noted, some environmental ethics take ecosystems to be individuals as opposed to mere aggregations of individuals of particular plants and animals. But considerations from ecology and other sciences might show, as Brennan urges in his contribution to this volume, that it is not clear that they are, except metaphorically, individuals. And an accurate ecology might call into question, as Clements shows in her contribution to this volume, certain alleged bases of environmental value, such as ecosystemic stability. Thus, it might not be clear that stability is in any sense a natural value typically exemplified by ecosystems. Similarly Sober, in his contribution to this volume, draws on biological phenomena to criticize some of the more radical environmental ethics.

Religious belief, which has a metaphysical dimension, also is likely to influence both environmental ethics and practice, as Passmore makes clear in his contribution to this volume.[29] The proper relationship between humankind and nature might be thought to be defined partly in terms of the requirements, preferences, or some such, of a divine creator. Those who think that nature was created for the use of humankind might be less sympathetic to deep environmentalism than those who think that humans are just one component of a creation which the divine being regards as having value as a whole. Indeed some might regard nature or the universe as the physical manifestation of the divine being, a view which might well encourage attitudes of respect for nature.

Metaphysical considerations of a more standardly philosophical kind also impact on the development of environmental ethics. For example, it is possible, as part of developing a systematic idealism, to question the very existence of one category of entity, non-conscious natural objects, to which some have wanted to extend moral concern or attribute value.[30] Perhaps many advocates of deep environmentalism will be unimpressed by systematic idealism but even for them a challenge remains. Many of the alleged value-adding properties of natural objects and of wild nature in general,

---

[29] See also Robin Attfield, 'Western Traditions and Environmental Traditions', in Elliot and Gare, *Environmental Philosophy*; and Passmore, *Man's Responsibility for Nature*.

[30] T. L. S. Sprigge, 'Non-Human Rights: An Idealist Perspective', *Inquiry*, 27 (1984), 439–61. See also Robert Elliot, 'Environmental Degradation, Vandalism and the Aesthetic Object Argument', *Australasian Journal of Philosophy*, 67 (1989), 191–204.

such as beauty, complexity, harmony, integrity seem to be primarily aesthetic properties and are arguably human projections on to the natural world. If this is so, we might ask whether such properties really provide a basis for a deep environmental ethic as against a more sensitive variant of human chauvinism.

CONCLUDING NOTE

The papers in this anthology are but a small sample from the growing literature in environmental ethics. But together they constitute an excellent introduction to environmental ethics, including as they do some of the very best, and most provocative, work in the area. They represent a range of views and focus on a range of issues and so convey the diversity of opinion and interests within environmental ethics. Despite their wide-ranging nature they do, as a group, have a thematic structure. To some extent this is revealed above, where the various articles are briefly discussed. It is useful, however, to conclude with a more explicit attempt to depict this structure.

The first four papers argue for particular normative positions. Williams's paper considers resource conservation issues in the context of utilitarian ethics. She extends a familiar ethical theory to a domain in which it has not been explicitly much discussed and its implications not adequately considered. The second paper, by Callicott, confronts traditional ethical theories, including utilitarianism, urging that they fail to provide the basis for an adequate environmental framework. Callicott's paper moves us on from an application of a traditional theory to an environmental issue to the much more provocative claim that traditional ethics need profound revision. The papers by Rolston and Elliot are more narrowly focused than Callicott's, seeking to establish the intrinsic value of species and natural objects respectively. Like Callicott's paper, although in a more subdued way, they argue for positions that involve more than the application of traditional patterns of thought to environmental issues.

The fifth and sixth papers, by R. and V. Routley, and Midgley respectively, both defuse a possible style of objection to environmental ethics that move beyond the traditional. Some have argued that such ethics are misconceived, or even incoherent, or that they entail meta-ethical views which are incorrect and so must themselves be flawed. The fifth and sixth papers counter such arguments, showing that there are no meta-ethical impediments to distinctively environmental ethics. These papers also advance and defend normative views that belong to a distinctively environmental ethic.

The seventh, eighth, and ninth papers make normative suggestions too but are distinctive in that in doing so they focus on metaphysical considerations. Thus Passmore impresses upon the reader the impact that metaphysical views have on the formation of ethical beliefs; the suggestion is that perhaps the chief impediment to a distinctively environmental ethic is a hostile metaphysical tradition that discourages the view of nature that would render such an ethic compelling. Mathews's paper outlines a metaphysical position, deriving from Spinoza and contemporary cosmology, which she thinks encourages a distinctively environmental ethic, even suggesting that it provides a basis for making our lives meaningful through some partial identification of our selves with the Self that is the universe. And Plumwood, drawing on some insights of feminist theory, provides a discussion of such notions of identification with nature or, more grandly, the universe. It is worth emphasizing a point which the editing of Plumwood's paper obscures: namely that she highlights the too often unnoticed parallel between deep ecology and rationalism.

The tenth paper, by Sagoff, draws connections between political philosophy and environmental ethics. It is a response to a style of argument that seeks to highlight tensions between environmentalism and political liberalism. The idea is that political liberalism has prima facie credibility but that the demands of environmentalists do not take seriously the requirement that the liberal state not legislate on questions of value as opposed to rights, that it remain neutral between competing conceptions of what is good. One response would be to urge that this tension is a reason for rejecting political liberalism, that it is just more evidence of the ethical impoverishment of the individualistic outlook of liberalism. There are elements of this response in Callicott's paper. Sagoff, however, shows that there are plausible ways of reconciling liberalism with environmentalism. So, Sagoff may be seen as rebutting an objection to environmentalism fuelled by views in the, perhaps, dominant Western political philosophy.

The final three papers, by Brennan, Clements, and Sober are, to varying degrees, sympathetic critiques of certain aspects, claims, or variants of environmental ethics. Brennan and Clements in particular draw on the ecological sciences to question certain claims made in environmental ethics. They are interesting not only because they pose challenges to environmental ethics but also because they show the relevance of scientific inquiry to ethical belief.

I

DISCOUNTING VERSUS MAXIMUM SUSTAINABLE YIELD

MARY B. WILLIAMS

Interest-bearing resources are those resources like crop species, fish species, draught animal species, topsoil, genetic variation, etc. which are instrumental in changing energy (ultimately solar energy) into energy available for consumption (as food, shelter, clothing, etc.) and which are such that their capacity to supply energy for future consumption is not decreased by utilization of some of the energy they supply. (Organisms tend to produce more offspring than can survive; the excess offspring can be utilized without damaging future productivity, so we can reap the interest without disturbing the capital.) Interest-bearing resources can be contrasted with exhaustible resources like fossil fuels, whose ability to supply energy for future consumption is decreased by every unit of energy consumed. Interest-bearing resources renew themselves and provide a bonus for us; they are usually called 'renewable' resources, but in this paper I want to direct more attention to the bonus provided for us.

Destructive utilization of an interest-bearing resource is utilization which results in a lowered capacity to provide energy for future consumption. Destructive utilization may be direct, as when whalers lower the productivity of their resources by catching too many whales, or when farmers lower the intrinsic productivity of their soil by poor soil conservation techniques. Destructive utilization may also be indirect, as when the productivity of a lake is reduced by industries that use it as a place to dump poisonous wastes, or when the productivity of prime farmland is reduced by developers who build suburban housing on it. The effects of such destruction may be irreversible, as when a species is made extinct; or they may be reversible at some cost, as when the closing of a fishery allows an overfished species to recover.

Reprinted from a longer article with permission from R. I. Sikora and Brian Barry eds., *Obligations to Future Generations* (Philadelphia: Temple University Press, 1978), 169–71, 177–85.

Do we have an obligation to stop our destructive behaviour pattern? In this paper I will try to show that such an obligation does follow from utilitarian theory. Since the practice of discounting the interests of future generations is inconsistent with the basic tenet of utilitarianism . . . the distant effects of an action are as important as the immediate effects; consequently the acceptability of a utilitarian method for determining subjective obligation will depend strongly on the acceptability of its method for treating distant effect. The method implicitly suggested by G. E. Moore[1] and J. J. C. Smart[2] depends strongly on the assumption that distant events are only negligibly affected by present actions. They argued for this assumption on the grounds that the distant consequences of an action are sufficiently small as to be negligible; that is, they argued that the actual values of both sets of unevaluable consequences are close enough to zero that their addition to the sum would make no difference to the result. Does this argument hold in the biological situations with which we are concerned?

There are three relevant biological properties. The first is the existence and ubiquity of homoeostatic mechanisms. These mechanisms tend to damp down the effect of any input that is small relative to the size of the system: they would thus support the possibility that the distant effects will be negligible. But if the input is large enough to break down the homoeostatic mechanisms, then the second property, that the death of a biological system is irreversible, will become important. And the third property, that biological systems live in an interdependent relationship with other biological systems, may cause the effect of the breakdown of one system to be magnified as it spreads through the interdependent systems. (Just as the kingdom was lost for the want of a horseshoe nail, so an ecosystem may be lost for the want of an apparently insignificant species.) In the latter two cases, the consequences are probably not negligible. The non-negligibility is made more likely if A (the input) is an unprecedented action, since this will greatly increase the probability of a significant unevaluable consequence. Actions of a type that has occurred frequently have fewer unevaluable consequences; if they have occurred frequently enough, the biological system will have adjusted to them so that whatever effects they have are less serious. Thus, although the assumption that distant consequences can be neglected was not made in order to justify discounting the interests of distant generations, the effect, in a significant number of biological situations, of acting on it is to make present utilities

[1] G. E. Moore, *Principia Ethica* (Cambridge: Cambridge University Press, 1971), 152–4.

[2] J. J. C. Smart and B. Williams, *Utilitarianism: For and Against* (Cambridge: Cambridge University Press, 1973), 33.

count more heavily than future utilities. And this is inconsistent with utilitarianism.

But if distant consequences cannot be assumed to be negligible, how should we put them into our utilitarian calculations? We can, of course, use the considerations outlined above to estimate the probable damage and enter it into the calculation, but it is virtually impossible to make such estimates. Fortunately, in the case of interest-bearing resources, the problem of estimating the utility of all effects into the distant future can be reduced to the problem of maximizing present sustainable yield. I will argue that utilitarian theory mandates maximum sustainable yield. The argument requires a knowledge of the relevant biology, so I will sketch the theory underlying the concept of maximum sustainable yield.[3] Consider a population of organisms which has just migrated into a new, favourable environment. At first, the growth rate of the population will be large and constant: the organisms will be producing as many offspring as their biology allows, and most of these offspring will survive. Denote this intrinsic growth rate of the population by r. As the population size increases, members of the population will begin competing with each other for the same resources, and the growth rate will slow down: some of those born will be unable to survive to adulthood, and others will be small and unhealthy because of malnutrition. As the population increases still further, it comes closer and closer to the environmental carrying capacity, K, for that population: the growth rate gets progressively lower as the competition gets fiercer. When the population size reaches K, no new organisms can survive to adulthood unless an existing member of the population dies; at this point the growth rate of the population, $F(x)$, is zero (x represents population size). The simplest example of a growth rate function which models this behaviour is $F(x) = rx(1 - x/K)$. Fig. 1 is a graph of this function; Fig. 2 is a graph showing how the size of our immigrant population would grow if this were its growth rate function.

Now let us consider a population, e.g. of fish, that we wish to harvest. Can we harvest an amount h without impairing the productivity of the population? Is there a maximum amount which can be harvested? Clearly, the amount that we can harvest at a given population size without driving the population size down is determined by the rate at which the population can replace the harvested organisms—that is, by the growth rate. Fig. 3 shows the effect of a harvest rate which is less than the maximum growth rate. It shows that: if the original population size is

---

[3] For a more detailed exposition of the maximum sustainable yield theory, see Colin Clark, *Mathematical Bioeconomics: The Optimal Management of Renewable Resources* (New York: John Wiley and Sons, 1976).

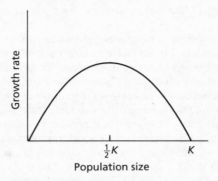

Fig. 1. Curve showing how the rate at which a population grows is dependent on the size of the population. Notice that, beyond a certain point, the rate of growth decreases as population size increases.

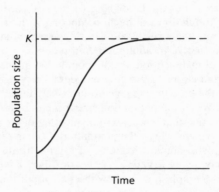

Fig. 2. Curve showing how the size of an immigrant population will increase until it reaches its environmental carrying capacity.

below the smaller size (x_1) with that growth rate, then harvesting at that rate will drive the population to extinction; if the original population size is between the two sizes with that growth rate, harvesting at that rate will allow the population to increase until it reaches the larger size (x_2) with that growth rate, and will cause the population to stabilize at that size. Clearly, there exists a maximum sustainable yield; it is equal to the maximum growth rate. The population has this maximum growth rate at size $1/2K$.

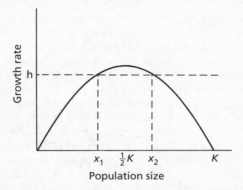

FIG. 3. Curve allowing us to assess the effect on a population with this growth curve of harvesting at rate h.

Now consider the relationship between maximum sustainable yield and destructive utilization. If the population size is greater than $\frac{1}{2}K$, then a harvest rate large enough to drive the size down to $\frac{1}{2}K$ is not destructive utilization, since the population produces more as its size moves toward $\frac{1}{2}K$. If the size is not greater than $\frac{1}{2}K$, then a harvest rate that drives the size down is destructive utilization. I have argued above that destructive utilization is inconsistent with energy maximization; for the same reason, any policy other than a policy of maximum sustainable yield is inconsistent with energy maximization. Thus, a maximum sustainable yield policy maximizes total energy.

Therefore, for a resource with this type of growth function, a first approximation to the policy which maximizes total utility is: if the population size is below $\frac{1}{2}K$, do not harvest until it reaches $\frac{1}{2}K$, and when it reaches $\frac{1}{2}K$ set the harvest rate equal to the maximum growth rate. If the population size is above or equal to $\frac{1}{2}K$, set the harvest rate at the maximum growth rate plus the excess above $\frac{1}{2}K$, and set the subsequent harvest rate at the maximum growth rate. Unfortunately, this is only a first approximation to the utility maximization policy. Because the costs of exploitation, as well as the benefits, must be considered in the utilitarian calculation, a better approximation to the desired policy will contain the costs of exploiting the resource. Because preventing harvest of the resource until it reaches $\frac{1}{2}K$ may cost more in economic dislocation, etc. than is gained by the speed of the increase to $\frac{1}{2}K$, a better approximation would take these factors into account. Because the interdependence of some harvestable resources will force us to use a multi-species model rather than the single species model presented above, a better approximation would use such a multi-species model. Other complicating factors will necessitate further revisions of the policy.

Finding the changes in the policy necessary to provide these better approximations will be an extremely difficult practical problem. But in each case the necessary data are data about the contemporary world. The obligation to consider the effects on all subsequent generations has been replaced by an obligation to maximize sustainable yield in the present generation. A policy of taking less than the maximum sustainable yield in order to increase the population size beyond $\frac{1}{2}K$ is clearly counterproductive; such a policy not only decreases the present harvest, it decreases the future productivity and thus decreases total production. So for these situations, the problem that, under a utilitarian theory, the present generation might have to sacrifice heavily because there are so many more future people does not arise; there are many more future people, but there are many more future cows and whales, too. There is no utility maximizing way to give distant generations a better heritage of interest-bearing resources than by giving the next generation a heritage of interest-bearing resources which are all at their maximum sustainable yield.

PROBLEMS

1. It must be admitted that this policy does not completely absolve us of the responsibility of considering unevaluable future consequences; these still exist. However, it does provide a powerful tool for those wishing to maximize total utility.

2. For those whose ethical system contains both the utilitarian principle and a principle of justice, the following may cause a problem: because generations previous to ours have practised destructive utilization, the generation which first institutes a maximum sustainable yield policy will bear an unfair burden as it decreases harvesting in order to bring species up to their maximum sustainable yield. (It might be appropriate to compensate that generation with more than its share of exhaustible resources.) In general, however, a maximum sustainable yield policy seems to mandate a just distribution over the generations.

3. The analysis in the previous section was of one type of interest-bearing resource–species. Its applicability to resources such as topsoil and genetic variation must be worked out.

4. The continued ability of a species to maintain its maximum sustainable yield is dependent on its continued ability to meet new environmental challenges; this is dependent on its genetic variation. Consideration of this problem forces us to realize that we may have to expand the meaning of the word 'sustainable'; the biological model we are using implicitly defines 'sustainable' as 'sustainable under present conditions'; we may need a biological model which includes factors of long-term sustainability.

5. Economic factors may also dictate the need for a model which ensures long-term sustainability rather than year-to-year sustainability. It could, for example, be more cost-efficient to build a new set of the machines used in exploiting a particular resource, operate it at a harvest level above the maximum sustainable yield until the machines are worn out, and then allow the resource to build back to $\frac{1}{2}K$ before building new machines.

6. Golding[4] has objected that, since people in the far distant future will be unlike us in unpredictable ways, we do not know what to desire for them. This is vitiated by the calculation given earlier, which shows that, for whales, our policy of maximum sustainable yield would be mandated even if we could foresee the relevant desires of people only twenty-one years in the future; for most interest-bearing resources (whose growth rate is larger than the growth rate of whales), we would need to foresee less than twenty-one years. In those cases in which it would be necessary to foresee a significant distance, it seems, in the absence of reason to think that desires or needs will change in a particular direction, reasonable to assume that the *best estimate* of future desires and needs is derived from the assumption that their needs and desires will be pretty much like ours.

CONCLUSION

The obligation to follow this policy does not exhaust our obligations concerning future generations; in particular, it does not cover whatever obligations we have concerning non-interest-bearing (exhaustible) resources. Nor does this policy tell us how to choose among the possible different ways of getting the same total yield of energy in a multi-species system. Nor does this policy provide complete escape from practical difficulties; the difficulties of determining the maximum sustainable yield of an

[4] Martin Golding, 'Obligations to Future Generations', *Monist*, 56 (1972), 85–99.

ecosystem will be formidable. However, this policy does provide guidance about a significant set of actions affecting future generations; by changing the problem from one of predicting all future consequences of an action to one of discovering facts about our contemporary ecosystem, it significantly reduces the difficulty of finding reasonably good answers to the problem.

The maximum sustainable yield policy has been presented in this paper as derivable from total utilitarian theory; it may also be derivable from other moral theories. Moral philosophers who claim that obligations can refer only to existing persons may find that, since a maximum sustainable yield policy can be justified by its effect on the next generation, their theory gives the same future-protecting effect as utilitarian theory. Such derivation from other major moral theories would greatly strengthen the claim that our social institutions should be changed to ensure a maximum sustainable yield policy.

II

ANIMAL LIBERATION: A TRIANGULAR AFFAIR

J. BAIRD CALLICOTT

PREFACE (1994)

I wrote 'A Triangular Affair' to sharply distinguish environmental ethics from animal liberation/rights when the former seemed to be overshadowed by the latter. Back in the late 1970s and early 1980s, when the piece was conceived and composed, many people seemed to conflate the two. In my youthful zeal to draw attention to the then unheralded Leopold land ethic, I made a few remarks that in retrospect appear irresponsible.

Most important, I no longer think that the land ethic is misanthropic. 'All ethics so far evolved', Leopold wrote, 'rest upon a single premiss: that the individual is a member of a community of interdependent parts. . . . The land ethic simply enlarges the boundaries of the community to include soils, waters, plants, and animals, or collectively: the land.' The biotic community and its correlative land ethic *does not replace* our several human communities and their correlative ethics—our duties and obligations to family and family members, to municipality and fellow-citizens, to country and countrymen, to humanity and human beings. Rather it *supplements* them. Hence the land ethic leaves our traditional human morality quite intact and pre-emptive.

Second in importance, I now think that we do in fact have duties and obligations—implied by the essentially communitarian premises of the land ethic—to domestic animals, as well as to wild fellow-members of the biotic community and to the biotic community as a whole. Farm animals, work animals, and pets have long been members of what Mary Midgley calls the 'mixed' community. They have entered into a kind of implicit social contract with us which lately we have abrogated. Think of it this way. Each of us belongs to several hierarchically ordered human com-

From *Environmental Ethics*, 2 (1980), 311–38. Reprinted with permission.

munities, each with its peculiar set of duties and obligations; to various mixed human–animal domestic communities, with their peculiar sets of duties and obligations; and to the biotic community, with its peculiar set of duties and obligations (which in sum Leopold called the land ethic). The land ethic no more eclipses our moral responsibilities in regard to domestic animals than it does our moral responsibilities in regard to other people.

Further, I now think that a vegetarian diet is indicated by the land ethic, no less than by the animal welfare ethics. Rainforests are felled to make pasture for cattle. Better for the environment if we ate forest fruits instead of beef. Livestock ruin watercourses and grasslands. And raising field crops for animal feed increases soil erosion and ground-water depletion.

Finally, though certainly I still wish there were far more bears than actually there are, a target ratio of one bear for every two people seems a bit extravagant.

'A Triangular Affair' clearly distinguishes between holistic environmental ethics, on the one hand, and individualistic 'moral humanism' and 'humane moralism', on the other. And that remains a serviceable distinction. Moralists of every stripe, however, must make common cause against the forces that are often simultaneously destroying human, mixed, and biotic communities. The differences between human, humane, and environmental concerns are real, and sometimes conflictive. But just as often they are convergent and mutually reinforcing. And all our ethical concerns can be theoretically unified, I am convinced, by a communitarian moral philosophy, thus enabling conflicts, when they do arise, to be adjudicated rationally.

ENVIRONMENTAL ETHICS AND ANIMAL LIBERATION

Partly because it is so new to Western philosophy (or at least heretofore only scarcely represented) *environmental ethics* has no precisely fixed conventional definition in glossaries of philosophical terminology. Aldo Leopold, however, is universally recognized as the father or founding genius of recent environmental ethics. His 'land ethic' has become a modern classic and may be treated as the standard example, the paradigm case, as it were, of what an environmental ethic is. Environmental ethics then can be defined ostensively by using Leopold's land ethic as the exemplary type. I do not mean to suggest that all environmental ethics should necessarily conform to Leopold's paradigm, but the extent to which an ethical system resembles Leopold's land ethic might be used, for want of anything better, as a criterion to measure the extent to which it is or is not of the environmental sort.

It is Leopold's opinion, and certainly an overall review of the prevailing traditions of Western ethics, both popular and philosophical, generally confirms it, that traditional Western systems of ethics have not accorded moral standing to non-human beings.[1] Animals and plants, soils and waters, which Leopold includes in his community of ethical beneficiaries, have traditionally enjoyed no moral standing, no rights, no respect, in sharp contrast to human persons whose rights and interests ideally must be fairly and equally considered if our actions are to be considered 'ethical' or 'moral'. One fundamental and novel feature of the Leopold land ethic, therefore, is the extension of *direct* ethical considerability from people to non-human natural entities.

At first glance, the recent ethical movement, usually labelled 'animal liberation' or 'animal rights', seems to be squarely and centrally a kind of environmental ethics.[2] The more uncompromising among the animal liberationists have demanded equal moral consideration on behalf of cows, pigs, chickens, and other apparently enslaved and oppressed non-human

---

[1] Aldo Leopold, *A Sand County Almanac* (New York: Oxford University Press, 1949), 202–3. Some traditional Western systems of ethics, however, have accorded moral standing to non-human beings. The Pythagorean tradition did, followed by Empedocles of Acragas; Saint Francis of Assisi apparently believed in the animal soul; in modern ethics, Jeremy Bentham's hedonic utilitarian system is also an exception to the usual rule. John Passmore ('The Treatment of Animals', *Journal of the History of Ideas*, 36 (1975), 196–218) provides a well-researched and eye-opening study of historical ideas about the moral status of animals in Western thought. Though exceptions to the prevailing attitudes have existed, they are exceptions indeed and represent but a small minority of Western religious and philosophical points of view.

[2] The tag 'animal liberation' for this moral movement originates with Peter Singer whose book *Animal Liberation* (New York: New York Review, 1975) has been widely influential. 'Animal rights' have been most persistently and unequivocally championed by Tom Regan in various articles, among them: 'The Moral Basis of Vegetarianism', *Canadian Journal of Philosophy*, 5 (1975), 181–214; 'Exploring the Idea of Animal Rights', in D. Patterson and R. Ryder, eds., *Animal Rights: A Symposium* (London: Centaur, 1979); 'Animal Rights, Human Wrongs', *Environmental Ethics*, 2 (1980), 99–120. A more complex and qualified position respecting animal rights has been propounded by Joel Feinberg, 'The Rights of Animals and Unborn Generations', in William T. Blackstone, ed., *Philosophy and Environmental Crisis* (Athens: University of Georgia Press, 1974), 43–68, and 'Human Duties and Animal Rights', in R. K. Morris and M. W. Fox, eds., *On the Fifth Day* (Washington: Acropolis Books, 1978), 45–69. Lawrence Haworth ('Rights, Wrongs and Animals', *Ethics*, 88 (1978): 95–105), in the context of the contemporary debate, claims limited rights on behalf of animals. S. R. L. Clark's *The Moral Status of Animals* (Oxford: Clarendon Press, 1975) has set out arguments which differ in some particulars from those of Singer, Regan, and Feinberg with regard to the moral considerability of some non-human animals. In this discussion, as a tribute to Singer, I use the term *animal liberation* generically to cover the several philosophical rationales for a humane ethic. Singer has laid particular emphasis on the inhumane usage of animals in agribusiness and scientific research. Two thorough professional studies from the humane perspective of these institutions are Ruth Harrison's *Animal Machines* (London: Stuart, 1964) and Richard Ryder's *Victims of Science* (London: Davis-Poynter, 1975), respectively.

animals.[3] The theoreticians of this new hyper-egalitarianism have coined such terms as *speciesism* (on analogy with *racism* and *sexism*) and *human chauvinism* (on analogy with *male chauvinism*), and have made animal liberation seem, perhaps not improperly, the next and most daring development of political liberalism.[4] Aldo Leopold also draws upon metaphors of political liberalism when he tells us that his land ethic 'changes the role of *Homo sapiens* from conqueror of the land community to plain member and citizen of it'.[5] For animal liberationists it is as if the ideological battles for equal rights and equal consideration for women and for racial minorities have been all but won, and the next and greatest challenge is to purchase equality, first theoretically and then practically, for all (actually only *some*) animals, regardless of species. This more rhetorically implied than fully articulated historical progression of moral rights from fewer to greater numbers of 'persons' (allowing that animals may also be persons) as advocated by animal liberationists, also parallels Leopold's scenario in 'The Land Ethic' of the historical extension of 'ethical criteria' to more and more 'fields of conduct' and to larger and larger groups of people during the past three thousand or so years.[6] As Leopold develops it, the land ethic is a cultural 'evolutionary possibility,' the next 'step in a sequence'.[7] For Leopold, however, the next step is much more sweeping, much more inclusive than the animal liberationists envision, since it 'enlarges the boundaries of the [moral] community to include soils, waters, [and] plants . . .' as well as animals.[8] Thus, the animal liberation movement *could* be construed as partitioning Leopold's perhaps undigestable and totally inclusive environmental ethic into a series of more assimilable stages:

[3] Peter Singer and Tom Regan especially insist upon *equal* moral *consideration* for non-human animals. Equal moral *consideration* does not necessarily imply equal *treatment*, however, as Singer points out, cf. Singer, *Animal Liberation*, 3, 17–24, and Singer, 'The Fable of the Fox and the Unliberated Animals', *Ethics*, 88 (1978), 119–20. Regan provides an especially clear summary of both his position and Singer's in 'Animal Rights, Human Wrongs', 108–12.

[4] We have Richard Ryder to thank for coining the term *speciesism*. See his *Speciesism: The Ethics of Vivisection* (Edinburgh: Scottish Society for the Prevention of Vivisection, 1974). Richard Routley introduced the term *human chauvinism* in 'Is There a Need for a New, an Environmental Ethic?', *Proceedings of the Fifteenth World Congress of Philosophy*, 1 (1973), 205–10. Peter Singer ('All Animals Are Equal', in Tom Regan and Peter Singer, eds., *Animal Rights and Human Obligations* (Englewood Cliffs, NJ: Prentice-Hall, 1976), 148–62) developed the egalitarian comparison of speciesism with racism and sexism in detail. To extend the political comparison further, animal liberation is also a reformist and activist movement. We are urged to act, to become vegetarians, to boycott animal products, and so forth. The concluding paragraph of Regan's 'Animal Rights, Human Wrongs', 120, is especially zealously hortatory.

[5] Leopold, *Sand County Almanac*, 204.

[6] Ibid. 201–3. A more articulate historical representation of the parallel expansion of legal rights appears in C. D. Stone's *Should Trees have Standing?* (Los Altos: William Kaufman, 1972), 3–10, however without specific application to animal liberation.

[7] Leopold, *Sand County Almanac*, 203.   [8] Ibid. 204.

today animal rights, tomorrow equal rights for plants, and after that full moral standing for rocks, soil, and other earthy compounds, and perhaps sometime in the still more remote future, liberty and equality for water and other elemental bodies.

Put just this way, however, there is something jarring about such a graduated progression in the exfoliation of a more inclusive environmental ethic, something that seems absurd. A more or less reasonable case might be made for rights for some animals, but when we come to plants, soils, and waters, the frontier between plausibility and absurdity appears to have been crossed. Yet, there is no doubt that Leopold sincerely proposes that *land* (in his inclusive sense) be ethically regarded. The beech and chestnut, for example, have in his view as much 'biotic right' to life as the wolf and the deer, and the effects of human actions on mountains and streams for Leopold is an ethical concern as genuine and serious as the comfort and longevity of battery hens.[9] In fact, Leopold to all appearances never considered the treatment of battery hens on a factory farm or steers in a feed lot to be a pressing moral issue. He seems much more concerned about the integrity of the farm wood lot and the effects of clear-cutting steep slopes on neighbouring streams.

Animal liberationists put their ethic into practice (and display their devotion to it) by becoming vegetarians, and the moral complexities of vegetarianism have been thoroughly debated in the recent literature as an adjunct issue to animal rights.[10] (No one, however, has yet expressed, as among Butler's Erewhonians, qualms about eating plants, though such sentiments might be expected to be latently present if the rights of plants are next to be defended.) Aldo Leopold, by contrast, did not even condemn hunting animals, let alone eating them, nor did he personally abandon hunting, for which he had had an enthusiasm since boyhood, upon becoming convinced that his ethical responsibilities extended beyond the human sphere.[11] There are several interpretations for this behavioural peculiarity. One is that Leopold did not see that his land ethic actually ought to prohibit hunting, cruelly killing, and eating animals. A corollary of this interpretation is that Leopold was so unperspicacious as deservedly to be thought stupid—a conclusion hardly comporting with the intellectual

---

[9] Ibid. 221 (trees); 129–33 (mountains); 209 (streams).

[10] John Benson ('Duty and the Beast', *Philosophy*, 53 (1978), 547–8) confesses that in the course of considering issues raised by Singer *et al.* he was 'obliged to change my own diet as a result'. An elaborate critical discussion is Philip E. Devine's 'The Moral Basis of Vegetarianism' (*Philosophy*, 53 (1978), 481–505).

[11] For a biography of Leopold including particular reference to Leopold's career as a 'sportsman', see Susan L. Flader, *Thinking Like a Mountain* (Columbia: University of Missouri Press, 1974).

subtlety he usually evinces in most other respects. If not stupid, then perhaps Leopold was hypocritical. But if a hypocrite, we should expect him to conceal his proclivity for blood sports and flesh eating and to treat them as shameful vices to be indulged secretively. As it is, bound together between the same covers with 'The Land Ethic' are his unabashed reminiscences of killing and consuming *game*.[12] This term (like *stock*) when used of animals, moreover, appears to be morally equivalent to referring to a sexually appealing young woman as a 'piece' or to a strong, young black man as a 'buck'—if animal rights, that is, are to be considered as on a par with women's rights and the rights of formerly enslaved races. A third interpretation of Leopold's approbation of regulated and disciplined sport hunting (and *a fortiori* meat eating) is that it is a form of human and animal behaviour not inconsistent with the land ethic as he conceived it. A corollary of this interpretation is that Leopold's land ethic and the environmental ethic of the animal liberation movement rest upon very different theoretical foundations, and that they are thus two very different forms of environmental ethics.

The urgent concern of animal liberationists for the suffering of domestic animals, toward which Leopold manifests an attitude which can only be described as indifference, and the urgent concern of Leopold, on the other hand, for the disappearance of species of plants as well as animals, and for soil erosion and stream pollution, appear to be symptoms not only of very different ethical perspectives, but of profoundly different cosmic visions as well. The neat similarities, noted at the beginning of this discussion, between the environmental ethic of the animal liberation movement and the classical Leopold land ethic appear in light of these observations to be rather superficial and to conceal substrata of thought and value which are not at all similar. The theoretical foundations of the animal liberation movement and those of the Leopold land ethic may even turn out not to be companionable, complementary, or mutually consistent. The animal liberationists may thus find themselves not only engaged in controversy with the many conservative philosophers upholding *apartheid* between man and 'beast', but also faced with an unexpected dissent from another, very different, system of environmental ethics.[13] Animal liberation and

---

[12] See especially, Leopold, *Sand County Almanac*, 54–8; 62–6; 120–2; 149–54; 177–87.

[13] A most thorough and fully argued dissent is provided by John Rodman in 'The Liberation of Nature', *Inquiry*, 20 (1977), 83–131. It is surprising that Singer, whose book is the subject of Rodman's extensive critical review, or some of Singer's philosophical allies, have not replied to these very penetrating and provocative criticisms. Another less specifically targeted dissent is Paul Shepard's 'Animal Rights and Human Rites' (*North American Review* (Winter, 1974), 34–41). More recently Kenneth Goodpaster ('From Egoism to Environmentalism', in K. Goodpaster and K. Sayre, eds., *Ethics and Problems of the 21st Century* (Notre Dame: Notre

animal rights may well prove to be a triangular rather than, as it has so far been represented in the philosophical community, a polar controversy.

ETHICAL HUMANISM AND HUMANE MORALISM

The orthodox response of 'ethical humanism' (as this philosophical perspective may be styled) to the suggestion that non-human animals should be accorded moral standing is that such animals are not worthy of this high perquisite. Only human beings are rational, or capable of having interests, or possess *self*-awareness, or have linguistic abilities, or can represent the future, it is variously argued.[14] These essential attributes taken singly or in various combinations make people somehow exclusively deserving of moral consideration. The so-called 'lower animals', it is insisted, lack the crucial qualification for ethical considerability and so may be treated (albeit humanely, according to some, so as not to brutalize man) as things or means, not as persons or as ends.[15]

The theoreticians of the animal liberation movement ('humane moralists' as they may be called) typically reply as follows.[16] Not all human beings qualify as worthy of moral regard, according to the various criteria specified. Therefore, by parity of reasoning, human persons who do not so

Dame University Press, 1979), 21–35) has expressed complaints about the animal liberation and animal rights movement in the name of environmental ethics. 'The last thing we need', writes Goodpaster, 'is simply another "liberation movement"' (p. 29).

[14] Singer, 'All Animals Are Equal', 159, uses the term *humanist* to convey a speciesist connotation. Rationality and future-conceiving capacities as criteria for rights holding have been newly revived by Michael E. Levin with specific reference to Singer in 'Animal Rights Evaluated', *Humanist* (July/Aug., 1977), 14–15. John Passmore, in *Man's Responsibility for Nature* (London: Duckworth, 1974), cf. 116, has recently insisted upon having interests as a criterion for having rights and denied that non-human beings have interests. L. P. Francis and R. Norman ('Some Animals are More Equal than Others', *Philosophy*, 53 (1978), 507–27) have argued, again with specific reference to animal liberationists, that linguistic abilities are requisite for moral status. H. J. McCloskey ('The Right to Life', *Mind*, 84 (1975), 410–13, and 'Moral Rights and Animals', *Inquiry*, 22 (1979), 23–54), adapting an idea of Kant's, defends, among other exclusively human qualifications for rights holding, *self*-awareness. Richard A. Watson ('Self-Consciousness and the Rights of Nonhuman Animals and Nature', *Environmental Ethics*, 1 (1979), 99–129) also defends self-consciousness as a criterion for rights holding, but allows that some non-human animals also possess it.

[15] In addition to the historical figures, who are nicely summarized and anthologized in *Animal Rights and Human Obligations*, John Passmore has recently defended the reactionary notion that cruelty towards animals is morally reprehensible for reasons independent of any obligation or duties people have to animals as such (*Man's Responsibility*, cf. 117).

[16] 'Humane moralists' is perhaps a more historically accurate designation than 'animal liberationists'. John Rodman, 'The Liberation of Nature', 88–9, has recently explored in a programmatic way the connections between the contemporary animal liberation/rights movements and the historical humane societies movement.

qualify as moral patients may be treated, as animals often are, as mere things or means (for example, used in vivisection experiments, disposed of if their existence is inconvenient, eaten, hunted, and so forth). But the ethical humanists would be morally outraged if irrational and inarticulate infants, for example, were used in painful or lethal medical experiments, or if severely retarded people were hunted for pleasure. Thus, the double-dealing, the hypocrisy, of ethical humanism appears to be exposed.[17] Ethical humanism, though claiming to discriminate between worthy and unworthy ethical patients on the basis of objective criteria impartially applied, turns out after all, it seems, to be *speciesism*, a philosophically indefensible prejudice (analogous to racial prejudice) against animals. The tails side of this argument is that some animals, usually the 'higher' lower animals (cetaceans, other primates, and so forth), as ethological studies seem to indicate, may meet the criteria specified for moral worth, although the ethical humanists, even so, are not prepared to grant them full dignity and the rights of persons. In short, the ethical humanists' various criteria for moral standing do not include all or only human beings, humane moralists argue, although in practice ethical humanism wishes to make the class of morally considerable beings coextensive with the class of human beings.

The humane moralists, for their part, insist upon *sentience* as the only relevant capacity a being need possess to enjoy full moral standing. If animals, they argue, are conscious entities who, though deprived of reason, speech, forethought or even *self*-awareness (however that may be judged), are capable of suffering, then their suffering should be as much a matter of ethical concern as that of our fellow human beings, or strictly speaking, as our very own. What, after all, has rationality or any of the other allegedly uniquely human capacities to do with ethical standing? Why, in other words, should beings who reason or use speech (and so forth) qualify for moral status, and those who do not fail to qualify?[18] Isn't this just like saying that only persons with white skin should be free, or that only persons who beget and not those who bear should own property? The criterion seems utterly unrelated to the benefit for which it selects. On the other hand, the capacity to suffer is, it seems, a more relevant criterion for moral standing because—as Bentham and Mill, notable among modern

---

[17] Tom Regan styles more precise formulations of this argument, 'the argument from marginal cases', in 'An Examination and Defence of One Argument Concerning Animal Rights', *Inquiry*, 22 (1979), 190. Regan directs our attention to Andrew Linzey, *Animal Rights* (London: SCM Press, 1976) as well as to Singer, *Animal Liberation*, for paradigmatic employment of this argument on behalf of moral standing for animals (p. 144).

[18] A particularly lucid advocacy of this notion may be found in Feinberg, 'Human Duties and Animal Rights', especially 53 ff.

philosophers, and Epicurus, among the ancients, aver—pain is evil, and its opposite, pleasure and freedom from pain, good. As moral agents (and this seems axiomatic), we have a duty to behave in such a way that the effect of our actions is to promote and procure good, so far as possible, and to reduce and minimize evil. That would amount to an obligation to produce pleasure and reduce pain. Now pain is pain wherever and by whomever it is suffered. As a moral agent, I should not consider my pleasure and pain to be of greater consequence in determining a course of action than that of other persons. Thus, by the same token, if animals suffer pain—and among philosophers only strict Cartesians would deny that they do—then we are morally obliged to consider their suffering as much an evil to be minimized by conscientious moral agents as human suffering.[19] Certainly actions of ours which contribute to the suffering of animals, such as hunting them, butchering and eating them, and experimenting on them, are on these assumptions morally reprehensible. Hence, a person who regards himself or herself as not aiming in life to live most selfishly, conveniently, or profitably, but rightly and in accord with practical principle, if convinced by these arguments, should, among other things, cease to eat the flesh of animals, to hunt them, to wear fur, leather clothing, bone ornaments and other articles made from the bodies of animals, to eat eggs and drink milk, if the animal producers of these commodities are retained under inhumane circumstances, and to patronize zoos (as sources of psychological if not physical torment of animals). On the other hand, since certain very simple animals are almost certainly insensible to pleasure and pain, they may and indeed should be treated as morally inconsequential. Nor is there any *moral* reason why trees should be respected or rivers or mountains or anything which is, though living or tributary to life processes, unconscious. The humane moralists, like the moral humanists, draw a firm distinction between those beings worthy of moral consideration and those not. They simply insist upon a different but quite definite cut-off point on the spectrum of natural entities, and accompany their criterion with arguments to show that it is more ethically defensible (granting certain assumptions) and more consistently applicable than that of the moral humanists.[20]

---

[19] Again, Feinberg in 'Human Duties and Animal Rights', 57–9, expresses this point especially forcefully.

[20] John Rodman's comment in 'The Liberation of Nature', 91, is worth repeating here since it has to all appearances received so little attention elsewhere: 'If it would seem arbitrary . . . to find one species claiming a monopoly on intrinsic value by virtue of its allegedly exclusive possession of reason, free will, soul, or some other occult quality, would it not seem almost as arbitrary to find that same species claiming a monopoly on intrinsic value for itself and those species most resembling it (e.g. in type of nervous system and behaviour) by virtue of their common and allegedly exclusive possession of sentience?' Goodpaster ('From Egoism to

THE FIRST PRINCIPLE OF THE LAND ETHIC

The fundamental principle of humane moralism, as we see, is Benthamic. Good is equivalent to pleasure and, more pertinently, evil is equivalent to pain. The presently booming controversy between moral humanists and humane moralists appears, when all the learned dust has settled, to be essentially internecine; at least, the lines of battle are drawn along familiar watersheds of the conceptual terrain.[21] A classical ethical theory, Bentham's, has been refitted and pressed into service to meet relatively new and unprecedented ethically relevant situations—the problems raised especially by factory farming and ever more exotic and frequently ill-conceived scientific research employing animal subjects. Then, those with Thomist, Kantian, Lockian, Moorean, and so forth ethical affiliations have heard the bugle and have risen to arms. It is no wonder that so many academic philosophers have been drawn into the fray. The issues have an apparent newness about them; moreover, they are socially and politically avant-garde. But there is no serious challenge to cherished first prin-

Environmentalism', 29) remarks that in modern moral philosophy 'a fixation on egoism and a consequent loyalty to a model of moral sentiment or reason which in essence generalizes or universalizes that egoism . . . makes it particularly inhospitable to our recent felt need for an environmental ethic. . . . For such an ethic does not readily admit of being reduced to "humanism"—nor does it sit well with any class or generalization model of moral concern'.

[21] John Rodman, 'The Liberation of Nature', 95, comments: 'Why do our "new ethics" seem so old? . . . Because the attempt to produce a "new ethics" by the process of "extension" perpetuates the basic assumptions of the conventional modern paradigm, however much it fiddles with the boundaries.' When the assumptions remain conventional, the boundaries are, in my view, scalar. But they are triangular when both positions are considered in opposition to the land ethic. The scalar relation is especially clear when two other positions, not specifically discussed in the text, the reverence-for-life ethic and pan-moralism, are considered. The reverence-for-life ethic (as I am calling it in deference to Albert Schweitzer) seems to be the next step on the scale after the humane ethic. William Frankena considers it so in 'Ethics and the Environment', Ethics and Problems of the 21st Century, 3–20. W. Murry Hunt ('Are Mere Things Morally Considerable', Environmental Ethics, 2 (1980), 59–65) has gone a step past Schweitzer, and made the bold suggestion that everything should be accorded moral standing, pan-moralism. Hunt's discussion shows clearly that there is a similar logic ('slippery slope' logic) involved in taking each downward step and thus a certain commonality of underlying assumptions among all the ethical types to which the land ethic stands in opposition. Hunt is not unaware that his suggestion may be interpreted as a reductio ad absurdum of the whole matter, but insists that that is not his intent. The land ethic is not part of this linear series of steps and hence may be represented as a point off the scale. The principal difference, as I explain below, is that the land ethic is collective or 'holistic' while the others are distributive or 'atomistic'. Another relevant difference is that moral humanism, humane moralism, reverence-for-life ethics, and the limiting case, pan-moralism, either openly or implicitly espouse a pecking-order model of nature. The land ethic, founded upon an ecological model of nature emphasizing the contributing roles played by various species in the economy of nature, abandons the 'higher'/'lower' ontological and axiological schema, in favour of a functional system of value. The land ethic, in other words, is inclined to establish value distinctions not on the basis of higher and lower orders of being, but on the basis of the importance of organisms, minerals, and so on to

ciples.[22] Hence, without having to undertake any creative ethical reflection or exploration or any re-examination of historical ethical theory, a fresh debate has been stirred up. The familiar historical positions have simply been retrenched, applied, and exercised.

But what about the third (and certainly minority) party to the animal liberation debate? What sort of reasonable and coherent moral theory would at once urge that animals (and plants, soils, and waters) be included in the same class with people as beings to whom ethical consideration is owed and yet not object to some of them being slaughtered (whether painlessly or not) and eaten, others hunted, trapped, and in various other ways seemingly cruelly used? Aldo Leopold provides a concise statement of what might be called the categorical imperative or principal precept of the land ethic: 'A thing is right when it tends to preserve the integrity, stability, and beauty of the biotic community. It is wrong when it tends otherwise.'[23] What is especially noteworthy, and that to which attention should be directed in this proposition, is the idea that the good of the biotic *community* is the ultimate measure of the moral value, the rightness or wrongness, of actions. Thus, to hunt and kill a white-tailed deer in certain districts may not only be ethically permissible, it might actually be a moral requirement, necessary to protect the local environment, taken as a whole, from the disintegrating effects of a cervid population explosion. On the other hand, rare and endangered animals like the lynx should be especially nurtured and preserved. The lynx, cougar, and other wild feline predators, from the neo-Benthamite perspective (if consistently and even-handedly applied) should be regarded as merciless, wanton, and incorrigible murderers of their fellow creatures, who not only kill, it should be added, but cruelly toy with their victims, thus increasing the measure of pain in the world. From the perspective of the land ethic, predators generally should be nurtured and preserved as critically important members of the biotic communities to which they are native. Certain plants similarly, may be overwhelmingly important to the stability, integrity, and beauty of biotic communities, while some animals, such as domestic sheep (allowed perhaps by egalitarian and humane herdspersons to graze freely and to reproduce themselves without being harvested for lamb and mutton) could

---

the biotic community. Some bacteria, for example, may be of greater value to the health or economy of nature than dogs, and thus command more respect.

[22] Rodman, 'The Liberation of Nature', 86, says in reference to Singer's humane ethic that 'the weakness . . . lies in the limitation of its horizon to the late eighteenth and early nineteenth century Utilitarian humane movement [and] its failure to live up to its own noble declaration that "philosophy ought to question the basic assumptions of the age".'

[23] Leopold, *Sand County Almanac*, 224–5.

be a pestilential threat to the natural floral community of a given locale. Thus, the land ethic is logically coherent in demanding at once that moral consideration be given to plants as well as to animals and yet in permitting animals to be killed, trees felled, and so on. In every case the effect upon ecological systems is the decisive factor in the determination of the ethical quality of actions. Well-meaning actions from the point of view of neo-Benthamite ethics may be regarded as morally wanton from the point of view of land ethics, and vice versa. An example of the former, in addition to those already mentioned, is turning dairy cows out to pasture in a wood lot situated on a steep slope overlooking a trout stream (for the sake of the shady comfort and dietary variety of the cattle) with ruinous impact upon the floral and wildlife community native to the woods, the fish and benthic organisms of the stream, and the microbic life and the physiochemical structure of the soil itself. An example of the latter is trapping or otherwise removing beaver (to all appearances very sensitive and intelligent animals) and their dams to eliminate siltation in an otherwise free-flowing and clear-running stream (for the sake of the complex community of insects, native fish, heron, osprey, and other avian predators of aquatic life which on the anthropocentric scale of consciousness are 'lower' life forms than beaver).

THE LAND ETHIC AND THE ECOLOGICAL POINT OF VIEW

The philosophical context of the land ethic and its conceptual foundation is clearly the body of empirical experience and theory which is summed up in the term *ecology*. The spectre of the naturalistic fallacy hovers around any claim to discover values in facts (and/or, probably, in scientific theories as well), but notwithstanding the naturalistic fallacy (or the fact/value lacuna), which is essentially a logical problem for formal ethics, there appears very often to be at least a strongly compelling psychological connection between the way the world is imagined or conceived and what state of things is held to be good or bad, what ways of behaving are right or wrong, and what responsibilities and obligations we, as moral agents, acknowledge.[24]

---

[24] Anthropologist Clifford Geertz ('Ethos, World View, and the Analysis of Sacred Symbols', in Clifford Geertz, ed., *The Interpretation of Culture* (New York: Basic Books, 1973), 127) remarks that in cultures the world over 'the powerfully coercive "ought" is felt to grow out of a comprehensive factual "is".... The tendency to synthesize world view and ethos at some level, if not logically necessary, is at least empirically coercive; if it is not philosophically justified, it is at least pragmatically universal.' Rodman, 'The Liberation of Nature', 96, laments the preoccupation of modern moral philosophy with the naturalistic fallacy, and comments that 'thanks to this, the quest for an ethics is reduced to prattle about "values" taken in abstraction from the "facts" of "experience" the notion of an ethics as an organic ethos, a way of life, remains lost to us.'

Since ecology focuses upon the relationships between and among things, it inclines its students toward a more holistic vision of the world. Before the rather recent emergence of ecology as a science the landscape appeared to be, one might say, a collection of objects, some of them alive, some conscious, but all the same, an aggregate, a plurality of separate individuals. With this atomistic representation of things it is no wonder that moral issues might be understood as competing and mutually contradictory clashes of the 'rights' of separate individuals, each separately pursuing its 'interests'. Ecology has made it possible to apprehend the same landscape as an articulate unity (without the least hint of mysticism or ineffability). Ordinary organic bodies have articulated and discernible parts (limbs, various organs, myriad cells); yet, because of the character of the network of relations among those parts, they form in a perfectly familiar sense a second-order whole. Ecology makes it possible to see land, similarly, as a unified system of integrally related parts, as, so to speak, a third-order organic whole.[25]

Another analogy that has helped ecologists to convey the particular holism which their science brings to reflective attention is that land is integrated as a human community is integrated. The various parts of the 'biotic community' (individual animals and plants) depend upon one another *economically* so that the system as such acquires distinct characteristics of its own. Just as it is possible to characterize and define collectively peasant societies, agrarian communities, industrial complexes, capitalist, communist, and socialist economic systems, and so on, ecology characterizes and defines various biomes as desert, savanna, wetland, tundra, woodland, and other communities, each with its particular 'professions', or 'niches'.

Now we may think that among the duties we as moral agents have toward ourselves is the duty of self-preservation, which may be interpreted as a duty to maintain our own organic integrity. It is not uncommon in historical moral theory, further, to find that, in addition to those peculiar responsibilities we have in relation both to ourselves and to other persons severally, we also have a duty to behave in ways that do not harm the fabric of society *per se*. The land ethic, in similar fashion, calls our attention to the recently discovered integrity—in other words, the unity—of the biota and posits duties binding upon moral agents in relation to that whole. Whatever the strictly formal logical connections between the concept of a social community and moral responsibility, there appears to be a strong psychological bond between that idea and conscience. Hence, the repre-

---

[25] By 'first-', 'second-', and 'third-' order wholes I intend, paradigmatically, single cell organisms, multi-cell organisms, and biocenoses, respectively.

sentation of the natural environment as, in Leopold's terms, 'one humming community' (or, less consistently in his discussion, a third-order organic being) brings into play, whether rationally or not, those stirrings of conscience which we feel in relation to delicately complex, functioning social and organic systems.[26]

The neo-Benthamite humane moralists have, to be sure, digested one of the metaphysical implications of modern biology. They insist that human beings must be understood continuously with the rest of organic nature. People are (and are only) animals, and much of the rhetorical energy of the animal liberation movement is spent in fighting a rearguard action for this aspect of Darwinism against those philosophers who still cling to the dream of a special metaphysical status for people in the order of 'creation'. To this extent the animal liberation movement is biologically enlightened and argues from the taxonomical and evolutionary continuity of man and beast to moral standing for some non-human animals. Indeed, pain, in their view the very substance of evil, is something that is conspicuously common to people and other sensitive animals, something that we as people experience not in virtue of our meta-simian cerebral capabilities, but because of our participation in a more generally animal, limbic-based consciousness. *If* it is pain and suffering that is the ultimate evil besetting human life, and this not in virtue of our humanity but in virtue of our animality, then it seems only fair to promote freedom from pain for those animals who share with us in this mode of experience and to grant them rights similar to ours as a means to this end.

Recent ethological studies of other primates, cetaceans, and so on, are not infrequently cited to drive the point home, but the biological information of the animal liberation movement seems to extend no further than this—the continuity of human with other animal life forms. The more recent ecological perspective especially seems to be ignored by humane moralists. The holistic outlook of ecology and the associated value

[26] 'Some Fundamentals of Conservation in the Southwest', composed in the 1920s but unpublished until it appeared last year (*Environmental Ethics*, 1 (1979), 131–41), shows that the organic analogy, conceptually representing the nature of the whole resulting from ecological relationships, antedates the community analogy in Leopold's thinking, so far at least as its moral implications are concerned. 'The Land Ethic' of *Sand County Almanac* employs almost exclusively the community analogy but a rereading of 'The Land Ethic' in the light of 'Some Fundamentals' reveals that Leopold did not entirely abandon the organic analogy in favour of the community analogy. For example, toward the end of 'The Land Ethic' Leopold talks about 'land health' and 'land the collective organism' (p. 258). William Morton Wheeler, *Essays in Philosophical Biology* (New York: Russell and Russell, 1939), and Lewis Thomas, *Lives of a Cell* (New York: Viking Press, 1974), provide extended discussions of holistic approaches to social, ethical, and environmental problems. Kenneth Goodpaster, almost alone among academic philosophers, has explored the possibility of a holistic environmental ethical system in 'From Egoism to Environmentalism'.

premium conferred upon the biotic community, its beauty, integrity, and stability may simply not have penetrated the thinking of the animal liberationists, or it could be that to include it would involve an intolerable contradiction with the Benthamite foundations of their ethical theory. Bentham's view of the 'interests of the community' was bluntly reductive. With his characteristic bluster, Bentham wrote, 'The community is a fictitious *body* composed of the individual persons who are considered as constituting as it were its *members*. The interest of the community then is what?—the sum of the interests of the several members who compose it.'[27] Bentham's very simile—the community is like a body composed of members—gives the lie to his reduction of its interests to the sum of its parts taken severally. The interests of a person are not those of his or her cells summed up and averaged out. Our organic health and well-being, for example, requires vigorous exercise and metabolic stimulation which cause stress and often pain to various parts of the body and a more rapid turnover in the life cycle of our individual cells. For the sake of the person taken as whole, some parts may be, as it were, unfairly sacrificed. On the level of social organization, the interests of society may not always coincide with the sum of the interests of its parts. Discipline, sacrifice, and individual restraint are often necessary in the social sphere to maintain social integrity as within the bodily organism. A society, indeed, is particularly vulnerable to disintegration when its members become preoccupied totally with their own particular interests, and ignore those distinct and independent interests of the community as a whole. One example, unfortunately our own society, is altogether too close at hand to be examined with strict academic detachment. The United States seems to pursue uncritically a social policy of reductive utilitarianism, aimed at promoting the happiness of all its members severally. Each special interest accordingly clamours more loudly to be satisfied while the community as a whole becomes noticeably more and more infirm economically, environmentally, and politically.

The humane moralists, whether or not they are consciously and deliberately following Bentham on this particular, nevertheless, in point of fact, are committed to the welfare of certain kinds of animals distributively or reductively in applying their moral concern for non-human beings.[28] They

---

[27] Jeremy Bentham, *An Introduction to the Principles of Morals and Legislation* (Oxford: Clarendon Press, 1823), chap. 1, s. 4.

[28] This has been noticed and lamented by Alistaire S. Gunn ('Why Should We Care About Rare Species?', *Environmental Ethics*, 2 (1980), 36) who comments, 'Environmentalism seems incompatible with the "Western" obsession with individualism, which leads us to resolve questions about our treatment of animals by appealing to the essentially atomistic, competitive notion of rights.' John Rodman, 'The Liberation of Nature', 89, says practically the same thing:

lament the treatment of animals, most frequently farm and laboratory animals, and plead the special interests of these beings. We might ask, from the perspective of the land ethic, what the effect upon the natural environment taken as whole would be if domestic animals were actually liberated? There is, almost certainly, very little real danger that this might actually happen, but it would be instructive to speculate on the ecological consequences.

ETHICAL HOLISM

Before we take up this question, however, some points of interest remain to be considered on the matter of a holistic versus a reductive environmental ethic. To pit the one against the other as I have done without further qualification would be mistaken. A society is constituted by its members, an organic body by its cells, and the ecosystem by the plants, animals, minerals, fluids, and gases which compose it. One cannot affect a system as a whole without affecting at least some of its components. An environmental ethic which takes as its *summum bonum* the integrity, stability, and beauty of the biotic community is not conferring moral standing on something *else* besides plants, animals, soils, and waters. Rather, the former, the good of the community as a whole, serves as a standard for the assessment of the relative value and relative ordering of its constitutive parts and therefore provides a means of adjudicating the often mutually contradictory demands of the parts considered separately for *equal* consideration. If diversity does indeed contribute to stability, then specimens of rare and endangered species, for example, have a prima facie claim to preferential consideration from the perspective of the land ethic. Animals of those species, which, like the honey-bee, function in ways critically important to the economy of nature, moreover, would be granted a greater claim to moral attention than psychologically more complex and sensitive ones, say, rabbits and voles, which seem to be plentiful, globally distributed, reproductively efficient, and only routinely integrated into the natural

'The moral atomism that focuses on individual animals and their subjective experiences does not seem well adapted to coping with ecological systems.' Peter Singer has in fact actually stressed the individual focus of his humane ethic in 'Not for Humans Only: The Place of Non-humans in Environmental Issues' (*Ethics and Problems of the 21st Century*, 191–206) as if it were a virtue! More revealingly, the only grounds that he can discover for moral concern over species, since species are *per se* not sensible entities (and that is the extent of his notion of an ethically relevant consideration), are anthropocentric grounds, human aesthetics, environmental integrity for humans, and so forth.

economy. Animals and plants, mountains, rivers, seas, the atmosphere are the immediate practical beneficiaries of the land ethic. The well-being of the biotic community, the biosphere as a whole, cannot be logically separated from their survival and welfare.

Some suspicion may arise at this point that the land ethic is ultimately grounded in human interests, not in those of non-human natural entities. Just as we might prefer a sound and attractive house to one in the opposite condition, so the 'goodness' of a whole, stable, and beautiful environment seems rather to be of the instrumental, not the intrinsic, variety. The question of ultimate value is a very sticky one for environmental as well as for all ethics and cannot be fully addressed here. It is my view that there can be no value apart from an evaluator, that all value is as it were in the eye of the beholder. The value that is attributed to the ecosystem, therefore, is humanly dependent or (allowing that other living things may take a certain delight in the well-being of the whole of things, or that the gods may) at least dependent upon some variety of morally and aesthetically sensitive consciousness. Granting this, however, there is a further, very crucial distinction to be drawn. It is possible that while things may only have value because we (or someone) values them, they may nonetheless be valued for themselves as well as for the contribution they might make to the realization of our (or someone's) interests. Children are valued for themselves by most parents. Money, on the other hand, has only an instrumental or indirect value. Which sort of value has the health of the biotic community and its members severally for Leopold and the land ethic? It is especially difficult to separate these two general sorts of value, the one of moral significance, the other merely selfish, when something that may be valued in both ways at once is the subject of consideration. Are pets, for example, well-treated, like children, for the sake of themselves, or, like mechanical appliances, because of the sort of services they provide their owners? Is a healthy biotic community something we value because we are so utterly and (to the biologically well-informed) so obviously dependent upon it not only for our happiness but for our very survival, or may we also perceive it disinterestedly as having an independent worth? Leopold insists upon a non-instrumental value for the biotic community and *mutatis mutandis* for its constituents. According to Leopold, collective enlightened self-interest on the part of human beings does not go far enough; the land ethic in his opinion (and no doubt this reflects his own moral intuitions) requires 'love, respect, and admiration for land, and a high regard for its value'. The land ethic, in Leopold's view, creates 'obligations over and above self-interest'. And, 'obligations have no meaning without conscience, and the problem we face is the extension of social conscience from people to land'.[29] If, in other words, any genuine ethic is possible, if it is possible to value *people* for the sake of themselves, then it is equally possible to value *land* in the same way.

Some indication of the genuinely biocentric value orientation of ethical environmentalism is indicated in what otherwise might appear to be gratuitous misanthropy. The biospheric perspective does not exempt *Homo sapiens* from moral evaluation in relation to the well-being of the community of nature taken as a whole. The preciousness of individual deer, as of any other specimen, is inversely proportional to the population of the species. Environmentalists, however reluctantly and painfully, do not omit to apply the same logic to their own kind. As omnivores, the population of human beings should, perhaps, be roughly twice that of bears, allowing for differences of size. A global population of more than four billion persons and showing no signs of an orderly decline presents an alarming prospect to humanists, but it is at present a global disaster (the more per capita prosperity, indeed, the more disastrous it appears) for the biotic community. If the land ethic were only a means of managing nature for the sake of man, misleadingly phrased in moral terminology, then man would be considered as having an ultimate value essentially different from that of his 'resources'. The extent of misanthropy in modern environmentalism thus may be taken as a measure of the degree to which it is biocentric. Edward Abbey in his enormously popular *Desert Solitaire* bluntly states that he would sooner shoot a man than a snake.[30] Abbey may not be simply depraved; this is perhaps only his way of dramatically making the point that the human population has become so disproportionate from the biological point of view that if one had to choose between a specimen of *Homo sapiens* and a specimen of a rare even if unattractive species, the choice would be moot. Among academicians, Garrett Hardin, a human ecologist by discipline who has written extensively on ethics, environmental and otherwise, has shocked philosophers schooled in the preciousness of human life with his 'lifeboat' and 'survival' ethics and his 'wilderness economics'. In context of the latter, Hardin recommends limiting access to wilderness by criteria of hardiness and woodcraft and would permit no emergency roads or airborne rescue vehicles to violate the pristine purity of wilderness areas. If a wilderness adventurer should have a serious accident, Hardin recommends that he or she get out on his or her own or die in the attempt. Danger, from the strictly human-centred,

[29] Leopold, *Sand County Almanac*, 223 and 209.
[30] Edward Abbey, *Desert Solitaire* (New York: Ballantine Books, 1968), 20.

psychological perspective, is part of the wilderness experience, Hardin argues, but in all probability his more important concern is to protect from mechanization the remnants of wild country that remain even if the price paid is the incidental loss of human life, which, from the perspective once more of the biologist, is a commodity altogether too common in relation to wildlife and to wild landscapes.[31] Hardin's recommendation of harsh policies in relation to desperate, starving nations is based strictly upon a utilitarian calculus, but reading between the lines, one can also detect the biologist's chagrin concerning the ecological dislocations which a human population explosion have already created and which if permitted to continue unchecked could permanently impoverish (if not altogether extinguish) an already stressed and overburdened economy of nature.[32]

Finally, it may be wondered if anything ought properly to be denominated an 'ethic' which on the basis of an impersonal, not to say abstract, good, 'the integrity, stability, and beauty of the biotic community', permits and even requires *preferential* consideration. A 'decision procedure', to give it for the moment a neutral rubric, which lavishes loving and expensive care on whooping cranes and (from the Benthamite point of view, villainous) timber wolves while simultaneously calculating the correct quotas for 'harvesting' mallards and ruffed grouse should hardly be dignified, it might be argued, by the term *ethic*. Modern systems of ethics have, it must be admitted, considered the principle of the equality of persons to be inviolable. This is true, for example, of both major schools of modern ethics, the utilitarian school going back to Bentham and Mill, and the deontological, originating with Kant. The land ethic manifestly does not accord equal moral worth to each and every member of the biotic community; the moral worth of individuals (including, take note, human individuals) is relative, to be assessed in accordance with the particular relation of each to the collective entity which Leopold called 'land'.

There is, however, a classical Western ethic, with the best philosophical credentials, which assumes a similar holistic posture (with respect to the social moral sphere). I have in mind Plato's moral and social philosophy. Indeed, two of the same analogies figuring in the conceptual foundations of the Leopold land ethic appear in Plato's value theory.[33] From the

---

[31] Garrett Hardin, 'The Economics of Wilderness', *Natural History*, 78 (1969), 173–7. Hardin is blunt: 'Making great and spectacular efforts to save the life of an individual makes sense only when there is a shortage of people. I have not lately heard that there is a shortage of people', 176.

[32] See e.g. Garrett Hardin, 'Living on a Lifeboat', *BioScience*, 24 (1974), 561–8.

[33] In *Republic*, 5 Plato directly says that 'the best governed state most nearly resembles an organism' (462d) and that there is no 'greater evil for a state than the thing that distracts it and makes it many instead of one, or a greater good than that which binds it together and makes it

ecological perspective, according to Leopold as I have pointed out, land is like an organic body or like a human society. According to Plato, body, soul, and society have similar structures and corresponding virtues.[34] The goodness of each is a function of its structure or organization and the relative value of the parts or constituents of each is calculated according to the contribution made to the integrity, stability, and beauty of each, whole.[35] In the *Republic*, Plato, in the very name of virtue and justice, is notorious for, among other things, requiring infanticide for a child whose only offence was being born without the sanction of the state, making presents to the enemy of guardians who allow themselves to be captured alive in combat, and radically restricting the practice of medicine to the dressing of wounds and the curing of seasonal maladies on the principle that the infirm and chronically ill not only lead miserable lives but contribute nothing to the good of the polity.[36] Plato, indeed, seems to regard individual human life and certainly human pain and suffering with complete indifference. On the other hand, he shrinks from nothing so long as it seems to him to be in the interest of the community. Among the apparently inhuman recommendations that he makes to better the community are a programme of eugenics involving a phoney lottery (so that those whose natural desires are frustrated, while breeding proceeds from the best stock as in a kennel or stable, will blame chance, not the design of the rulers), the destruction of the pair-bond and nuclear family (in the interests of greater military and bureaucratic efficiency and group solidarity), and the utter abolition of private property.[37]

When challenged with the complaint that he is ignoring individual human happiness (and the happiness of those belonging to the most privileged class at that), he replies that it is the well-being of the community as a whole, not that of any person or special class, at which his legislation aims.[38] This principle is readily accepted, first of all, in our attitude toward

one' (462a). Goodpaster in 'From Egoism to Environmentalism', 30, has in a general way anticipated this connection: 'The oft-repeated plea by some ecologists and environmentalists that our thinking needs to be less atomistic and more "holistic" translates in the present context into a plea for a more embracing object of moral consideration. In a sense it represents a plea to return to the richer Greek conception of man by nature social and not intelligibly removable from his social and political context though it goes beyond the Greek conception in emphasizing that societies too need to be understood in a context, an ecological context, and that it is this larger whole that is the "bearer of value".'

[34] See especially *Republic* 4.444a–e.
[35] For a particularly clear statement by Plato of the idea that the goodness of anything is a matter of the fitting order of the parts in relation to respective wholes see *Gorgias* 503d–507a.
[36] Cf., *Republic* 5.461c (infanticide); 468a (disposition of captives); 3.416d–406e (medicine).
[37] Cf., *Republic* 5.459a–406e (eugenics, non-family life and child rearing), *Republic* 3.416d–417b (private property).
[38] Cf., *Republic* 4.419a–421c and *Republic* 7.419d–521b.

the body, he reminds us—the separate interests of the parts of which we acknowledge to be subordinate to the health and well-being of the whole—and secondly, assuming that we accept his faculty psychology, in our attitude toward the soul, whose multitude of desires must be disciplined, restrained, and, in the case of some, altogether repressed in the interest of personal virtue and a well-ordered and morally responsible life. Given these formal similarities to Plato's moral philosophy, we may conclude that the land ethic—with its holistic good and its assignment of differential values to the several parts of the environment irrespective of their intelligence, sensibility, degree of complexity, or any other characteristic discernible in the parts considered separately—is somewhat foreign to modern systems of ethical philosophy, but perfectly familiar in the broader context of classical Western ethical philosophy. If, therefore, Plato's system of public and private justice is properly an 'ethical' system, then so is the land ethic in relation to environmental virtue and excellence.[39]

REAPPRAISING DOMESTICATION

Among the last philosophical remarks penned by Aldo Leopold before his untimely death in 1948 is the following: 'Perhaps such a shift of values [as implied by the attempt to weld together the concepts of ethics and ecology] can be achieved by reappraising things unnatural, tame, and confined in terms of things natural, wild, and free.'[40] John Muir, in a similar spirit of reappraisal, had noted earlier the difference between the wild mountain sheep of the Sierra and the ubiquitous domestic variety. The latter, which

---

[39] After so much strident complaint has been registered here about the lack of freshness in self-proclaimed 'new' environmental ethics (which turn out to be 'old' ethics retreaded) there is surely an irony in comparing the (apparently brand new) Leopold land ethic to Plato's ethical philosophy. There is, however, an important difference. The humane moralists have simply revived and elaborated Bentham's historical application of hedonism to questions regarding the treatment of animals with the capacity of sensibility. There is nothing new but the revival and elaboration. Plato, on the other hand, never develops anything faintly resembling an *environmental* ethic. Plato never reached an ecological view of living nature. The wholes of his universe are body, soul, society and cosmos. Plato is largely concerned, if not exclusively, with moral problems involving individual human beings in a political context and he has the temerity to insist that the good of the whole transcends individual claims. (Even in the *Crito* Plato is sympathetic to the city's claim to put Socrates to death, however unjust the verdict against him.) Plato thus espouses a holistic ethic which is valuable as a (very different) paradigm to which the Leopold land ethic, which is also holistic but in a relation to a very different whole, may be compared. It is interesting further that some (but not all) of the analogies which Plato finds useful to convey his holistic social values are also useful to Leopold in his effort to set out a land ethic.

[40] Leopold, *Sand County Almanac*, ix.

Muir described as 'hooved locusts', were only, in his estimation, 'half alive' in comparison with their natural and autonomous counterparts.[41] One of the more distressing aspects of the animal liberation movement is the failure of almost all its exponents to draw a sharp distinction between the very different plights (and rights) of wild and domestic animals.[42] But this distinction lies at the very centre of the land ethic. Domestic animals are creations of man. They are living artefacts, but artefacts nevertheless, and they constitute yet another mode of extension of the works of man into the ecosystem. From the perspective of the land ethic a herd of cattle, sheep, or pigs is as much or more a ruinous blight on the landscape as a fleet of four-wheel-drive off-road vehicles. There is thus something profoundly incoherent (and insensitive as well) in the complaint of some animal liberationists that the 'natural behaviour' of chickens and male calves is cruelly frustrated on factory farms. It would make almost as much sense to speak of the natural behaviour of tables and chairs.

Here a serious disanalogy (which no one to my knowledge has yet pointed out) becomes clearly evident between the liberation of Blacks from slavery (and more recently, from civil inequality) and the liberation of animals from a similar sort of subordination and servitude. Black slaves remained, as it were, metaphysically autonomous: they were by nature, if not by convention, free beings quite capable of living on their own. They could not be enslaved for more than a historial interlude; the strength of the force of their freedom was too great. They could, in other words, be retained only by a continuous counterforce, and only temporarily. This

---

[41] See John Muir, 'The Wild Sheep of California', *Overland Monthly*, 12 (1874), 359.

[42] Roderick Nash (*Wilderness and the American Mind*, rev. edn. (New Haven and London: Yale University Press, 1973), 2) suggests that the English word *wild* is ultimately derived from *will*. A wild being is thus a willed one—'self-willed, wilful, or uncontrollable'. The humane moralists' indifference to this distinction is rather dramatically represented in Regan's 'Animal Rights, Human Wrongs' (99–104) which begins with a bid for the reader's sympathy through a vivid description of four concrete episodes of human cruelty toward animals. I suspect that Regan's intent is to give examples of four principal categories of animal abuse at the hands of man: whaling, traffic in zoo captives, questionable scientific experimentation involving unquestionable torture, and intensive meat production. But his illustrations, divided according to precepts central to land ethics, concern two episodes of wanton slaughter of *wild* animals, a blue whale and a gibbon, aggravated by the consideration that both are specimens of disappearing species, and two episodes of routine cruelty toward *domestic* animals, a 'bobby calf' (destined to become veal) and a laboratory rabbit. The misery of the calf and the agony of the rabbit are, to be sure, reprehensible, from the perspective of the land ethic, for reasons I explain shortly, but it is, I think, a trivialization of the deeper environmental and ecological issues involved in modern whaling and wildlife traffic to discuss the exploitation and destruction of blue whales and gibbon apes as if they are wrong for the same reasons that the treatment of laboratory rabbits and male dairy calves is wrong. The inhumane treatment of penned domestics should not be, I suggest, even discussed in the same context as whaling and wildlife traffic; it is a disservice to do so.

is equally true of caged wild animals. African cheetahs in American and European zoos are captive, not indentured, beings. But this is not true of cows, pigs, sheep, and chickens. They have been bred to docility, tractability, stupidity, and dependency. It is literally meaningless to suggest that they be liberated. It is, to speak in hyperbole, a logical impossibility. Certainly it is a practical impossibility. Imagine what would happen if the people of the world became morally persuaded that domestic animals were to be regarded as oppressed and enslaved persons and accordingly set free. In one scenario we might imagine that like former American black slaves they would receive the equivalent of forty acres and a mule and be turned out to survive on their own. Feral cattle and sheep would hang around farm outbuildings waiting forlornly to be sheltered and fed, or would graze aimlessly through their abandoned and deteriorating pastures. Most would starve or freeze as soon as winter settled in. Reproduction, which had been assisted over many countless generations by their former owners, might be altogether impossible in the feral state for some varieties, and the care of infants would be an art not so much lost as never acquired. And so in a very short time, after much suffering and agony, these species would become abruptly extinct. Or, in another scenario beginning with the same simple emancipation from human association, survivors of the first massive die-off of untended livestock might begin to recover some of their remote wild ancestral genetic traits and become smaller, leaner, heartier, and smarter versions of their former selves. An actual contemporary example is afforded by the feral mustangs ranging over parts of the American West. In time such animals as these would become (just as the mustangs are now) competitors both with their former human masters and (with perhaps more tragic consequences) indigenous wildlife for food and living space.

Foreseeing these and other untoward consequences of immediate and unplanned liberation of livestock, a human population grown morally more perfect than at present might decide that they had a duty, accumulated over thousands of years, to continue to house and feed as before their former animal slaves (whom they had rendered genetically unfit to care for themselves), but not to butcher them or make other ill use of them, including frustrating their 'natural' behaviour, their right to copulate freely, reproduce, and enjoy the delights of being parents. People, no longer having meat to eat, would require more vegetables, cereals, and other plant foods, but the institutionalized animal incompetents would still consume all the hay and grains (and more since they would no longer be slaughtered) than they did formerly. This would require clearing more land and bringing it into agricultural production with further loss of wildlife habitat and ecological destruction. Another possible scenario might be a decision on the part of people not literally to liberate domestic animals but simply to cease to breed and raise them. When the last livestock have been killed and eaten (or permitted to die 'natural' deaths), people would become vegetarians and domestic livestock species would thus be rendered deliberately extinct (just as they had been deliberately created). But there is surely some irony in an outcome in which the beneficiaries of a humane extension of conscience are destroyed in the process of being saved.[43]

The land ethic, it should be emphasized, as Leopold has sketched it, provides for the *rights* of non-human natural beings to a share in the life processes of the biotic community. The conceptual foundation of such rights, however, is less conventional than natural, based as one might say, upon evolutionary and ecological entitlement. Wild animals and native plants have a particular place in nature, according to the land ethic, which domestic animals (because they are products of human art and represent an extended presence of human beings in the natural world) do not have. The land ethic, in sum, is as much opposed, though on different grounds, to commercial traffic in wildlife, zoos, the slaughter of whales and other marine mammals, and so forth, as is the humane ethic. Concern for animal (and plant) rights and well-being is as fundamental to the land ethic as to the humane ethic, but the difference between naturally evolved and humanly bred species is an essential consideration for the one, though not for the other.

The 'shift of values' which results from our 'reappraising things unnatural, tame, and confined in terms of things natural, wild, and free' is especially dramatic when we reflect upon the definitions of *good* and *evil* espoused by Bentham and Mill and uncritically accepted by their contemporary followers. Pain and pleasure seem to have nothing at all to do with good and evil if our appraisal is taken from the vantage point of ecological biology. Pain in particular is primarily information. In animals, it informs the central nervous system of stress, irritation, or trauma in outlying regions of the organism. A certain level of pain under optimal organic circumstances is indeed desirable as an indicator of exertion—of the degree of exertion needed to maintain fitness, to stay in shape, and of a level of exertion beyond which it would be dangerous to go. An arctic wolf in pursuit of a caribou may experience pain in her feet or chest because of the rigours of the chase. There is nothing bad or wrong in that.

---

[43] John Rodman, 'The Liberation of Nature', 101, castigates Singer for failing to consider what the consequences of wholesale animal liberation might be. With tongue in cheek he congratulates Singer for taking a step toward the elimination of a more subtle evil, the genetic debasement of other animal beings, that is, domestication *per se*.

Or, consider a case of injury. Suppose that a person in the course of a wilderness excursion sprains an ankle. Pain informs him or her of the injury and by its intensity the amount of further stress the ankle may endure in the course of getting to safety. Would it be better if pain were not experienced upon injury or, taking advantage of recent technology, anaesthetized? Pleasure appears to be, for the most part (unfortunately it is not always so) a reward accompanying those activities which contribute to organic maintenance, such as the pleasures associated with eating, drinking, grooming, and so on, or those which contribute to social solidarity like the pleasures of dancing, conversation, teasing, and so forth, or those which contribute to the continuation of the species, such as the pleasures of sexual activity and of being parents. The doctrine that life is the happier the freer it is from pain and that the happiest life conceivable is one in which there is continuous pleasure uninterrupted by pain is biologically preposterous. A living mammal which experienced no pain would be one which had a lethal dysfunction of the nervous system. The idea that pain is evil and ought to be minimized or eliminated is as primitive a notion as that of a tyrant who puts to death messengers bearing bad news on the supposition that thus his well-being and security is improved.[44]

More seriously still, the value commitments of the humane movement seem at bottom to betray a world-denying or rather a life-loathing philosophy. The natural world, as actually constituted, is one in which one being lives at the expense of others.[45] Each organism, in Darwin's metaphor, struggles to maintain its own organic integrity. The more complex animals seem to experience (judging from our own case, and reasoning from analogy) appropriate and adaptive psychological accompaniments to organic existence. There is a palpable passion for self-preservation. There are desire, pleasure in the satisfaction of desires, acute agony attending injury, frustration, and chronic dread of death. But these experiences are the psychological substance of living. To live *is* to be anxious about life, to

---

[44] A particularly strong statement of the ultimate commitment of the neo-Benthamites is found in Feinberg's 'Human Duties and Animal Rights', 57: 'We regard pain and suffering as an intrinsic evil . . . simply because they are pain and suffering. . . . The question "What's wrong with pain anyway?" is never allowed to arise.' I shall raise it. I herewith declare in all soberness that I see nothing wrong with pain. It is a marvellous method, honed by the evolutionary process, of conveying important organic information. I think it was the late Alan Watts who somewhere remarks that upon being asked if he did not think there was too much pain in the world replied, 'No, I think there's just enough.'

[45] Paul Shepard, 'Animal Rights and Human Rites', 37, comments that 'the humanitarian's projection onto nature of illegal murder and the rights of civilized people to safety not only misses the point but is exactly contrary to fundamental ecological reality: the structure of nature is a sequence of killings.'

feel pain and pleasure in a fitting mixture, and sooner or later to die. That is the way the system works. If nature as a whole is good, then pain and death are also good. Environmental ethics in general require people to play fair in the natural system. The neo-Benthamites have in a sense taken the uncourageous approach. People have attempted to exempt themselves from the life–death reciprocities of natural processes and from ecological limitations in the name of a prophylactic ethic of maximizing rewards (pleasure) and minimizing unwelcome information (pain). To be fair, the humane moralists seem to suggest that we should attempt to project the same values into the non-human animal world and to widen the charmed circle—no matter that it would be biologically unrealistic to do so or biologically ruinous if, per impossible, such an environmental ethic were implemented.

There is another approach. Rather than imposing our alienation from nature and natural processes and cycles of life on other animals, we human beings could reaffirm our participation in nature by accepting life as it is given without a sugar coating. Instead of imposing artificial legalities, rights, and so on on nature, we might take the opposite course and accept and affirm natural biological laws, principles, and limitations in the human personal and social spheres. Such appears to have been the posture toward life of tribal peoples in the past. The chase was relished with its dangers, rigours, and hardships as well as its rewards; animal flesh was respectfully consumed; a tolerance for pain was cultivated; virtue and magnanimity were prized; lithic, floral, and faunal spirits were worshipped; population was routinely optimized by sexual continency, abortion, infanticide, and stylized warfare; and other life forms, although certainly appropriated, were respected as fellow players in a magnificent and awesome, if not altogether idyllic, drama of life. It is impossible today to return to the symbiotic relationship of Stone Age man to the natural environment, but the ethos of this by far the longest era of human existence could be abstracted and integrated with a future human culture seeking a viable and mutually beneficial relationship with nature. Personal, social, and environmental health would, accordingly, receive a premium value rather than comfort, self-indulgent pleasure, and anaesthetic insulation from pain. Sickness would be regarded as a worse evil than death. The pursuit of health or wellness at the personal, social, and environmental levels would require self-discipline in the form of simple diet, vigorous exercise, conservation, and social responsibility.

Leopold's prescription for the realization and implementation of the land ethic—the reappraisal of things unnatural, tame, and confined in terms of things natural, wild, and free—does not stop, in other words, with a reappraisal of non-human domestic animals in terms of their wild (or willed) counterparts; the human ones should be similarly reappraised. This means, among other things, the reappraisal of the comparatively recent values and concerns of 'civilized' *Homo sapiens* in terms of those of our 'savage' ancestors.[46] Civilization has insulated and alienated us from the rigours and challenges of the natural environment. The hidden agenda of the humane ethic is the imposition of the anti-natural prophylactic ethos of comfort and soft pleasure on an even wider scale. The land ethic, on the other hand, requires a shrinkage, if at all possible, of the domestic sphere; it rejoices in a recrudescence of wilderness and a renaissance of tribal cultural experience.

The converse of those goods and evils, axiomatic to the humane ethic, may be illustrated and focused by the consideration of a single issue raised by the humane morality: a vegetarian diet. Savage people seem to have had, if the attitudes and values of surviving tribal cultures are representative, something like an intuitive grasp of ecological relationships and certainly a morally charged appreciation of eating. There is nothing more intimate than eating, more symbolic of the connectedness of life, and more mysterious. What we eat and how we eat is by no means an insignificant ethical concern.

From the ecological point of view, for human beings universally to become vegetarians is tantamount to a shift of trophic niche from omnivore with carnivorous preferences to herbivore. The shift is a downward one on the trophic pyramid, which in effect shortens those food-chains terminating with man. It represents an increase in the efficiency of the conversion of solar energy from plant to human biomass, and thus, by bypassing animal intermediates, increases available food resources for human beings. The human population would probably, as past trends overwhelmingly suggest, expand in accordance with the potential thus afforded. The net result would be fewer non-human beings and more human beings, who, of course, have requirements of life far more elaborate than even those of domestic animals, requirements which would tax other 'natural resources' (trees for shelter, minerals mined at the expense of topsoil and its vegetation, and so on) more than under present circumstances. A vegetarian human population is therefore *probably* ecologically catastrophic.

Meat eating, as implied by the foregoing remarks, may be more *ecologically* responsible than a wholly vegetable diet. Meat, however, purchased

---

[46] This matter has been ably and fully explored by Paul Shepard, *The Tender Carnivore and the Sacred Game* (New York: Scribner's Sons, 1973). A more empirical study has been carried out by Marshall Sahlins, *Stone Age Economics* (Chicago: Aldine/Atherton, 1972).

at the supermarket, externally packaged and internally laced with petro-chemicals, fattened in feed lots, slaughtered impersonally, and, in general, mechanically processed from artificial insemination to microwave roaster, is an affront not only to physical metabolism and bodily health but to conscience as well. From the perspective of the land ethic, the immoral aspect of the factory farm has to do far less with the suffering and killing of non-human animals than with the monstrous transformation of living things from an organic to a mechanical mode of being. Animals, begin-ning with the Neolithic Revolution, have been debased through selective breeding, but they have nevertheless remained animals. With the Indus-trial Revolution an even more profound and terrifying transformation has overwhelmed them. They have become, in Ruth Harrison's most apt de-scription, 'animal machines'. The very presence of animals, so emblematic of delicate, complex organic tissue, surrounded by machines, connected to machines, penetrated by machines in research laboratories or crowded together in space-age 'production facilities' is surely the more real and visceral source of our outrage at vivisection and factory farming than the contemplation of the quantity of pain that these unfortunate beings experience. I wish to denounce as loudly as the neo-Benthamites this ghastly abuse of animal life, but also to stress that the pain and suffering of research and agribusiness animals is not greater than that endured by free-living wildlife as a consequence of predation, disease, starvation, and cold—indicating that there is something immoral about vivisection and factory farming which is not an ingredient in the natural lives and deaths of wild beings. That immoral something is the transmogrification of organic to mechanical processes.

Ethical vegetarianism to all appearances insists upon the human con-sumption of plants (in a paradoxical moral gesture toward those animals whose very existence is dependent upon human carnivorousness), even when the tomatoes are grown hydroponically, the lettuce generously coated with chlorinated hydrocarbons, the potatoes pumped up with chemical fertilizers, and the cereals stored with the help of chemical pre-servatives. The land ethic takes as much exception to the transmogrifi-cation of plants by mechanico-chemical means as to that of animals. The important thing, I would think, is not to eat vegetables as opposed to animal flesh, but to resist factory farming in all its manifestations, including especially its liberal application of pesticides, herbicides, and chemical fertilizers to maximize the production of vegetable crops.

The land ethic, with its ecological perspective, helps us to recognize and affirm the organic integrity of self and the untenability of a firm distinction between self and environment. On the ethical question of what to eat, it answers, not vegetables instead of animals, but organically as opposed to mechanico-chemically produced food. Purists like Leopold prefer, in his expression, to get their 'meat from God', that is, to hunt and consume wildlife and to gather wild plant foods, and thus to live within the parameters of the aboriginal human ecological niche.[47] Second best is eating from one's own orchard, garden, hen-house, pigpen, and barnyard. Third best is buying or bartering organic foods from one's neighbours and friends.

CONCLUSION

Philosophical controversy concerning animal liberation/rights has been most frequently represented as a polar dispute between traditional moral humanists and seemingly avant-garde humane moralists. Further, animal liberation has been assumed to be closely allied with environmental ethics, possibly because in Leopold's classical formulation moral standing and indeed rights (of some unspecified sort) are accorded non-human beings, among them animals. The purpose of this discussion has been to distinguish sharply environmental ethics from the animal liberation/rights movement both in theory and practical application and to suggest, thereupon, that there is an underrepresented, but very important, point of view respecting the problem of the moral status of non-human animals. The debate over animal liberation, in short, should be conceived as triangular, not polar, with land ethics or environmental ethics, the third and, in my judgement, the most creative, interesting, and practicable alternative. Indeed, from this third point of view moral humanism and humane moralism appear to have much more in common with one another than either have with environmental or land ethics. On reflection one might even be led to suspect that the noisy debate between these parties has served to drown out the much deeper challenge to 'business-as-usual' ethical philosophy represented by Leopold and his exponents, and to keep ethical philosophy firmly anchored to familiar modern paradigms.

Moral humanism and humane moralism, to restate succinctly the most salient conclusions of this essay, are *atomistic* or distributive in their theory

[47] The expression 'meat from God' occurs twice in *Sand County Almanac*, viii and 166. The expression is usually given a spiritual-metaphorical interpretation: In the Foreword Leopold writes, 'It is here [at the shack] that we seek—and still find—our meat from God'—that is, spiritual satisfaction. Read in light of the second occurrence its meaning more probably is: It is here at the shack that we go hunting—successfully—despite the general decline in game elsewhere. Leopold mentions 'organic farming' as something intimately connected with the land ethic; in the same context he also speaks of 'biotic farming', 222.

of moral value, while environmental ethics (again, at least, as set out in Leopold's outline) is *holistic* or collective. Modern ethical theory, in other words, has consistently located moral value in individuals and set out certain metaphysical reasons for including some individuals and excluding others. Humane moralism remains firmly within this modern convention and centres its attention on the competing criteria for moral standing and rights holding, while environmental ethics locates ultimate value in the biotic community and assigns differential moral value to the constitutive individuals relatively to that standard. This is perhaps the most fundamental theoretical difference between environmental ethics and the ethics of animal liberation.

Allied to this difference are many others. One of the more conspicuous is that in environmental ethics, plants are included within the parameters of the ethical theory as well as animals. Indeed, inanimate entities such as oceans and lakes, mountains, forest, and wetlands are assigned a greater value than individual animals and in a way quite different from systems which accord them moral considerability through a further multiplication of competing individual loci of value and holders of rights.

There are intractable practical differences between environmental ethics and the animal liberation movement. Very different moral obligations follow in respect, most importantly, to domestic animals, the principal beneficiaries of the humane ethic. Environmental ethics sets a very low priority on domestic animals as they very frequently contribute to the erosion of the integrity, stability, and beauty of the biotic communities into which they have been insinuated. On the other hand, animal liberation, if pursued at the practical as well as rhetorical level, would have ruinous consequences on plants, soils, and waters, consequences which could not be directly reckoned according to humane moral theory. As this last remark suggests, the animal liberation/animal rights movement is in the final analysis utterly unpracticable. An imagined society in which all animals capable of sensibility received equal consideration or held rights to equal consideration would be so ludicrous that it might be more appropriately and effectively treated in satire than in philosophical discussion. The land ethic, by contrast, even though its ethical purview is very much wider, is nevertheless eminently practicable, since, by reference to a single good, competing individual claims may be adjudicated and relative values and priorities assigned to the myriad components of the biotic community. This is not to suggest that the implementation of environmental ethics as social policy would be easy. Implementation of the land ethic would require discipline, sacrifice, retrenchment, and massive economic reform, tantamount to a virtual revolution in prevailing attitudes and lifestyles.

Nevertheless, it provides a unified and coherent practical principle and thus a decision procedure at the practical level which a distributive or atomistic ethic may achieve only artificially and so imprecisely as to be practically indeterminate.

III

DUTIES TO ENDANGERED SPECIES

HOLMES ROLSTON III

In the Endangered Species Act, Congress has lamented the lack of 'adequate concern [for] and conservation [of]' species.[1] But neither scientists nor ethicists have fully realized how developing this concern requires an unprecedented mix of biology and ethics. What logic underlies duties involving forms of life? Looking to the past for help, one searches in vain through 3,000 years of philosophy (back at least to Noah!) for any serious reference to endangered species. Among present theories of justice, Harvard philosopher John Rawls asserts, 'The destruction of a whole species can be a great evil,' but also admits that in his theory 'no account is given of right conduct in regard to animals and the rest of nature.'[2] Meanwhile there is an urgency to the issue. The *Global 2000 Report* projects a massive loss of species, up to 20 per cent within a few decades.[3]

DUTIES TO PERSONS CONCERNING SPECIES

The usual way to approach a concern for species is to say that there are no duties directly to endangered species, only duties to other persons concerning species. From a utilitarian standpoint, summarized by Hampshire, the protection of nature and 'the preservation of species are to be aimed at and commended only in so far as human beings are, or will be, emotionally and sentimentally interested'.[4] In an account based on rights, Feinberg reaches a similar conclusion. 'We do have duties to protect threatened species, not duties to the species themselves as such, but rather duties to

Reprinted by permission from *BioScience*, 35 (1985), 718–26. © 1985 American Institute of Biological Sciences.

[1] US Congress, *Endangered Species Act of 1973*, s. 2(a)(1) (Public Law 93–205).

[2] John Rawls, *A Theory of Justice* (Cambridge, Mass.: Harvard University Press, 1971), 512.

[3] G. O. Barney, study director, *The Global 2000 Report to the President* (Washington: Government Printing Office, 1980–1), i. 37.

[4] Stuart Hampshire, *Morality and Pessimism* (New York: Cambridge University Press, 1972), 3–4.

future human beings.[5] Using traditional ethics to confront the novel threat of extinctions, we can reapply familiar duties to persons and see whether this is convincing. This line of argument can be impressive but seems to leave deeper obligations untouched.

Persons have a strong duty not to harm others and a weaker, though important, duty to help others. Arguing the threat of harm, the Ehrlichs maintain, in a blunt metaphor, that species are rivets in the Earthship in which humans are flying.[6] Extinctions are maleficent rivet-popping. In this model, non-rivet species, if there are any, would have no value; humans desire only the diversity that prevents a crash. The care is not for particular species but, in a variant metaphor, for the sinking ark.[7] To worry about a sinking ark seems a strange twist on the Noah story. Noah built the ark to preserve each species. In the Ehrlich–Myers account, the species-rivets are preserved to keep the ark from sinking! The reversed justification is revealing.

On the benefits side, species that are not rivets may prove resources. Thomas Eisner testified to Congress that only 2 per cent of the flowering plants have been tested for alkaloids, which often have medical value.[8] A National Science Foundation report advocated saving the Devil's Hole Pupfish, *Cyprinodon diabolis*, because it thrives in extremes and 'can serve as useful biological models for future research on the human kidney—and on survival in a seemingly hostile environment'.[9] Myers further urges 'conserving our global stock'.[10] At first this advice seems wise, yet later somewhat demeaning for humans to regard all other species as *stock*.

Destroying species is like tearing pages out of an unread book, written in a language humans hardly know how to read, about the place where they live. No sensible person would destroy the Rosetta Stone, and no self-respecting persons will destroy the mouse lemur, endangered in Madagascar and thought to be the nearest modern animal to the relatively unspecialized primates from which the human line evolved. Still, following this logic, humans do not have duties to the book, the stone, or the species, but to ourselves, duties of prudence and education. Humans need insight into the full text of ecosystem evolution. It is not endangered species

[5] Joel Feinberg, 'The Rights of Animals and Unborn Generations', in W. T. Blackstone, ed., *Philosophy and Environmental Crisis* (Athens: University of Georgia Press, 1974), 43–68, cit. 56.

[6] Paul R. and Anne Ehrlich, *Extinction* (New York: Random House, 1981).

[7] Norman Myers, *The Sinking Ark* (Oxford: Pergamon Press, 1979).

[8] 'Statement of Thomas Eisner', in *Endangered Species Act Oversight*, Hearings 8 and 10 Dec. 1981 (Washington: Government Printing Office, 1982), 295–7.

[9] National Science Foundation, 'The Biology of Aridity', *Mosaic*, 8/1 (Jan./Feb. 1977), 28–35, cit. 28.

[10] Norman Myers, 'Conserving Our Global Stock', *Environment*, 21/9 (Nov. 1979), 25–33.

but an endangered human future that is of concern. Such reasons are pragmatic and impressive. They are also moral, since persons are benefited or hurt. But are they exhaustive?

One problem is that pragmatic reasons get overstated. Peter H. Raven testified before Congress that a dozen dependent species of insects, animals, or other plants typically become extinct with each plant that goes extinct.[11] But Raven knows that such cascading, disastrous extinction is true only on statistical average, since a plant named for him, Raven's manzanita, *Arctostaphylos hookeri* ssp. *ravenii*, is known from a single wild specimen, and its extinction is unlikely to trigger others. Rare species add some back-up resilience. Still, if all seventy-nine plants on the endangered species list disappeared, it is doubtful that the regional ecosystems involved would measurably shift their stability. Few cases can be cited where the removal of a rare species damaged an ecosystem.

Let's be frank. A substantial number of endangered species have no resource value. Beggar's ticks, *Bidens* spp., with their stick-tight seeds, are a common nuisance through much of the USA. One species, tidal shore beggar's tick, *B. bidentoides*, which differs little in appearance from the others, is endangered. It seems unlikely to be a potential resource. As far as humans are concerned, its extinction might be good riddance.

We might say that humans ought to preserve for themselves an environment adequate to match their capacity to wonder. But this is to value the *experience* of wonder, rather than the *objects* of wonder. Valuing merely the experience seems to commit a fallacy of misplaced wonder, for speciation is itself among the wonderful things on Earth. Valuing speciation directly, however, seems to attach value to the evolutionary process, not merely to subjective experiences that arise when humans reflect over it.

We might say that humans of decent character will refrain from needless destruction of all kinds, including destruction of species. Vandals destroying art objects do not so much hurt statues as cheapen their own character. But is the American shame at destroying the passenger-pigeon only a matter of self-respect? Or is it shame at our ignorant insensitivity to a form of life that (unlike a statue) had an intrinsic value that placed some claim on us?

The deeper problem with the anthropocentric rationale, beyond overstatement, is that its justifications are submoral and fundamentally exploitative even if subtly. This is not true, intraspecifically, among humans, when out of a sense of duty an individual defers to the values of fellows.

---

[11] 'Statement of Peter H. Raven', in *Endangered Species Act Oversight*, 290–5.

But it is true interspecifically, since *Homo sapiens* treats all other species as rivets, resources, study materials, or entertainments. Ethics has always been about partners with entwined destinies. But it has never been very convincing when pleaded as enlightened self-interest (that one ought always to do what is in one's intelligent self-interest), including class self-interest, even though in practice genuinely altruistic ethics often needs to be reinforced by self-interest. To value all other species only for human interest is like a nation's arguing all its foreign policy in terms of national interest. Neither seems fully moral.

Perhaps an exploiting attitude, and the tendency to justify it ethically, has been naturally selected in *Homo sapiens*, at least in the population that has become dominant in the West. But humans—scientists who have learned to be disinterested and ethicists who have learned to consider the interests of others—ought to be able to see further. Humans have learned some intraspecific altruism. The challenge now is to learn interspecific altruism. Utilitarian reasons for saving species may be good ones, necessary for policy. But can we not also discover the best reasons, the full extent of human duties? Dealing with a problem correctly requires an appropriate way of thinking about it. What is offensive in the impending extinctions is not the loss of rivets and resources, but the maelstrom of killing and insensitivity to forms of life and the forces producing them. What is required is not prudence but principled responsibility to the biospheric Earth.

SPECIFIC FORMS OF LIFE

There are many barriers to thinking of duties to species, however, and scientific ones precede ethical ones. It is difficult enough to argue from the fact that a species exists to the value judgement that a species ought to exist—what philosophers call an argument from *is* to *ought*. Matters grow worse if the concept of species is rotten to begin with. Perhaps the concept is arbitrary and conventional, a mapping device that is only theoretical. Perhaps it is unsatisfactory theoretically in an evolutionary ecosystem. Perhaps species do not exist. Duties to them would be as imaginary as duties to contour lines or to lines of latitude and longitude. Is there enough factual reality in species to base duty there?

Betula lenta uber, round-leaf birch, is known from only two locations on nearby Virginia creeks and differs from the common *B. lenta* only in having rounded leaf tips. For thirty years it was described as a subspecies or merely a mutation. But M. L. Fernald pronounced it a species, *B. uber*, and for forty years it has been considered one. High fences have been built around all known specimens. If a greater botanist were to redesignate it a subspecies, would this change in alleged facts affect our alleged duties? Ornithologists recently reassessed an endangered species, the Mexican duck, *Anas diazi*, and lumped it with the common mallard, *A. platy-rhynchos*, as subspecies *diazi*. US Fish and Wildlife authorities took if off the endangered species list partly as a result. Did a duty cease? Was there never one at all?

If a species is only a category, or class, boundary lines may be arbitrarily drawn. Darwin wrote, 'I look at the term species, as one arbitrarily given for the sake of convenience to a set of individuals closely resembling each other.'[12] Some natural properties are used to delimit species—reproductive structures, bones, teeth. But which properties are selected and where the lines are drawn vary with taxonomists. When A. J. Shaw recently 'discovered' a new species of moss, *Pohlia tundrae*, in the alpine Rocky Mountains, he did not find any hitherto unknown plants at all, he just regrouped herbarium material that had been known for decades under other names.[13] Indeed, biologists routinely put after a species the name of the 'author' who, they say, 'erected' the taxon.

Individual organisms exist, but if species are merely classes, they are inventions. A. B. Shaw claims, 'The species concept is entirely subjective,' and, concluding a presidential address to palaeontologists, even exclaims, 'Help stamp out species!'[14] He refers, of course, to the artefacts of taxonomists, not to living organisms. But if species do not exist except embedded in a theory in the minds of classifiers, it is hard to see how there can be duties to save them. No one proposes duties to genera, families, orders, or phyla; everyone concedes that these do not exist in nature.

But a biological 'species' is not just a class. A species is a living historical 'form' (Latin: *species*), propagated in individual organisms, that flows dynamically over generations. Simpson concludes, 'An evolutionary species is a lineage (an ancestral-descendant sequence of populations) evolving separately from others and with its own unitary evolutionary role and tendencies.'[15] Mayr holds, 'Species are groups of interbreeding natural

---

[12] Charles Darwin, *The Origin of Species by Means of Natural Selection* (Baltimore: Penguin Books, 1968), 108.

[13] A. J. Shaw, '*Pohlia andrewsii* and *P. tundrae*, Two New Arctic-Alpine Propaguliferous Species from North America', *Bryologist*, 84 (1981), 65–74.

[14] A. B. Shaw, 'Adam and Eve, Palaeontology, and the Non-objective Arts', *Journal of Palaeontology*, 43 (1969), 1085–98, cit. 1098.

[15] G. G. Simpson, *Principles of Animal Taxonomy* (New York: Columbia University Press, 1961), 153.

populations that are reproductively isolated from other such groups.'[16] He can even emphasize, though many biologists today would deny this, that '*species are the real units of evolution*, they are the entities which specialize, which become adapted, or which shift their adaptation.'[17] Recently, Mayr has sympathized with Ghiselin and Hull who hold that species are integrated individuals, and species names proper names, with organisms related to their species as part is to whole.[18] Eldredge and Cracraft find that 'a species is a diagnosable cluster of individuals within which there is a parental pattern of ancestry and descent, beyond which there is not, and which exhibits a pattern of phylogenetic ancestry and descent among units of like kind.' Species, they insist with emphasis, are '*discrete entities in time as well as space*'.[19]

It is admittedly difficult to pinpoint precisely what a species is, and there may be no single, quintessential way to define species; a polythetic or polytypic gestalt of features may be required. All we need for this discussion, however, is that species be objectively there as living processes in the evolutionary ecosystem; the varied criteria for defining them (descent, reproductive isolation, morphology, gene pool) come together at least in providing evidence that species are really there. In this sense, species are dynamic natural kinds, if not corporate individuals. A species is a coherent, ongoing form of life expressed in organisms, encoded in gene flow, and shaped by the environment.

The claim that there are specific forms of life historically maintained in their environments over time does not seem arbitrary or fictitious at all but, rather, as certain as anything else we believe about the empirical world, even though at times scientists revise the theories and taxa with which they map these forms. Species are not so much like lines of latitude and longitude as like mountains and rivers, phenomena objectively there to be mapped. The edges of all these natural kinds will sometimes be fuzzy, to some extent discretionary. We can expect that one species will slide into another over evolutionary time. But it does not follow from the fact that speciation is sometimes in progress that species are merely made up,

[16] Ernst Mayr, *Principles of Systematic Zoology* (New York: McGraw Hill, 1969), 26.

[17] Ernst Mayr, 'The Biological Meaning of Species', *Biological Journal of the Linnean Society*, 1 (1969), 311–20, cit. 318.

[18] Ernst Mayr, *The Growth of Biological Thought* (Cambridge, Mass.: Harvard University Press, 1982), 253; M. T. Ghiselin, 'A Radical Solution to the Species Problem', *Systematic Zoology*, 23 (1974), 536–44; David L. Hull, 'Are Species Really Individuals?', *Systematic Zoology*, 25 (1976), 174–91.

[19] Niles Eldredge and Joel Cracraft, *Phylogenetic Patterns and the Evolutionary Process* (New York: Columbia University Press, 1980), 92.

instead of found as evolutionary lines articulated into diverse forms, each with its more or less distinct integrity, breeding population, gene pool, and role in its ecosystem.

At this point, we can anticipate how there can be duties to species. What humans ought to respect are dynamic life forms preserved in historical lines, vital informational processes that persist genetically over millions of years, overleaping short-lived individuals. It is not *form* (species) as mere morphology, but the *formative* (speciating) process that humans ought to preserve, although the process cannot be preserved without its products. Nor should humans want to protect the labels they use, but the living process in the environment. Endangered 'species' is a convenient and realistic way of tagging this process, but protection can be interpreted (as the Endangered Species Act permits) in terms of subspecies, variety, or other taxa or categories that point out the diverse forms of life.

DUTIES TO SPECIES

The easiest conclusion to reach from prevailing theories of justice, which involve tacit or explicit 'contracts' between persons, is that duties and rights are reciprocal. But reciprocally claiming, recognizing, exercising, and enjoying rights and duties can only be done by reflective rational agents. Humans have entered no contract with other species; certainly they have not with us. There is no ecological contract parallel to the social contract; all the capacities for deliberate interaction so common in culture vanish in nature. Individual animals and plants, to say nothing of species, cannot be reasoned with, blamed, or educated into the prevailing contract.

But to make rights and duties reciprocal supposes that only moral agents count in the ethical calculus. Duties exist as well to those persons who cannot argue back—to the mute and the powerless—and perhaps this principle extends to other forms of life. Morality is needed wherever the vulnerable must be protected from the powerful.

The next easiest conclusion to reach, either from rights-based or utilitarian theories, is that humans have duties wherever there are psychological interests involving the capacity for experience. That moves a minimal criterion for duty past rational moral agency to sentience. The question is not whether animals can reciprocate the contract but whether they can suffer. Singer thinks that the only reason to be concerned about endangered species is the interests of humans and other sentient animals at stake in their loss.[20] Only they can enjoy benefits or suffer harm, so only they can be treated justly or unjustly.

But species, not sentience, generate some duties. On San Clemente Island, the US Fish and Wildlife Service and the California Department of Fish and Game asked the Navy to shoot 2,000 feral goats to save three endangered plant species, *Malacothamnus clementinus*, *Castilleja grisea*, and *Delphinium kinkiense*. That would kill several goats for each known surviving plant. (Happily, the Fund for Animals rescued most of the goats; unhappily they could not trap them all and the issue is unresolved.) The National Park Service did kill hundreds of rabbits on Santa Barbara Island to protect a few plants of *Dudleya traskiae*, once thought extinct and curiously called the Santa Barbara live-forever. Hundreds of elk starve in Yellowstone National Park each year, and the Park Service is not alarmed, but the starving of an equal number of grizzly bears, which would involve about the same suffering in psychological experience, would be of great concern.

A rather difficult claim to make under contemporary ethical theory is that duty can arise toward any living organism. Such duties, if they exit, could be easy to override, but by this account humans would have at least a minimal duty not to disrupt living beings without justification.

Here the question about species, beyond individuals, is both revealing and challenging because it offers a biologically based counter-example to the focus on individuals—typically sentient and usually persons—so characteristic in Western ethics. In an evolutionary ecosystem, it is not mere individuality that counts, but the species is also significant because it is a dynamic life form maintained over time by an informed genetic flow. The individual represents (re-presents) a species in each new generation. It is a token of a type, and the type is more important than the token.

It is as logical to say that the individual is the species' way of propagating itself as to say that the embryo or egg is the individual's way of propagating itself. We can think of the cognitive processing as taking place not merely in the individual but in the gene pool. Genetically, though not neurally, a species over generations 'learns' (discovers) pathways previously unknown. A form of life reforms itself, tracks its environment, and sometimes passes over to a new species. There is a specific groping for a valued *ought*-to-be beyond what now *is* in any individual. Though species are not moral agents, a biological identity—a kind of value—is here defended. The dignity resides in the dynamic form; the individual inherits this, instan-

---

[20] Peter Singer, 'Not for Humans Only', in K. E. Goodpaster and K. M. Sayre, eds., *Ethics and Problems of the 21st Century* (Notre Dame, Ind.: University of Notre Dame Press, 1979), 191–206, especially 204.

tiates it, and passes it on. To borrow a metaphor from physics, life is both a particle (the individual) and a wave (the specific form).

A species lacks moral agency, reflective self-awareness, sentience, or organic individuality. So we may be tempted to say that specific-level processes cannot count morally. But each ongoing species defends a form of life, and these are on the whole good things, arising in a process out of which humans have evolved. All ethicists say that in *Homo sapiens* one species has appeared that not only exists but ought to exist. But why say this exclusively of a late-coming, highly developed form? Why not extend this duty more broadly to the other species (though perhaps not with equal intensity over them all, in view of varied levels of development)? These kinds defend their forms of life too. Only the human species contains moral agents, but perhaps conscience *ought not* to be used to exempt every other form of life from consideration, with the resulting paradox that the single moral species acts only in its collective self-interest toward all the rest.

Extinction shuts down the generative processes. The wrong that humans are doing, or allowing to happen through carelessness, is stopping the historical flow in which the vitality of life is laid. Every extinction is an incremental decay in stopping life processes—no small thing. Every extinction is a kind of superkilling. It kills forms (*species*), beyond individuals. It kills 'essences' beyond 'existences', the 'soul' as well as the 'body'. It kills collectively, not just distributively. It is not merely the loss of potential human information that is tragic, but the loss of biological information, present independently of instrumental human uses for it.

'Ought species x to exist?' is a single increment in the collective question, 'Ought life on Earth to exist?' The answer to the question about one species is not always the same as the answer to the bigger question, but since life on Earth is an aggregate of many species, the two are sufficiently related that the burden of proof lies with those who wish deliberately to extinguish a species and simultaneously to care for life on Earth. To kill a species is to shut down a unique story; and, although all specific stories must eventually end, we seldom want unnatural ends. Humans ought not to play the role of murderers. The duty to species can be overriden, for example with pests or disease organisms. But a prima facie duty stands nevertheless.

One form of life has never endangered so many others. Never before has this level of question—superkilling by a superkiller—been faced. Humans have more understanding than ever of the speciating processes, more predictive power to foresee the intended and unintended results of their actions, and more power to reverse the undesirable consequences. The duties that such power and vision generate no longer attach simply to individuals or persons but are emerging duties to specific forms of life. If, in this world of uncertain moral convictions, it makes any sense to claim that one ought not to kill individuals without justification, it makes more sense to claim that one ought not to superkill the species, without superjustification.

INDIVIDUALS AND SPECIES

Many will be uncomfortable with this claim because their ethical theory does not allow duty to a collection. Feinberg writes, 'A whole collection, as such, cannot have beliefs, expectations, wants, or desires. . . . Individual elephants can have interests, but the species elephant cannot.'[21] Singer asserts, 'Species as such are not conscious entities and so do not have interests above and beyond the interests of the individual animals that are members of the species.'[22] Regan maintains, 'The rights view is a view about the moral rights of individuals. Species are not individuals, and the rights view does not recognize the moral rights of species to anything, including survival.'[23] Rescher says, 'Moral obligation is thus always interest-oriented. But only individuals can be said to have interests; one only has moral obligations to particular individuals or particular groups thereof. Accordingly, the duty to save a species is not a matter of moral duty toward it, because moral duties are only oriented to individuals. A species as such is the wrong sort of target for a moral obligation.'[24]

Even those who recognize that organisms, non-sentient as well as sentient, can be benefited or harmed may see the good of a species as the sum of and reducible to the goods of individuals. The species is well off when and because its members are; species well-being is just aggregated individual well-being. The 'interests of a species' constitute only a convenient device, something like a centre of gravity in physics, for speaking of an aggregated focus of many contributing individual member units.

But duties to a species are not duties to a class or category, not to an aggregation of sentient interests, but to a lifeline. An ethic about species needs to see how the species *is* a bigger event than individual interests or

[21] Feinberg, 'Rights of Animals and Unborn Generations', 55–6.
[22] Singer, 'Not for Humans Only', 203.
[23] Tom Regan, *The Case for Animal Rights* (Berkeley: University of California Press, 1983), 359.
[24] Nicholas Rescher, *Unpopular Essays on Technological Progress* (Pittsburgh: University of Pittsburgh Press, 1980), 83.

sentience. Making this clearer can support the conviction that a species *ought* to continue.

Events can be good for the well-being of the species, considered collectively, although they are harmful if considered as distributed to individuals. This is one way to interpret what is often called a genetic 'load', genes that somewhat reduce health, efficiency, or fertility in most individuals but introduce enough variation to permit improving the specific form.[25] Less variation and better repetition in reproduction would, on average, benefit more individuals in any one next generation, since individuals would have less 'load'. But on a longer view, variation can confer stability in a changing world. A greater experimenting with individuals, although this typically makes individuals less fit and is a disadvantage from that perspective, benefits rare, lucky individuals selected in each generation with a resulting improvement in the species. Most individuals in any particular generation carry some (usually slightly) detrimental genes, but the variation is good for the species. Note that this does not imply species selection; selection perhaps operates only on individuals. But it does mean that we can distinguish between the goods of individuals and the larger good of the species.

Predation on individual elk conserves and improves the species *Cervus canadensis*. A forest fire harms individual aspen trees, but it helps *Populus tremuloides* because fire restarts forest succession without which the species would go extinct. Even the individuals that escape demise from external sources die of old age; their deaths, always to the disadvantage of those individuals, are a necessity for the species. A finite life-span makes room for those replacements that enable development to occur, allowing the population to improve in fitness or adapt to a shifting environment. Without the 'flawed' reproduction that permits variation, without a surplus of young, or predation and death, which all harm individuals, the species would soon go extinct in a changing environment, as all environments eventually are. The individual is a receptacle of the form, and the receptacles are broken while the form survives; but the form cannot otherwise survive.

When a biologist remarks that a breeding population of a rare species is dangerously low, what is the danger to? Individual members? Rather, the remark seems to imply a specific-level, point-of-no-return threat to the continuing of that form of life. No individual crosses the extinction threshold; the species does.

[25] G. R. Fraser, 'Our Genetical "Load": A Review of Some Aspects of Genetical Variation', *Annals of Human Genetics*, 25 (1962), 387–415.

Reproduction is typically assumed to be a need of individuals, but since any particular individual can flourish somatically without reproducing at all, indeed may be put through duress and risk or spend much energy reproducing, by another logic we can interpret reproduction as the species keeping up its own kind by re-enacting itself again and again, individual after individual. In this sense a female grizzly does not bear cubs to be healthy herself, any more than a woman needs children to be healthy. Rather, her cubs are *Ursus arctos*, threatened by non-being, recreating itself by continuous performance. A species in reproduction defends its own kind from other species, and this seems to be some form of 'caring'.

Biologists have often and understandably focused on individuals, and some recent trends interpret biological processes from the perspective of genes. A consideration of species reminds us that many events can be interpreted at this level too. An organism runs a directed course through the environment, taking in materials, using them resourcefully, discharging wastes. But this single, directed course is part of a bigger picture in which a species via individuals maintains its course over longer spans of time. Thinking this way, the life the individual has is something passing through the individual as much as something it intrinsically possesses. The individual is subordinate to the species, not the other way round. The genetic set, in which is coded the *telos*, is as evidently a 'property' of the species as of the individual.

Biologists and linguists have learned to accept the concept of information in the genetic set without any subject who speaks or understands. Can ethicists learn to accept value in, and duty to, an informed process in which centred individuality or sentience is absent? Here events can be significant at the specific level, an additional consideration to whether they are beneficial to individuals. The species-in-environment is an interactive complex, a selective system where individuals are pawns on a chessboard. When human conduct endangers these specific games of life, duties may appear.

A species has no self. It is not a bounded singular. Each organism has its own centredness, but there is no specific analogue to the nervous hook-ups or circulatory flows that characterize the organism. But, like the market in economics, an organized system does not have to have a controlling centre to have identity. Having a biological identity reasserted genetically over time is as true of the species as of the individual. Individuals come and go; the marks of the species collectively remain much longer.

A consideration of species strains any ethic focused on individuals, much less on sentience or persons. But the result can be a biologically sounder ethic, though it revises what was formerly thought logically permissible or

ethically binding. The species line is quite fundamental. It is more important to protect this integrity than to protect individuals. Defending a form
of life, resisting death, regeneration that maintains a normative identity
over time—all this is as true of species as of individuals. So what prevents
duties arising at that level? The appropriate survival unit is the appropriate
level of moral concern.

SPECIES AND ECOSYSTEM

A species is what it is inseparably from its environment. The species
defends its kind against the world, but at the same time interacts with its
environment, functions in the ecosystem, and is supported and shaped
by it. The species and the community are complementary processes in
synthesis, somewhat parallel to, but a level above, the way the species and
the individual have distinguishable but entwined identities. Neither the
individual nor the species stands alone; both are embedded in a system. It
is not preservation of *species* but of *species in the system* that we desire. It
is not just what they are but where they are that we must value correctly.

The species *can* only be preserved *in situ*; the species *ought* to be
preserved *in situ*. Zoos and botanical gardens can lock up a collection of
individuals, but they cannot begin to simulate the ongoing dynamism of
gene flow under the selection pressures in a wild biome. The full integrity
of the species must be integrated into the ecosystem. *Ex situ* preservation,
while it may save resources and souvenirs, does not preserve the generative process intact. Again, the appropriate survival unit is the appropriate
level of moral concern.

It might seem that ending the history of a species now and again is not
far out of line with the routines of the universe. But artificial extinction,
caused by human encroachments, is radically different from natural extinction. Relevant differences make the two as morally distinct as death by
natural causes is from murder. Though harmful to a species, extinction in
nature is no evil in the system; it is rather the key to tomorrow. Such
extinction is a normal turnover in ongoing speciation.

Anthropogenic extinction has nothing to do with evolutionary speciation. Hundreds of thousands of species will perish because of culturally
altered environments radically differing from the spontaneous environments in which such species were naturally selected and in which they
sometimes go extinct. In natural extinctions, nature takes away life when it
has become unfit in habitat, or when the habitat alters, and supplies other
life in its place. Artificial extinction shuts down tomorrow because it shuts

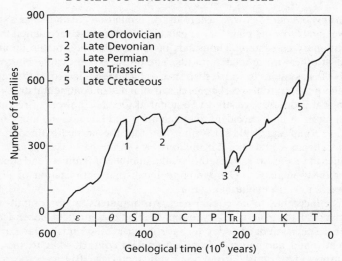

Fig. 1. Standing diversity through time for families of marine vertebrates and invertebrates, with standard geological symbols, and catastrophic extinctions numbered.
Source: Raup and Sepkoski, 'Mass Extinctions in the Marine Fossil Record'.

down speciation. Natural extinction typically occurs with transformation, either of the extinct line or related or competing lines. Artificial extinction is without issue. One opens doors; the other closes them. Humans generate and regenerate nothing; they only dead-end these lines.

From this perspective, humans have no duty to preserve rare species from natural extinctions, although they might have a duty to other humans to save such species as resources or museum pieces. Humans cannot and need not save the product without the process.

Through evolutionary time, nature has provided new species at a higher rate than the extinction rate; hence, the accumulated diversity. In one of the best documented studies of the marine fossil record, Raup and Sepkoski summarize a general increase in standing diversity (Fig. 1).[26] Regardless of differing details on land or biases in the fossil record, a graph of the increase of diversity on Earth must look something like this.

There have been four or five catastrophic extinctions, each succeeded by a recovery of previous diversity. These anomalies so deviate from the trends that many palaeontologists look for extraterrestrial causes. If due to

[26] D. M. Raup and J. J. Sepkoski, Jr., 'Mass Extinctions in the Marine Fossil Record', *Science*, 215 (1982), 1501–3.

supernovae, collisions with asteroids, or oscillations of the solar system above and below the plane of the galaxy, such events are accidental to the evolutionary ecosystem. Thousands of species perished at the impingement of otherwise unrelated events. The disasters were irrelevant to the kinds of ecosystems in which such species had been selected. If the causes were more terrestrial—cyclic changes in climates or continental drift—the biological processes are still to be admired for their powers of recovery. Even interrupted by accident, they maintain and increase the numbers of species. Raup and Sepkoski further find that the normal extinction rate declines from 4.6 families per million years in the early Cambrian to 2.0 families in recent times, even though the number of families (and species) enormously increases. This seems to mean that optimization of fitness increases through evolutionary time.

An ethicist has to be circumspect. An argument might commit what logicians call the genetic fallacy to suppose that present value depended on origins. Species judged today to have intrinsic value might have arisen anciently and anomalously from a valueless context, akin to the way life arose mysteriously from non-living materials. But in a historical ecosystem, what a thing is differentiates poorly from the generating and sustaining matrix. The individual and the species have what value they have, to some extent, in the context of the forces that beget them.

Imagine that Fig. 1 is the graph of the performance of a 600-million-year-old business. Is it not a healthy one? But this record is of the business of life, and the long-term performance deserves ethical respect. There is something awesome about an Earth that begins with zero and runs up toward 5 to 10 million species in several billion years, set-backs notwithstanding.

What is valuable about species is not to be isolated in them for what they are in themselves. Rather, the dynamic account evaluates species as process, product, and instrument in the larger drama toward which humans have duties, reflected in duties to species. Whittaker finds that on continental scales and for most groups, 'increase of species diversity . . . is a self-augmenting process without any evident limit.' There is a tendency toward 'species packing'.[27] Nature seems to produce as many species as it can, not merely enough to stabilize an ecosystem or only species that can directly or indirectly serve human needs. Humans ought not to inhibit this exuberant lust for kinds. That process, along with its product, is about as near to ultimacy as humans can come in their relationship with the natural world.

[27] R. H. Whittaker, 'Evolution and Measurement of Species Diversity', *Taxon*, 21 (1972), 213–51, cit. 214.

Several billion years worth of creative toil, several million species of teeming life, have been handed over to the care of this late-coming species in which mind has flowered and morals have emerged. Ought not those of this sole moral species do something less self-interested than to count all the produce of an evolutionary ecosystem as rivets in their spaceship, resources in their larder, laboratory materials, recreation for their ride? Such an attitude hardly seems biologically informed, much less ethically adequate. Its logic is too provincial for moral humanity. Or, in a biologist's term, it is ridiculously territorial. If true to their specific epithet, ought not *Homo sapiens* value this host of species as something with a claim to care in its own right?

AN ENDANGERED ETHIC?

The contemporary ethical systems seem misfits in the role most recently demanded of them. There is something overspecialized about an ethic, held by the dominant class of *Homo sapiens*, that regards the welfare of only one of several million species as an object of duty. If this requires a paradigm change about the sorts of things to which duty can attach, so much the worse for those ethics no longer functioning in, nor suited to, their changing environment. The anthropocentrism associated with them was fiction anyway. There is something Newtonian, not yet Einsteinian, besides something morally naïve, about living in a reference frame where one species takes itself as absolute and values everything else relative to its utility.

IV

FAKING NATURE

ROBERT ELLIOT

I

Consider the following case. There is a proposal to mine beach sands for rutile. Large areas of dune are to be cleared of vegetation and the dunes themselves destroyed. It is agreed, by all parties concerned, that the dune area has value quite apart from a utilitarian one. It is agreed, in other words, that it would be a bad thing, considered in itself, for the dune area to be dramatically altered. Acknowledging this the mining company expresses its willingness, indeed its desire, to restore the dune area to its original condition after the minerals have been extracted.[1] The company goes on to argue that any loss of value is merely temporary and that full value will in fact be restored. In other words they are claiming that the destruction of what has value is compensated for by the later creation (re-creation) of something of equal value. I shall call this 'the restoration thesis'.

In the actual world many such proposals are made, not because of shared conservationist principles, but as a way of undermining the arguments of conservationists. Such proposals are in fact effective in defeating environmentalist protest. They are also notoriously ineffective in putting right, or indeed even seeming to put right, the particular wrong that has been done to the environment. The sand-mining case is just one of a number of similar cases involving such things as open-cut mining, clear-felling of forests, river diversion, and highway construction. Across a range of such cases some concession is made by way of acknowledging the value of pieces of landscape, rivers, forests, and so forth, and a suggestion is made that this value can be restored once the environmentally disruptive process has been completed.

From *Inquiry*, 25 (1982), 81–93. Reprinted by permission of Scandinavian Press, Oslo, Norway.

---

[1] In this case *full* restoration will be literally impossible because the minerals are not going to be replaced.

Imagine, contrary to fact, that restoration projects are largely successful; that the environment is brought back to its original condition and that even a close inspection will fail to reveal that the area has been mined, clear-felled, or whatever. If this is so, then there is temptation to think that one particular environmentalist objection is defeated. The issue is by no means merely academic. I have already claimed that restoration promises do in fact carry weight against environmental arguments. Thus Mr Doug Anthony, the Australian Deputy Prime Minister, saw fit to suggest that sand-mining on Fraser Island could be resumed once 'the community becomes more informed and more enlightened as to what reclamation work is being carried out by mining companies . . .'.[2] Or consider how the protests of environmentalists might be deflected in the light of the following report of environmental engineering in the United States.

. . . about 2 km of creek 25 feet wide has been moved to accommodate a highway and in doing so engineers with the aid of landscape architects and biologists have rebuilt the creek to the same standard as before. Boulders, bends, irregularities and natural vegetation have all been designed into the new section. In addition, special log structures have been built to improve the habitat as part of a fish development program.[3]

Not surprisingly the claim that revegetation, rehabilitation, and the like restore value has been strongly contested. J. G. Mosley reports that:

The Fraser Island Environmental Inquiry Commissioners did in fact face up to the question of the relevance of successful rehabilitation to the decision on whether to ban exports (of beach sand minerals) and were quite unequivocal in saying that if the aim was to protect a natural area such success was irrelevant. . . . The Inquiry said: '. . . even if, contrary to the overwhelming weight of evidence before the Commission, successful rehabilitation of the flora after mining is found to be eco-logically possible on all mined sites on the Island . . . the overall impression of a wild, uncultivated island refuge will be destroyed forever by mining'.[4]

I want to show both that there is a rational, coherent ethical system which supports decisive objections to the restoration thesis, and that that system is not lacking in normative appeal. The system I have in mind will make valuation depend, in part, on the presence of properties which cannot survive the disruption-restoration process. There is, however, one point that needs clarifying before discussion proceeds. Establishing that restoration projects, even if empirically successful, do not fully restore value does not by any means constitute a knock-down argument against

---

[2] J. G. Mosley, 'The Revegetation "Debate": A Trap For Conservationists', *Australian Conservation Foundation Newsletter*, 12/8 (1980), 1.
[3] Peter Dunk, 'How New Engineering Can Work with the Environment', *Habitat Australia*, 7/5 (1979), 12.
[4] See Mosley, 'The Revegetation "Debate"', 1.

some environmentally disruptive policy. The value that would be lost if such a policy were implemented may be just one value among many which conflict in this situation. Countervailing considerations may be decisive and the policy thereby shown to be the right one. If my argument turns out to be correct it will provide an extra, though by no means decisive, reason for adopting certain environmentalist policies. It will show that the resistance which environmentalists display in the face of restoration promises is not merely silly, or emotional, or irrational. This is important because so much of the debate assumes that settling the dispute about what is ecologically possible automatically settles the value question. The thrust of much of the discussion is that if restoration is shown to be possible, and economically feasible, then recalcitrant environmentalists are behaving irrationally, being merely obstinate or being selfish.

There are indeed familiar ethical systems which will serve to explain what is wrong with the restoration thesis in a certain range of cases. Thus preference utilitarianism will support objections to some restoration proposal if that proposal fails to maximally satisfy preferences. Likewise, classical utilitarianism will lend support to a conservationist stance provided that the restoration proposal fails to maximize happiness and pleasure. However, in both cases the support offered is contingent upon the way in which the preferences and utilities line up. And it is simply not clear that they line up in such a way that the conservationist position is even usually vindicated. While appeal to utilitarian considerations might be strategically useful in certain cases they do not reflect the underlying motivation of the conservationists. The conservationists seem committed to an account of what has value which allows that restoration proposals fail to compensate for environmental destruction despite the fact that such proposals would maximize utility. What then is this distinct source of value which motivates and underpins the stance taken by, among others, the Commissioners of the Fraser Island Environmental Inquiry?

II

It is instructive to list some reasons that might be given in support of the claim that something of value would be lost if a certain bit of the environment were destroyed. It may be that the area supports a diversity of plant and animal life, it may be that it is the habitat of some endangered species, it may be that it contains striking rock formations or particularly fine specimens of mountain ash. If it is only considerations such as these that contribute to the area's value then perhaps opposition to the environmentally disruptive project would be irrational provided certain firm guarantees were available; for instance that the mining company or timber company would carry out the restoration and that it would be successful. Presumably there are steps that could be taken to ensure the continuance of species diversity and the continued existence of the endangered species. Some of the other requirements might prove harder to meet, but in some sense or other it is possible to recreate the rock formations and to plant mountain ash that will turn out to be particularly fine specimens. If value consists of the presence of objects of these various kinds, independently of what explains their presence, then the restoration thesis would seem to hold. The environmentalist needs to appeal to some feature which cannot be replicated as a source of some part of a natural area's value.

Putting the point thus indicates the direction the environmentalist could take. He might suggest that an area is valuable, partly, because it is a natural area, one that has not been modified by human hand, one that is undeveloped, unspoilt, or even unsullied. This suggestion is in accordance with much environmentalist rhetoric, and something like it at least must be at the basis of resistance to restoration proposals. One way of teasing out the suggestion and giving it a normative basis is to take over a notion from aesthetics. Thus we might claim that what the environmental engineers are proposing is that we accept a fake or a forgery instead of the real thing. If the claim can be made good then perhaps an adequate response to restoration proposals is to point out that they merely fake nature; that they offer us something less than was taken away.[5] Certainly there is a weight of opinion to the effect that, in art at least, fakes lack a value possessed by the real thing.[6]

One way in which this argument might be nipped in the bud is by claiming that it is bound to exploit an ultimately unworkable distinction between what is natural and what is not. Admittedly the distinction between the natural and the non-natural requires detailed working out. This is something I do not propose doing. However, I do think the distinction can be made good in a way sufficient to the present need. For present purposes I shall take it that 'natural' means something like 'un-

---

[5] Offering something less is not, of course, always the same as offering nothing. If diversity of animal and plant life, stability of complex ecosystems, tall trees, and so on are things that we value in themselves, then certainly we are offered something. I am not denying this, and I doubt that many would qualify their valuations of the above-mentioned items in a way that leaves the restored environment devoid of value. Environmentalists would count as of worth programmes designed to render polluted rivers re-inhabitable by fish species. The point is rather that they may, as I hope to show, rationally deem it less valuable than what was originally there.

[6] See e.g. Colin Radford, 'Fakes', *Mind*, 87/345 (1978) 66–76, and Nelson Goodman, *Languages of Art* (New York: Bobbs-Merrill, 1968), 99–122, though Radford and Goodman have different accounts of why genesis matters.

modified by human activity'. Obviously some areas will be more natural than others according to the degree to which they have been shaped by human hand. Indeed most rural landscapes will, on this view, count as non-natural to a very high degree. Nor do I intend the natural/non-natural distinction to exactly parallel some dependent moral evaluations; that is, I do not want to be taken as claiming that what is natural is good and what is non-natural is not. The distinction between natural and non-natural connects with valuation in a much more subtle way than that. This is something to which I shall presently return. My claim then is that restoration policies do not always fully restore value because part of the reason that we value bits of the environment is because they are natural to a high degree. It is time to consider some counter-arguments.

An environmental engineer might urge that the exact similarity which holds between the original and the perfectly restored environment leaves no room for a value discrimination between them. He may urge that if they are *exactly* alike, down to the minutest detail (and let us imagine for the sake of argument that this is a technological possibility), then they must be *equally* valuable. The suggestion is that value-discriminations depend on there being intrinsic differences between the states of affairs evaluated. This begs the question against the environmentalist, since it simply discounts the possibility that events temporally and spatially outside the immediate landscape in question can serve as the basis of some valuation of it. It discounts the possibility that the manner of the landscape's genesis, for example, has a legitimate role in determining its value. Here are some examples which suggest that an object's origins do affect its value and our valuations of it.

Imagine that I have a piece of sculpture in my garden which is too fragile to be moved at all. For some reason it would suit the local council to lay sewerage pipes just where the sculpture happens to be. The council engineer informs me of this and explains that my sculpture will have to go. However, I need not despair because he promises to replace it with an exactly similar artefact, one which, he assures me, not even the very best experts could tell was not the original. The example may be unlikely, but it does have some point. While I may concede that the replica would be better than nothing at all (and I may not even concede that), it is utterly improbable that I would accept it as full compensation for the original. Nor is my reluctance entirely explained by the monetary value of the original work. My reluctance springs from the fact that I value the original as an aesthetic object, as an object with a specific genesis and history.

Alternatively, imagine I have been promised a Vermeer for my birthday. The day arrives and I am given a painting which looks just like a

Vermeer. I am understandably pleased. However, my pleasure does not last for long. I am told that the painting I am holding is not a Vermeer but instead an exact replica of one previously destroyed. Any attempt to allay my disappointment by insisting that there just is no difference between the replica and the original misses the mark completely. There is a difference and it is one which affects my perception, and consequent valuation, of the painting. The difference of course lies in the painting's genesis.

I shall offer one last example which perhaps bears even more closely on the environmental issue. I am given a rather beautiful, delicately constructed, object. It is something I treasure and admire, something in which I find considerable aesthetic value. Everything is fine until I discover certain facts about its origin. I discover that it is carved out of the bone of someone killed especially for that purpose. This discovery affects me deeply and I cease to value the object in the way that I once did. I regard it as in some sense sullied, spoilt by the facts of its origin. The object itself has not changed but my perceptions of it have. I now know that it is not quite the kind of thing I thought it was, and that my prior valuation of it was mistaken. The discovery is like the discovery that a painting one believed to be an original is in fact a forgery. The discovery about the object's origin changes the valuation made of it, since it reveals that the object is not of the kind that I value.

What these examples suggest is that there is at least a prima facie case for partially explaining the value of objects in terms of their origins, in terms of the kinds of processes that brought them into being. It is easy to find evidence in the writings of people who have valued nature that things extrinsic to the present, immediate environment determine valuations of it. John Muir's remarks about Hetch Hetchy Valley are a case in point.[7] Muir regarded the valley as a place where he could have direct contact with primeval nature; he valued it, not just because it was a place of great beauty, but because it was also a part of the world that had not been shaped by human hand. Muir's valuation was conditional upon certain facts about the valley's genesis; his valuation was of a, literally, natural object, of an object with a special kind of continuity with the past. The news that it was a carefully contrived elaborate *ecological* artefact would have transformed that valuation immediately and radically.

The appeal that many find in areas of wilderness, in natural forests and wild rivers depends very much on the naturalness of such places. There may be similarities between the experience one has when confronted with

---

[7] See Ch. 10 of Roderick Nash, *Wilderness and the American Mind* (New Haven: Yale University Press, 1973).

the multi-faceted complexity, the magnitude, the awesomeness of a very large city, and the experience one has walking through a rain forest. There may be similarities between the feeling one has listening to the roar of water over the spillway of a dam, and the feeling one has listening to a similar roar as a wild river tumbles down rapids. Despite the similarities there are also differences. We value the forest and river in part because they are representative of the world outside our dominion, because their existence is independent of us. We may value the city and the dam because of what they represent of human achievement. Pointing out the differences is not necessarily to denigrate either. However, there will be cases where we rightly judge that it is better to have the natural object than it is to have the artefact.

It is appropriate to return to a point mentioned earlier concerning the relationship between the natural and the valuable. It will not do to argue that what is natural is necessarily of value. The environmentalist can comfortably concede this point. He is not claiming that all natural phenomena have value in virtue of being natural. Sickness and disease are natural in a straightforward sense and are certainly not good. Natural phenomena such as fires, hurricanes, volcanic eruptions can totally alter landscapes and alter them for the worse. All of this can be conceded. What the environmentalist wants to claim is that, within certain constraints, the naturalness of a landscape is a reason for preserving it, a determinant of its value. Artificially transforming an utterly barren, ecologically bankrupt landscape into something richer and more subtle may be a good thing. That is a view quite compatible with the belief that replacing a rich natural environment with a rich artificial one is a bad thing. What the environmentalist insists on is that naturalness is one factor in determining the value of pieces of the environment. But that, as I have tried to suggest, is no news. The castle by the Scottish loch is a very different kind of object, value-wise, from the exact replica in the appropriately shaped environment of some Disneyland of the future. The barrenness of some Cycladic island would stand in a different, better perspective if it were not brought about by human intervention.

As I have glossed it, the environmentalist's complaint concerning restoration proposals is that nature is not replaceable without depreciation in one aspect of its value which has to do with its genesis, its history. Given this, an opponent might be tempted to argue that there is no longer any such thing as 'natural' wilderness, since the preservation of those bits of it which remain is achievable only by deliberate policy. The idea is that by placing boundaries around national parks, by actively discouraging grazing, trail-biking and the like, by prohibiting sand-mining, we are turning the wilderness into an artefact, that in some negative or indirect way we are creating an environment. There is some truth in this suggestion. In fact we need to take notice of it if we do value wilderness, since positive policies *are* required to preserve it. But as an argument against my overall claim it fails. What is significant about wilderness is its causal continuity with the past. This is something that is not destroyed by demarcating an area and declaring it a national park. There is a distinction between the 'naturalness' of the wilderness itself and the means used to maintain and protect it. What remains within the park boundaries is, as it were, the real thing. The environmentalist may regret that such positive policy is required to preserve the wilderness against human, or even natural, assault.[8] However, the regret does not follow from the belief that what remains is of depreciated value. There is a significant difference between preventing damage and repairing damage once it is done. That is the difference that leaves room for an argument in favour of a preservation policy over and above a restoration policy.

There is another important issue which needs highlighting. It might be thought that naturalness only matters in so far as it is perceived. In other words it might be thought that if the environmental engineer could perform the restoration quickly and secretly, then there would be no room for complaint. Of course, in one sense there would not be, since the knowledge which would motivate complaint would be missing. What this shows is that there can be loss of value without the loss being perceived. It allows room for valuations to be mistaken because of ignorance concerning relevant facts. Thus my Vermeer can be removed and secretly replaced with the perfect replica. I have lost something of value without knowing that I have. This is possible because it is not simply the states of mind engendered by looking at the painting, by gloatingly contemplating my possession of it, by giving myself over to aesthetic pleasure, and so on which explain why it has value. It has value because of the kind of thing that it is, and one thing that it is is a painting executed by a man with certain intentions, at a certain stage of his artistic development, living in a certain aesthetic *milieu*. Similarly, it is not just those things which make me feel the joy that wilderness makes me feel, that I value. That would be a reason for desiring such things, but that is a distinct consideration. I value the forest because it is of a specific kind, because there is a certain kind of causal history which explains its existence. Of course I can be deceived into thinking that a piece of landscape has that kind of history, has developed

---

[8] For example protecting the Great Barrier Reef from damage by the crown-of-thorns starfish.

in the appropriate way. The success of the deception does not elevate the restored landscape to the level of the original, anymore than the success of the deception in the previous example confers on the fake the value of a real Vermeer. What has value in both cases are objects which are of the kind that I value, not merely objects which I think are of that kind. This point, it should be noted, is appropriate independently of views concerning the subjectivity or objectivity of value.

An example might bring the point home. Imagine that John is someone who values wilderness. John may find himself in one of the following situations:

1. He falls into the clutches of a utilitarian-minded super-technologist. John's captor has erected a rather incredible device which he calls an experience machine. Once the electrodes are attached and the right buttons pressed one can be brought to experience anything whatsoever. John is plugged into the machine, and, since his captor knows full well John's love of wilderness, given an extended experience as of hiking through a spectacular wilderness. This is environmental engineering at its most extreme. Quite assuredly John is being short-changed. John wants there to be wilderness and he wants to experience it. He wants the world to be a certain way and he wants to have experiences of a certain kind; veridical.

2. John is abducted, blindfolded, and taken to a simulated, plastic wilderness area. When the blindfold is removed John is thrilled by what he sees around him: the tall gums, the wattles, the lichen on the rocks. At least that is what he thinks is there. We know better: we know that John is deceived, that he is once again being short-changed. He has been presented with an environment which he thinks is of value but isn't. If he knew that the leaves through which the artificially generated breeze now stirred were synthetic he would be profoundly disappointed, perhaps even disgusted at what at best is a cruel joke.

3. John is taken to a place which was once devastated by strip-mining. The forest which had stood there for some thousands of years had been felled and the earth torn up, and the animals either killed or driven from their habitat. Times have changed, however, and the area has been restored. Trees of the species which grew there before the devastation grow there again, and the animal species have returned. John knows nothing of this and thinks he is in pristine forest. Once again, he has been short-changed, presented with less than what he values most.

In the same way that the plastic trees may be thought a (minimal) improvement on the experience machine, so too the real trees are an improvement on the plastic ones. In fact in the third situation there is incomparably more of value than in the second, but there could be more. The forest, though real, is not genuinely what John wants it to be. If it were not the product of contrivance he would value it more. It is a product of contrivance. Even in the situation where the devastated area regenerates rather than is restored, it is possible to understand and sympathize with John's claim that the environment does not have the fullest possible value. Admittedly in this case there is not so much room for that claim, since the environment has regenerated of its own accord. Still, the regenerated environment does not have the right kind of continuity with the forest that stood there initially; that continuity has been interfered with by the earlier devastation. (In actual fact the regenerated forest is likely to be perceivably quite different to the kind of thing originally there.)

III

I have argued that the causal genesis of forests, rivers, lakes, and so on is important in establishing their value. I have also tried to give an indication of why this is. In the course of my argument I drew various analogies, implicit rather than explicit, between faking art and faking nature. This should not be taken to suggest, however, that the concepts of aesthetic evaluation and judgement are to be carried straight over to evaluations of, and judgements about, the natural environment. Indeed there is good reason to believe that this cannot be done. For one thing an apparently integral part of aesthetic evaluation depends on viewing the aesthetic object as an intentional object, as an artefact, as something that is shaped by the purposes and designs of its author. Evaluating works of art involves explaining them, and judging them, in terms of their author's intentions; it involves placing them within the author's corpus of work; it involves locating them in some tradition and in some special *milieu*. Nature is not a work of art though works of art (in some suitably broad sense) may look very much like natural objects.

None of this is to deny that certain concepts which are frequently deployed in aesthetic evaluation cannot usefully and legitimately be deployed in evaluations of the environment. We admire the intricacy and delicacy of colouring in paintings as we might admire the intricate and delicate shadings in a eucalypt forest. We admire the solid grandeur of a building as we might admire the solidity and grandeur of a massive rock outcrop. And of course the ubiquitous notion of *the beautiful* has a purchase in environmental evaluations as it does in aesthetic evaluations.

Even granted all this there are various arguments which might be developed to drive a wedge between the two kinds of evaluation which would weaken the analogies between faking art and faking nature. One such argument turns on the claim that aesthetic evaluation has, as a central component, a judgemental factor, concerning the author's intentions and the like in the way that was sketched above.[9] The idea is that nature, like works of art, may elicit any of a range of emotional responses in viewers. We may be awed by a mountain, soothed by the sound of water over rocks, excited by the power of a waterfall, and so on. However, the judgemental element in aesthetic evaluation serves to differentiate it from environmental evaluation and serves to explain, or so the argument would go, exactly what it is about fakes and forgeries in art which discounts their value with respect to the original. The claim is that if there is no judgemental element in environmental evaluation, then there is no rational basis to preferring real to faked nature when the latter is a good replica. The argument can, I think, be met.

Meeting the argument does not require arguing that responses to nature count as aesthetic responses. I agree that they are not. Nevertheless there are analogies which go beyond emotional content, and which may persuade us to take more seriously the claim that faked nature is inferior. It is important to make the point that only in fanciful situations dreamt up by philosophers are there no detectable differences between fakes and originals, both in the case of artefacts and in the case of natural objects. By taking a realistic example where there are discernible, and possibly discernible, differences between the fake and the real thing, it is possible to bring out the judgemental element in responses to, and evaluations of, the environment. Right now I may not be able to tell a real Vermeer from a Van Meegaran, though I might learn to do so. By the same token I might not be able to tell apart a naturally evolved stand of mountain ash from one which has been planted, but might later acquire the ability to make the requisite judgement. Perhaps an anecdote is appropriate here. There is a particular stand of mountain ash that I had long admired. The trees were straight and tall, of uniform stature, neither densely packed nor too open-spaced. I then discovered what would have been obvious to a more expert eye, namely that the stand of mountain ash had been planted to replace original forest which had been burnt out. This explained the uniformity in size, the density and so on: it also changed my attitude to that piece of landscape. The evaluation that I make now of that landscape is to a certain

---

[9] See e.g. Don Mannison, 'A Prolegomenon to a Human Chauvinist Aesthetic', in D. S. Mannison, M. A. McRobbie, R. Routley, eds., *Environmental Philosophy* (Canberra: Research School of Social Sciences, Australian National University, 1980), 212–16.

extent informed, the response is not merely emotive but cognitive as well. The evaluation is informed and directed by my beliefs about the forest, the type of forest it is, its condition as a member of that kind, its causal genesis and so on. What is more, the judgemental element affects the emotive one. Knowing that the forest is not a naturally evolved forest causes me to feel differently about it: it causes me to perceive the forest differently and to assign it less value than naturally evolved forests.

Val Routley has eloquently reminded us that people who value wilderness do not do so merely because they like to soak up pretty scenery.[10] They see much more and value much more than this. What they do see, and what they value, is very much a function of the degree to which they understand the ecological mechanisms which maintain the landscape and which determine that it appears the way it does. Similarly, knowledge of art history, of painting techniques, and the like will inform aesthetic evaluations and alter aesthetic perceptions. Knowledge of this kind is capable of transforming a hitherto uninteresting landscape into one that is compelling. Holmes Rolston has discussed at length the way in which an understanding and appreciation of ecology generates new values.[11] He does not claim that ecology reveals values previously unnoticed, but rather that the understanding of the complexity, diversity, and integration of the natural world which ecology affords us, opens up a new area of valuation. As the facts are uncovered, the values are generated. What the remarks of Routley and Rolston highlight is the judgemental factor which is present in environmental appraisal. Understanding and evaluation do go hand in hand; and the responses individuals have to forests, wild rivers, and the like are not merely raw, emotional responses.

IV

Not all forests are alike, not all rain forests are alike. There are countless possible discriminations that the informed observer may make. Comparative judgements between areas of the natural environment are possible with regard to ecological richness, stage of development, stability, peculiar local circumstance, and the like. Judgements of this kind will very often underlie hierarchical orderings of environments in terms of their intrinsic worth. Appeal to judgements of this kind will frequently strengthen the

---

[10] Val Routley, 'Critical Notice of Passmore's *Man's Responsibility for Nature*', *Australasian Journal of Philosophy*, 53/2 (1975), 171–85.
[11] Holmes Rolston III, 'Is There An Ecological Ethic', *Ethics*, 85/2 (1975), 93–109.

case for preserving some bit of the environment. Thus one strong argument against the Tasmanian Hydroelectricity Commission's proposal to dam the Lower Gordon River turns on the fact that it threatens the inundation of an exceedingly fine stand of Huon pine. If the stand of Huon pines could not justifiably be ranked so high on the appropriate ecological scale then the argument against the dam would be to that extent weakened.

One reason that a faked forest is not just as good as a naturally evolved forest is that there is always the possibility that the trained eye will tell the difference.[12] It takes some time to discriminate areas of Alpine plain which are naturally clear of snow gums from those that have been cleared. It takes some time to discriminate regrowth forest which has been logged from forest which has not been touched. These are discriminations which it is possible to make and which are made. Moreover, they are discriminations which affect valuations. The reasons why the 'faked' forest counts for less, more often than not, than the real thing are similar to the reasons why faked works of art count for less than the real thing.

Origin is important as an integral part of the evaluation process. It is important because our beliefs about it determine the valuations we make. It is also important in that the discovery that something has an origin quite different to the origin we initially believe that it has, can literally alter the way we perceive that thing.[13] The point concerning the possibility of detecting fakes is important in that it stresses just how much detail must be written into the claim that environmental engineers can replicate nature. Even if environmental engineering could achieve such exactitude, there is, I suggest, no compelling reasons for accepting the restoration thesis. It is worth stressing though that, as a matter of strategy, environmentalists must argue the empirical inadequacy of restoration proposals. This is the strongest argument against restoration ploys, because it appeals to diverse value-frameworks, and because such proposals are promises to deliver a specific good. Showing that the good won't be delivered is thus a useful move to make.

[12] For a discussion of this point with respect to art forgeries, see Goodman, *Languages of Art*, esp. 103–12.

[13] For an excellent discussion of this same point with respect to artefacts, see Radford, 'Fakes', esp. 73–6.

V

DUTIES CONCERNING ISLANDS

MARY MIDGLEY

Had Robinson Crusoe any duties?

When I was a philosophy student, this used to be a familiar conundrum, which was supposed to pose a very simple question; namely, can you have duties to yourself? Mill, they correctly told us, said no. 'The term duty to oneself, when it means anything more than prudence, means self-respect or self-development, and for none of these is anyone accountable to his fellow-creatures.'[1] Kant, on the other hand, said yes. 'Duties to ourselves are of primary importance and should have pride of place . . . nothing can be expected of a man who dishonours his own person.'[2] There is a serious disagreement here, not to be sneezed away just by saying, 'it depends on what you mean by duty'. Much bigger issues are involved—quite how big has, I think, not yet been fully realized. To grasp this, I suggest that we rewrite a part of Crusoe's story, in order to bring in sight a different range of concerns.

19 Sept. 1685. This day I set aside to devastate my island. My pinnace being now ready on the shore, and all things prepared for my departure, Friday's people also expecting me, and the wind blowing fresh away from my little harbour, I had a mind to see how all would burn. So then, setting sparks and powder craftily among certain dry spinneys which I had chosen, I soon had it ablaze, nor was there left, by the next dawn, any green stick among the ruins. . . .

Now, work on the style how you will, you cannot make that into a convincing paragraph. Crusoe was not the most scrupulous of men, but he would have felt an invincible objection to this senseless destruction. So would the rest of us. Yet the language of our moral tradition has tended strongly, ever since the Enlightenment, to make that objection unstateable. All the terms which express that an obligation is serious or binding—

Reprinted with permission from R. Elliot and A. Gare, eds., *Environmental Philosophy* (St. Lucia: University of Queensland Press, 1983), 166–81.

[1] John Stuart Mill, *Essay on Liberty* (London: Dent, Everyman's Library, 1910), 135.

[2] Immanuel Kant, 'Duties to Oneself', in *Lectures on Ethics*, tr. Louis Infield (London: Methuen, 1930), 118.

duty, right, law, morality, obligation, justice—have been deliberately narrowed in their use so as to apply only in the framework of contract, to describe only relations holding between free and rational agents. Since it has been decided a priori that rationality admits of no degrees and that cetaceans are not rational, it follows that, unless you take either religion or science fiction seriously, we can only have duties to humans, and sane, adult, responsible humans at that. Now the morality we live by certainly does not accept this restriction. In common life we recognize many other duties as serious and binding, though of course not necessarily overriding. If philosophers want to call these something else instead of duties, they must justify their move.

We have here one of those clashes between the language of common morality (which is of course always to some extent confused and inarticulate) and an intellectual scheme which arose in the first place from a part of that morality, but has now taken off on its own claims of authority to correct other parts of its source. There are always real difficulties here. As ordinary citizens, we have to guard against dismissing such intellectual schemes too casually; we have to do justice to the point of them. But, as philosophers, we have to resist the opposite temptation of taking the intellectual scheme as decisive, just because it is elegant and satisfying, or because the moral insight which is its starting-point is specially familiar to us. Today, this intellectualist bias is often expressed by calling the insights of common morality mere 'intuitions'. This is quite misleading, since it gives the impression that they have been reached without thought, and that there is, by contrast, a scientific solution somewhere else to which they ought to bow—as there might be if we were contrasting commonsense 'intuitions' about the physical world with physics or astronomy. Even without that word, philosophers often manage to give the impression that whenever our moral views clash with any simple, convenient scheme, it is our *duty* to abandon them. Thus, Grice states:

It is an inescapable consequence of the thesis presented in these pages that certain classes cannot have natural rights: animals, the human embryo, future generations, lunatics and children under the age of, say, ten. In the case of young children at least, my experience is that this consequence is found hard to accept. But it is a consequence of the theory; it is, I believe, true; and I think we should be willing to accept it. At first sight it seems a harsh conclusion, but it is not nearly so harsh as it appears.[3]

But it is in fact extremely harsh, since what he is saying is that the treatment of children ought not to be determined by their interests but by

---

[3] G. R. Grice, *Grounds for Moral Sentiments* (Cambridge: Cambridge University Press, 1967), 147–9.

the interests of the surrounding adults capable of contract, which, of course, can easily conflict with them. In our society, he explains, this does not actually make much difference, because parents here are so benevolent that they positively want to benefit their children, and accordingly here 'the interests of children are reflected in the interests of their parents.' But this, he adds, is just a contingent fact about us. 'It is easy to imagine a society where this is not so', where, that is, parents are entirely exploitative. 'In this circumstance, the morally correct treatment of children would no doubt be harsher than it is in our society. But the conclusion has to be accepted.' Grice demands that we withdraw our objections to harshness, in deference to theoretical consistency. But 'harsh' here does not mean just 'brisk and bracing', like cold baths and a plain diet. (There might well be more of those where parents do feel bound to consider their children's interests.) It means 'unjust'. Our objection to unbridled parental selfishness is not a mere matter of tone or taste; it is a moral one. It therefore requires a moral answer, an explanation of the contrary *value* which the contrary theory expresses. Grice, and those who argue like him, take the ascetic, disapproving tone of those who have already displayed such a value, and who are met by a slovenly reluctance to rise to it. But they have not displayed that value. The ascetic tone cannot be justified merely by an appeal to consistency. An ethical theory which, when consistently followed through, has iniquitous consequences, is a bad theory and must be changed. Certainly we can ask whether these consequences really are iniquitous, but this question must be handled seriously. We cannot directly conclude that the consequences cease to stink the moment they are seen to follow from our theory.

The theoretical model which has spread blight in this area is, of course, that of social contract, and, to suit it, that whole cluster of essential moral terms—right, duty, justice and the rest—has been progressively narrowed. This model shows human society as a spread of standard social atoms, originally distinct and independent, each of which combines with others only at its own choice and in its own private interest. This model is drawn from physics, and from seventeenth-century physics, at that, where the ultimate particles of matter were conceived as hard, impenetrable, homogeneous little billiard-balls, with no hooks or internal structure. To see how such atoms could combine at all was very hard. Physics, accordingly, moved on from this notion to one which treats atoms and other particles as complex items, describable mainly in terms of forces, and those the same kind of forces which operate outside them. It has abandoned the notion of ultimate, solitary, independent individuals. Social-contract theory, however, retains it.

On this physical—or archaeo-physical—model, all significant moral relations between individuals are the symmetrical ones expressed by contract. If, on the other hand, we use a biological or 'organic' model, we can talk also of a variety of asymmetrical relations found within a whole. Leaves relate not only to other leaves, but to fruit, twigs, branches, and the whole tree. People appear not only as individuals, but as members of their groups, families, tribes, species, ecosystems, and biosphere, and have moral relations as parts to these wholes. The choice between these two ways of thinking is not, of course, a simple once-and-for-all affair. Different models are useful for different purposes. We can, however, reasonably point out, firstly, that the old physical pattern does make all attempts to explain combination extremely difficult; and, secondly, that since human beings actually are living creatures, not crystals or galaxies, it is reasonable to expect that biological ways of thinking will be useful in understanding them.

In its own sphere, the social contract model has of course been of enormous value. Where we deal with clashes of interest between free and rational agents already in existence, and particularly where we want to disentangle some of them from some larger group that really does not suit them, it is indispensable. And for certain political purposes during the last three centuries these clashes have been vitally important. An obsession with contractual thinking, and a conviction that it is a cure-all, are therefore understandable. But the trouble with such obsessions is that they distort the whole shape of thought and language in a way which makes them self-perpetuating, and constantly extends their empire. Terms come to be defined in a way which leaves only certain moral views expressible. This can happen without any clear intention on the part of those propagating them, and even contrary to their occasional declarations, simply from mental inertia. Thus, John Rawls, having devoted most of his long book to his very subtle and exhaustive contractual view of justice, remarks without any special emphasis near the end that 'we should recall here the limits of a theory of justice. Not only are many aspects of morality left aside, but no account can be given of right conduct in regard to animals and the rest of nature.'[4] He concedes that these are serious matters. 'Certainly it is wrong to be cruel to animals and the destruction of a whole species can be a great evil. The capacity for feelings of pleasure and pain and for the forms of life of which animals are capable clearly impose duties of compassion and humanity in their case.' All this is important, he says, and it calls for a wider metaphysical enquiry, but it is not his subject. Earlier in the same passage

---

[4] John Rawls, *A Theory of Justice* (Oxford: Oxford University Press, 1972), 512.

he touches on the question of permanently irrational human beings, and remarks that it 'may present a difficulty. I cannot examine this problem here, but I assume that the account of equality would not be materially affected.'[5] Won't it though? It is a strange project to examine a single virtue—justice—without at least sketching in one's view of the vast background of general morality which determines its shape and meaning, including, of course, such awkward and non-contractual virtues as 'compassion and humanity'. It isolates the duties which people owe each other *merely as thinkers* from those deeper and more general ones which they owe each other as beings who feel. It cannot, therefore, fail both to split a man's nature and to isolate him from the rest of the creation to which he belongs.

Such an account may not be *Hamlet* without the prince, but it is *Hamlet* with half the cast missing, and without the state of Denmark. More exactly, it is like a history of Poland which regards Russia, Germany, Europe, and the Roman Church as not part of its subject. I am not attacking Rawls's account on its own ground. I am simply pointing out what the history of ethics shows all too clearly—how much our thinking is shaped by what our sages *omit* to mention. The Greek philosophers never really raised the problem of slavery till towards the end of their epoch, and then few of them did so with conviction. This happened even though it lay right in the path of their inquiries into political justice and the value of the individual soul. Christianity did raise that problem, because its class background was different and because the world in the Christian era was already in turmoil, so that men were not presented with the narcotic of a happy stability. But Christianity itself did not, until quite recently, raise the problem of the morality of punishment, and particularly of eternal punishment. This failure to raise central questions was not, in either case, complete. One can find very intelligent and penetrating criticisms of slavery occurring from time to time in Greek writings—even in Aristotle's defence of that institution.[6] But they are mostly like Rawls's remark here. They conclude that 'this should be investigated some day'. The same thing happens with Christian writings concerning punishment, except that the consideration, 'this is a great mystery,' acts as an even more powerful paralytic to thought. Not much more powerful, however. Natural inertia, when it coincides with vested interest or the illusion of vested interest, is as strong as gravitation.

It is important that Rawls does not, like Grice, demand that we toe a line which would make certain important moral views impossible. Like Hume,

---

[5] Ibid. 510.
[6] Aristotle, *Politics*, 1. 3–8; cf., idem, *Nichomachean Ethics*, 7. 2.

who similarly excluded animals from justice, he simply leaves them out of his discussion. This move ought in principle to be harmless. But when it is combined with an intense concentration of discussion on contractual justice, and a corresponding neglect of compassion and humanity, it inevitably suggests that the excluded problems are relatively unimportant. This suggestion is still more strongly conveyed by rulings which exclude the non-human world from rights, duties, and morality. Words like 'rights' and 'duties' are awkward because they do indeed have narrow senses approximating to the legal, but they also have much wider ones in which they cover the whole moral sphere. To say 'they do not have rights,' or 'you do not have duties to them' conveys to any ordinary hearer a very simple message; namely, 'they do not matter'. This is an absolution, a removal of blame for ill-treatment of 'them', whoever they may be.

To see how strong this informal, moral usage of 'rights' is, we need only look at the history of that powerful notion, the 'rights of man'. These rights were not supposed to be ones conferred by law, since the whole point of appealing to them was to change laws so as to embody them. They were vague, but vast. They did not arise, as rights are often said to do, only within a community, since they were taken to apply in principle everywhere. The immense, and on the whole coherent, use which has been made of this idea by reform movements shows plainly that the tension between the formal and the informal idea of 'right' is part of the word's meaning, a fruitful connection of thought, not just a mistake. It is therefore hard to adopt effectively the compromise which some philosophers now favour, of saying that it is indeed wrong to treat animals in certain ways, but that we have no duties to them or that they have no rights.[7] 'Animal rights' may be hard to formulate, as indeed are the rights of humans. But 'no rights' will not do. The word may need to be dropped entirely. The compromise is still harder with the word 'duty', which is rather more informal, and is more closely wedded to a private rather than political use.

Where the realm of right and duty stops, there, to ordinary thinking, begins the realm of the optional. What is not a duty may be a matter of taste, style or feeling, of aesthetic sensibility, of habit and nostalgia, of etiquette and local custom, but it cannot be something which demands our attention whether we like it or not. When claims get into this area, they can scarcely be taken seriously. This becomes clear when Kant tries to straddle the border. He says that we have no direct duties to animals, because they are not rational, but that we should treat them properly all the same

---

[7] For example, John Passmore, *Man's Responsibility for Nature* (London: Duckworth, 1974), 116–17; H. J. McCloskey, 'Rights', *Philosophical Quarterly*, 15 (1965).

because of 'indirect' duties which are really duties to our own humanity.[8] This means that ill-treating them (a) might lead us to ill-treat humans, and (b) is a sign of a bad or inhumane disposition. The whole issue thus becomes a contingent one of spiritual style or training, like contemplative exercises, intellectual practice or, indeed, refined manners.[9] Some might need practice of this kind to make them kind to people, others might not, and, indeed, might get on better without it. (Working off one's ill-temper on animals might make one treat people *better*.) But the question of cruelty to animals cannot be like this, because it is of the essence of such training exercises that they are internal. Anything that affects some other being is not just practice, it is real action. Anyone who refrained from cruelty *merely* from a wish not to sully his own character, without any direct consideration for the possible victims, would be frivolous and narcissistic.

A similar trivialization follows where theorists admit duties of compassion and humanity to non-contractors, but deny duties of justice. Hume and Rawls, in making this move, do not explicitly subordinate these other duties, or say that they are less binding. But because they make the contract element so central to morality, this effect appears to follow. The priority of justice is expressed in such everyday proverbs as 'be just before you're generous'. We are therefore rather easily persuaded to think that compassion, humanity and so forth are perhaps emotional luxuries, to be indulged only after all debts are paid. A moment's thought will show that this is wrong. Someone who receives simultaneously a request to pay a debt and another to comfort somebody bereaved or on their deathbed is not as a matter of course under obligation to treat the debt as the more urgent. He has to look at circumstances on both sides, but in general we should probably expect the other duties to have priority. This is still more true if, on his way to pay the debt, he encounters a stranger in real straits, drowning or lying on the road. To give the debt priority, we probably need to think of his creditor as also being in serious trouble—which brings compassion and humanity in on both sides of the case.

What makes it so hard to give justice a different clientele from the other virtues, as Hume and Rawls do, is simply the fact that justice is such a pervading virtue. In general, all serious cases of cruelty, meanness, inhumanity, and the like are also cases of injustice. If we are told that a certain set of these cases does not involve injustice, our natural thought is that these cases must be *trivial*. Officially, Hume's and Rawls's restriction is not supposed to mean this. What, however, is it supposed to mean? It is

---

[8] Nor will it help for philosophers to say 'it is not the case that they have rights'. Such pompous locutions have either no meaning at all, or the obvious one.

[9] Immanuel Kant, 'Duties towards Animals and Spirits', in *Lectures on Ethics*, 240.

forty years since I first read Hume's text, and I find his thought as obscure now as I did then. I well remember double-taking then, going back over the paragraph for a point which, I took it, I must have missed. Can anyone see it?

> Were there a species of creatures intermingled with men, which, though rational, were possessed of such inferior strength, both of body and mind, that they were incapable of all resistance, and could never, upon the highest provocation, make us feel the effects of their resentment; the necessary consequence, I think, is that we should be bound by the laws of humanity to give gentle usage to these creatures, but should not, properly speaking, lie under any restraint of justice with regard to them, nor could they possess any right or property, exclusive of such arbitrary lords. Our intercourse with them could not be called society, which supposes a degree of equality, but absolute command on one side and servile obedience on the other. . . . This is plainly the situation of men with regard to animals.[10]

I still think that the word 'justice', so defined, has lost its normal meaning. In ordinary life we think that duties of justice become *more* pressing, not less so, when we are dealing with the weak and inarticulate, who cannot argue back. It is the boundaries of prudence which depend on power, not those of justice. Historically, Hume's position becomes more understandable when one sees its place in the development of social-contract thinking. The doubtful credit for confining justice to the human species seems to belong to Grotius, who finally managed to ditch the Roman notion of *jus naturale*, natural right or law, common to all species. I cannot here discuss his remarkably unimpressive arguments for this.[11] The point I want to make here is simply in reference to the effect of these restrictive definitions of terms like 'justice' on people's view of the sheer size of the problems raised by what falls outside them.

Writers who treat morality as primarily contractual tend to discuss non-contractual cases briefly, casually, and parenthetically, as though they were rather rare. Rawls's comments on the problem of mental defectives are entirely typical here. We have succeeded, they say, in laying most of the carpet; why are you making this fuss about those little wrinkles behind the sofa? This treatment confirms a view, already suggested by certain aspects of current politics in the United States, that those who fail to clock in as normal rational agents and make their contracts are just occasional exceptions, constituting one more 'minority' group—worrying, no doubt, to the scrupulous, but not a central concern of any society. Let us, then,

---

[10] David Hume 'An Enquiry Concerning the Principles of Morals', in *Hume's Moral and Political Philosophy*, ed. H. E. Aiben (New York: Hafner, 1949), app. 3, 190–1.

[11] A point well discussed by Stephen R. L. Clark, *The Moral Status of Animals* (Oxford: Clarendon Press, 1977), 12–13.

glance briefly at their scope, by roughly listing some cases which seem to involve us in non-contractual duties. (The order is purely provisional and the numbers are added just for convenience.)

Human sector	1. The dead
	2. Posterity
	3. Children
	4. The senile
	5. The temporarily insane
	6. The permanently insane
	7. Defectives, ranging down to 'human vegetables'
	8. Embryos, human and otherwise
Animal sector	9. Sentient animals
	10. Non-sentient animals
Inanimate sector	11. Plants of all kinds
	12. Artefacts, including works of art
	13. Inanimate but structured objects—crystals, rivers, rocks, etc.
Comprehensive	14. Unchosen groups of all kinds, including families and species
	15. Ecosystems, landscapes, villages, warrens, cities, etc.
	16. Countries
	17. The biosphere
Miscellaneous	18. Oneself
	19. God

No doubt I have missed a few, but that will do to go on with. The point is this; if we look only at a few of these groupings, and without giving them full attention, it is easy to think that we can include one or two as honorary contracting members by a slight stretch of our conceptual scheme, and find arguments for excluding the others from serious concern entirely. But if we keep our eye on the size of the range, this stops being plausible. As far as sheer numbers go, this is no minority of the beings with whom we have to deal. We are a small minority of them. As far as importance goes, it is certainly possible to argue that some of these sorts of beings should concern us more and others less: we need a priority system. But, to build it, *moral* arguments are required. The various kinds of claims have to be understood and compared, not written off in advance. We cannot rule that those who, in our own and other cultures, suppose that there is a direct objection to injuring or destroying some of them, are always just confused, and mean only, in fact, that this item will be needed for rational human consumption.[12]

The blank antithesis which Kant made between rational persons (having value) and mere things (having none) will not serve us to map out this vast continuum. And the idea that, starting at some given point on this list, we have a general licence for destruction, is itself a moral view which would have to be justified. Western culture differs from most others in the breadth of destructive licence which it allows itself, and, since the seventeenth century, that licence has been greatly extended. Scruples about rapine have been continually dismissed as irrational, but it is not always clear with what rational principles they are supposed to conflict. Western destructiveness has not in fact developed in response to a new set of disinterested intellectual principles demonstrating the need for more people and less redwoods, but mainly as a by-product of greed and increasing commercial confidence. Humanistic hostility to superstition has played some part in the process, because respect for the non-human items on our list is often taken to be religious. It does not have to be. Many scientists who are card-carrying atheists can still see the point of preserving the biosphere. So can the rest of us, religious or otherwise. It is the whole of which we are parts, and its other parts concern us for that reason.

But the language of rights is rather ill-suited to expressing this, because it has been developed mainly for the protection of people who, though perhaps oppressed, are in principle articulate. This makes it quite reasonable for theorists to say that rights belong only to those who understand them and can claim them. When confronted with the 'human sector' of our list, these theorists can either dig themselves in, like Grice, and exclude the lot, or stretch the scheme, like Rawls, by including the hypothetical rational choices which these honorary members *would* make if they were not unfortunately prevented. Since many of these people seem less rational than many animals, zoophiles have, then, a good case for calling this second device arbitrary or specious, and extending rights to the border of sentience. Here, however, the meaning of the term 'rights' does become thin, and when we reach the inanimate area, usage will scarcely cover it. (It is worth noticing that long before this, when dealing merely with the 'rights of man', the term often seems obscure, because to list and specify these rights is so much harder than to shout for them. The word is probably of more use as a slogan, indicating a general direction, than as a detailed

---

[12] For details, see John Rodman, 'Animal Justice: The Counter-Revolution in Natural Right and Law', *Inquiry*, 22/1–2 (Summer 1979).

conceptual tool.) There may be a point in campaigning to extend usage. But to me it seems wiser on the whole not to waste energy on this verbal point, but instead to insist on the immense variety of kinds of beings with which we have to deal. Once we grasp this, we ought not to be surprised that we are involved in many different kinds of claim or duty. The dictum that 'rights and duties are correlative' is misleading, because the two words keep rather different company, and one may be narrowed without affecting the other.

What, then, about duties? I believe that this term can properly be used over the whole range. We have quite simply got many kinds of duties to animals,[13] to plants, and to the biosphere. But to speak in this way we must free the term once and for all from its restrictive contractual use, or irrelevant doubts will still haunt us. If we cannot do this, we shall have to exclude the word 'duty', along with 'rights' from all detailed discussion, using wider words like 'wrong', 'right', and 'ought' instead. This gymnastic would be possible but inconvenient. The issue about duty becomes clear as soon as we look at the controversy from which I started, between Kant's and Mill's views on duties to oneself. What do we think about this? Are there duties of integrity, autonomy, self-knowledge, self-respect? It seems that there are. Mill is right, of course, to point out that they are not duties *to* someone in the ordinary sense. The divided self is a metaphor. It is as natural and necessary a metaphor here as it is over, say, self-deception or self-control, but it certainly is not literal truth. The form of the require-ment is different. Rights, for instance, certainly do not seem to come in here as they often would with duties to other persons; we would scarcely say, 'I have a right to my own respect'. And the *kind* of things which we can owe ourselves are distinctive. It is not just chance who they are owed to. You cannot owe it to somebody else, as you can to yourself, to force him to act freely or with integrity. He owes that to himself, the rest of us can only remove outside difficulties. As Kant justly said, our business is to promote our own perfection and the happiness of others; the perfection of others is an aim which belongs to them.[14] Respect, indeed, we owe both to ourselves and to others, but Kant may well be right to say that self-respect is really a different and deeper requirement, something without which all outward duties would become meaningless. (This may explain the paralyzing effect of depression.)

---

[13] A case first made by Jeremy Bentham, *An Introduction to the Principles of Morals and Legislation* (1784), Ch. 17, and well worked out by Peter Singer, *Animal Liberation* (New York: Avon, 1975), Chs. 1, 5, and 6.

[14] Immanuel Kant, *Preface to the Metaphysical Elements of Ethics*, 'Introduction to Ethics', 4 and 5, tr. Thomas K. Abbot.

Duties to oneself, in fact, are duties with a different *form*. They are far less close than outward duties to the literal model of debt, especially monetary debt. Money is a thing which can be owed in principle to any-body, it is the same whoever you owe it to, and if by chance you come to owe it to yourself, the debt vanishes. Not many of our duties are really of this impersonal kind; the attempt to commute other sorts of duties into money is a notorious form of evasion. Utilitarianism, however, wants to make all duties as homogeneous as possible. And that is the point of Mill's position. He views all our self-concerning motives as parts of the desire for happiness. Therefore he places all duty, indeed all morality, on the outside world, as socially required restriction of that desire—an expression, that is, of other people's desire for happiness.

We do not call anything wrong, unless we mean that a person ought to be punished in some way or another for doing it; if not by law, by the opinion of his fellow-creatures; if not by opinion, by the reproaches of his own conscience. This seems the real turning point of the distinction between morality and simple expediency. It is a part of the notion of Duty in every one of its forms, that a person may rightly be compelled to fulfil it. Duty is a thing which may be *exacted* from a person, as one exacts a debt.[15]

To make the notion of wrongness depend on punishment and public opinion in this way instead of the other way round is a bold step. Mill did not mind falling flat on his face from time to time in trying out a new notion for the public good. He did it for us, and we should, I think, take proper advantage of his generosity, and accept the impossibility which he demon-strates. The concepts cannot be connected this way round. Unless you think of certain acts as wrong, it makes no sense to talk of punishment. 'Punishing' alcoholics with aversion therapy or experimental rats with electric shocks is not really punishing at all; it is just deterrence. This 'punishment' will not make their previous actions wrong, nor has it any-thing to do with morality. The real point of morality returns to Mill's scheme in the Trojan horse of 'the reproaches of his own conscience'. Why do *they* matter? Unless the conscience is talking sense—that is, on Utilitarian principles, unless it is delivering the judgement of society—it should surely be silenced. Mill, himself a man of enormous integrity, deeply concerned about autonomy, would never have agreed to silence it. But, unless we do so, we shall have to complicate his scheme. It may well be true that, in the last resort and at the deepest level, conscience and the desire for happiness converge. But in ordinary life and at the everyday level they can diverge amazingly. We do want to be honest but we do not

[15] John Stuart Mill, *Utilitarianism* (London: Dent, Everyman's Library, 1910), ch. 5, 45; first published 1863.

want to be put out. What we know we ought to do is often most unwelcome to us, which is why we call it duty. And whole sections of that duty do not concern other people directly at all. A good example is the situation in Huxley's *Brave New World*, where a few dissident citizens have grasped the possibility of a fuller and freer life. Nobody else wants this. Happiness is already assured. The primary duty of change here seems to be that of each to himself. True, they may feel bound also to help others to change, but hardly in a way which those others would *exact*. In fact, we may do better here by dropping the awkward second party altogether and saying that they have a duty *of* living differently—one which will affect both themselves and others, but which does not require, as a debt does, a named person or people *to* whom it must be paid. Wider models like 'the whole duty of man' may be more relevant.

This one example from my list will, I hope, be enough to explain the point. I cannot go through all of them, nor ought it to be necessary. Duties need *not* be quasi-contractual relations between symmetrical pairs of rational human agents. There are all kinds of other obligations holding between asymmetrical pairs, or involving, as in this case, no outside beings at all. To speak of duties *to* things in the inanimate and comprehensive sectors of my list is not necessarily to personify them superstitiously, or to indulge in chatter about the 'secret life of plants'.[16] It expresses merely that there are suitable and unsuitable ways of behaving in given situations. People have duties *as* farmers, parents, consumers, forest dwellers, colonists, species members, shipwrecked mariners, tourists, potential ancestors, and actual descendants, etc. As such, it is the business of each not to forget his transitory and dependent position, the rich gifts which he has received, and the tiny part he plays in a vast, irreplaceable and fragile whole.

It is remarkable that we now have to state this obvious truth as if it were new, and invent the word 'ecological' to describe a whole vast class of duties. Most peoples are used to the idea. In stating it, and getting back into the centre of our moral stage, we meet various difficulties, of which the most insidious is possibly the temptation to feed this issue as fuel to

---

[16] P. Tompkins and C. Bird, *The Secret Life of Plants* (New York: Harper and Row, 1973), claimed to show, by various experiments involving electrical apparatus, that plants can feel. Attempts to duplicate their experiments have, however, totally failed to produce any similar results. (See A. W. Galston and C. L. Slayman, 'The Secret Life of Plants', *American Scientist*, 67 (1973), 337.) It seems possible that the original results were due to a fault in the electrical apparatus. The attempt shows, I think, one of the confusions which continually arise from insisting that all duties must be of the same form. We do not need to prove that plants are animals in order to have reason to spare them. The point is well discussed by Marian Dawkins in her book *Animal Suffering* (London: Chapman and Hall, 1981), 117–19.

long-standing controversies about religion. Is concern for the non-human aspects of our biosphere necessarily superstitious and therefore to be resisted tooth and nail? I have pointed out that it need not be religious. Certified rejectors of all known religions can share it. No doubt, however, there is a wider sense in which any deep and impersonal concern can be called religious—one in which Marxism is a religion. No doubt, too, all such deep concerns have their dangers, but certainly the complete absence of them has worse dangers. Moreover, anyone wishing above all to avoid the religious dimension should consider that the intense individualism which has focused our attention exclusively on the social-contract model is itself thoroughly mystical. It has glorified the individual human soul as an object having infinite and transcendent value; has hailed it as the only real creator; and bestowed on it much of the panoply of God. Nietzsche, who was responsible for much of this new theology,[17] took over from the old theology (which he plundered extensively) the assumption that all the rest of creation mattered only as a frame for humankind. This is not an impression which any disinterested observer would get from looking round at it, nor do we need it in order to take our destiny sufficiently seriously.

Crusoe then, I conclude, did have duties concerning his island, and with the caution just given we can reasonably call them duties *to* it. They were not very exacting, and were mostly negative. They differed, of course, from those which a long-standing inhabitant of a country has. Here the language of *fatherland* and *motherland*, which is so widely employed, indicates rightly a duty of care and responsibility which can go very deep, and which long-settled people commonly feel strongly. To insist that it is really only a duty to the exploiting human beings is not consistent with the emphasis often given to reverence for the actual trees, mountains, lakes, rivers and the like which are found there. A decision to inhibit all this rich area of human love is a special manœuvre for which reasons would need to be given, not a dispassionate analysis of existing duties and feelings. What happens, however, when you are shipwrecked on an entirely strange island? As the history of colonization shows, there is a tendency for people so placed to drop any reverence and become more exploitative. But it is not irresistible. Raiders who settle down can quite soon begin to feel at home, as the Vikings did in East Anglia, and can, after a while, become as possessive, proud, and protective towards their new land as the old

---

[17] See particularly, Friedrich Nietzsche, *Thus Spake Zarathustra*, 3, s. 'Of Old and New Tables'; and *The Joyful Wisdom* (otherwise called *The Gay Science*), 125 (the Madman's Speech). I have discussed this rather mysterious appointment of man to succeed God in a paper called 'Creation and Originality', to be published in a volume of my essays forthcoming from the Harvester Press.

inhabitants. Crusoe himself does, from time to time, show this pride rather touchingly, and it would, I think, certainly have inhibited any moderate temptation, such as that which I mentioned, to have a good bonfire. What keeps him sane through his stay is in fact his duty to God. If that had been absent, I should rather suppose that sanity would depend on a stronger and more positive attachment to the island itself and its creatures. It is interesting, however, that Crusoe's story played its part in developing that same icy individualism which has gone so far towards making both sorts of attachment seem corrupt or impossible. Rousseau delighted in *Robinson Crusoe*, and praised it as the only book fit to be given to a child, *not* because it showed a man in his true relation to animal and vegetable life, but because it was the bible of individualism. 'The surest way to raise him [the child] above prejudice and to base his judgements on the true relations of things, is to put him in the place of a solitary man, and to judge all things as they would be judged by such a man in relation to their own utility. . . . So long as only bodily needs are recognized, man is self-sufficing . . . the child knows no other happiness but food and freedom.'[18] That false atomic notion of human psychology—a prejudice above which nobody ever raised Rousseau—is the flaw in all social-contract thinking. If he were right, every member of the human race would need a separate island—and what, then, would our ecological problems be? Perhaps, after all, we had better count our blessings.

[18] Barbara Foxley, tr., *Emile* (London: Dent, Everyman's Library, 1966), 147–8.

VI

AGAINST THE INEVITABILITY OF
HUMAN CHAUVINISM

RICHARD ROUTLEY AND VAL ROUTLEY

I

In our enlightened times, when most forms of chauvinism have been
abandoned, at least in theory, by those who consider themselves progressive, Western ethics still appears to retain, at its very heart, a fundamental form of chauvinism, namely, human chauvinism. For both popular
Western thought and most Western ethical theories assume that both
value and morality can ultimately be reduced to matters of interest or
concern to the class of humans.

Class chauvinism, in the relevant sense, is substantially differential, discriminatory, and inferior treatment (characteristically, but not necessarily,
by members of the privileged class) of items outside the class, for which
there is not sufficient justification. Human chauvinism, like other varieties
of chauvinism, can take stronger and weaker forms; an example of the
weaker form is the Greater Value Thesis, the invariable allocation of
greater value or preference, on the basis of species, to humans, while not
however entirely excluding non-humans from moral consideration and
claims.[1] We will be concerned primarily with strong forms of human
chauvinism, which see value and morality as ultimately concerned entirely
with humans, and non-human items as having value or creating constraints
on human action only in so far as these items serve human interests or
purposes.

© University of Notre Dame Press, 1979. Reprinted with permission from K. Goodpaster and
K. Sayre, eds., *Ethics and Problems of the 21st Century* (Notre Dame: University of Notre Dame
Press, 1979), 36–59.

[1] This thesis has, among other unacceptable outcomes, the consequence that, if there is only
room in one's boat for one and one must choose between saving Adolf Hitler and a wombat
which has lived a decent and kindly life and never harmed a living creature, one is morally
obligated to choose the former. That would not be the choice of the authors.

In recent years, since the rise of the 'environmental consciousness', there has been increasing, if still tentative, questioning of this exclusive concern with, or at least heavy bias toward, human interests; and indeed, at a time when human beings are rapidly accelerating their impact on the natural world, the question as to the validity of this basic assumption is not merely an abstract one, but is of immediate and practical concern in its implications for human action. In reply to this questioning (which appears to originate largely from people with environmental interests), modern moral philosophers—fulfilling their now established function of providing a theoretical superstructure to explain and justify contemporary moral sensibilities rather than questioning fundamental assumptions—tend to argue that the bias toward human interests, which is an integral part of going ethical theories, is not just another form of class chauvinism which it is both possible and desirable to eliminate, but is rather a restriction dictated by the logic of evaluative and moral concepts, and that there is no coherent, possible, or viable alternative to the 'human chauvinism' of standard ethical theories. In this paper, we want to consider and reject a series of arguments in the theory of value designed to show that this is so and thereby to advance the cause of an alternative, non-chauvinistic, environmental ethic.

The orthodox defence of human chauvinism argues that it is inevitable that humans should be taken as the exclusive subjects of value and morality. Humans are uniquely and exclusively qualified for moral consideration and attributions of value, according to this defence either because the human species alone does, as a matter of fact, possess properties which are a precondition for such ascriptions or because, as a matter of the definition or the logic or the significance of moral concepts in natural language, such considerations are restricted as a matter of logic to the human species. In the first case the restriction of morality and value to the human species will be taken as contingent, in the second necessary. In either case, if the argument is correct, the bias in favour of humans in current theories is inescapable so that, depending on one's definition of chauvinism, either human chauvinism itself is inevitable, or human bias is, because justifiable, not a real chauvinism at all. We shall consider the logical or definitional approach first.

According to the definitional approach, moral and evaluative terms are, as a matter of their *definitions*, restricted in their application to members of the human species; only in a secondary way at best do such terms find a wider application, according as evaluated items are instrumental to human interests. The thesis is often backed up by the production of definitions which are so restricted, for example, 'the value of a thing is its capacity to confer a benefit on someone, to make a favorable difference to his life',[2] where in the intended context 'someone' is obviously restricted to humans. The attempt to preserve human chauvinism in an unchallengeable form through definitions involves the fallacy of taking definitions to be self-validating and unchallengeable, and appears to be based on the confusion of abbreviative definitions with those involving or presupposing substantive claims, such as creative definitions, which may be accepted or rejected. Such definitions as those above cannot be merely abbreviative because they attempt to characterize or explicate already understood terms, such as 'moral' or 'value'. Worse still, they do so in a way which is not dictated by prevailing usage—which does not require that moral and value terms be restricted in range to humans in order that they continue to apply to humans in the ordinary way. Alternative definitions which do not so restrict the range of application may be supplied; they can in fact be found by looking up dictionaries, and these alternatives quite properly do not close off genuine issues which natural language itself leaves open.

The fallacy of the definitional move is that of believing that by converting the substantive evaluative theses of human chauvinism to matters of definition they become somehow exempt from challenge or need for justification. This is comparable to justifying discriminatory membership for a club by referring to the rules, similarly conceived as self-validating and exempt from question or need of justification. Since a similar move could obviously be employed to limit membership of the Moral Club to, say, white male humans in place of humans generally, it is plain that such a definitional argument does far too much and is capable of use to produce completely unacceptable conclusions.

But of course substantive theses involved in definitions, like club rules, are not exempt from challenge and may be arbitrary, undesirable, restrictive, and in need of justification. Once this is grasped the definitional move can be seen as entirely question begging, since the question of the acceptability and inevitability of human chauvinism is simply transformed into the question of the acceptability and inevitability of the definition. The production of such human chauvinist definitions has done nothing to advance the case of human chauvinism other than to throw a spurious air of unchallengeability and necessity over the highly challengeable and arbitrary substantive theses they embody.

The attempt to settle substantive issues 'by definition' is both philosophically facile and methodologically unsound and is especially so when

---

[2] K. Baier, in K. Baier and N. Rescher, eds., *Values and the Future* (New York: The Free Press, 1969), 40.

there are clearly alternative definitions which would not settle the issue in the same way. What, however, of the substantive claim presupposed by the definitional move, namely, that as a matter of natural language usage, or the logic of moral and evaluative concepts, the meaning of moral and value terms, it is logically necessary that direct, non-instrumental application of such terms be restricted to the human (a claim made at least in the case of rights by Ritchie,[3] and subsequently by Passmore,[4] and by others). But usually, when it is asserted that non-humans cannot have rights, obligations and suchlike, what sort of 'cannot' is involved is not specified— whether it is a 'cannot' of logical impossibility, or of non-significance or absurdity, or something else again. The point is nicely illustrated by Feinberg's discussion of McCloskey,[5] and by McCloskey himself.[6] In any case, however, the thesis appears to be mistaken, for it rules out as logically impossible or absurd a number of positions and theses which are very plainly neither and which it may even, in some circumstances, be important to consider. For example, it is surely neither impossible nor absurd to consider moral questions concerning conduct of humans toward other species, for example, to a race of sensitive and intelligent extraterrestrial beings, and similarly moral questions arising from their conduct toward or concerning humans; indeed science fiction writers do this commonly without producing nonsense or contradicting themselves. Not only does the proposed restriction appear quite mistaken given current usage, but there seems indeed to be something logically unsound about the attempt to place a logical restriction to a particular species on such terms, just as there would be in restricting membership of the Moral Club to people with blue eyes and blond hair who are over six feet tall. The accident of being a zoological human, defined in terms of various physical characteristics, cannot be morally relevant. It is impossible to restrict moral terms to particular species, when species distinctions are defined in terms of physical characteristics which are not morally relevant.

More generally, any attempt to derive a logically necessary connection between humanity itself and the applicability of morality is bound to fail. For creatures anatomically and zoologically distinct from humans which are identical with humans in terms of all morally relevant features are logically possible, upsetting any logical linkage. But attempts to establish a

---

[3] D. G. Ritchie, *Natural Rights* (London: Allen and Unwin, 1894), 107.
[4] J. Passmore, 'The Treatment of Animals', *Journal of the History of Ideas*, 36 (1975): 212; and *Man's Responsibility for Nature* (London: Duckworth, 1974), 116, 189.
[5] J. Feinberg, 'Can Animals Have Rights', in T. Regan and P. Singer, eds., *Animal Rights and Human Obligations* (Englewood Cliffs: Prentice-Hall, 1976), 195.
[6] H. J. McCloskey, 'Rights', *Philosophical Quarterly*, 15 (1965): 115–27.

logical tie between humanity and morality through features which all and only humans possess and which are themselves linked logically to morality would, of course, involve a modal fallacy, namely, that of substituting a contingent equivalence within an opaque modal context of logical necessity. In order for such an argument to be valid, it would have to be logically necessary that non-humans do not possess such features, not merely a contingent fact that they do not; but this assumption must be incorrect for morally relevant characteristics.

The only proposal which has a chance of succeeding, then, is the factual one which makes the selection of just humans for the Moral Club a contingent matter, the claim being that as a matter of contingent fact all and only humans possess a certain set of characteristics, which characteristics themselves are logically tied with qualification for moral consideration and for direct attribution of value to the possessor.

What this contingent form of human chauvinism has to produce then, in order to establish its case, is a set of characteristics which satisfy the following conditions of adequacy:

1. The set of characteristics must be possessed by at least all properly functioning humans, since to omit any significant group usually considered subject to moral consideration, such as infants, young children, primitive tribesmen, etc., and to allow that it was permissible to treat these groups in the way it is considered permissible to treat non-humans, that is, as mere instruments, would certainly be repugnant to modern moral sensibilities and would offend common intuitions as to the brotherhood of man, the view that all humans are possessors of inalienable rights. Thus human chauvinism, if it is to produce a coherent theory which does not unacceptably rule out some groups of humans, must find some set of features common to the most diverse members of humankind, from Rio Tinto executives to hunter–gatherer tribes of Amazonian Indians, from those who engage in highly abstract activities such as logic and mathematics to those who cannot, from the literate and cultured to the illiterate and uncouth, from the poet and professor to the infant. This alone will be no easy task.

2. In order for human chauvinism to be justified, this set of characteristics must not be possessed by any non-human.

3. The set of characteristics must be not merely morally relevant but sufficient to justify, in a non-circular way, the cut-off of moral consideration at exactly the right point. If human chauvinism is to avoid the charge of arbitrariness and unjustifiability and to demonstrate its inevitability and the impossibility of alternatives, it must emerge from the characteristics

why items not having them may be used as mere instruments to serve the interests of those which do possess them. There must be some explanatory logical connection between the set of characteristics and membership of the Moral Club.

Chauvinists are always anxious to stress distinguishing points between the privileged class and those outside it—and there is no lack of characteristics which distinguish humans from non-humans, at least functioning healthy adult ones. The point is that these distinctions usually do not warrant the sort of radically inferior treatment for which they are proposed as a rationale. On the basis of the characteristics, then, the proposed radical difference in treatment between the privileged and non-privileged class and the purely instrumental treatment of the non-privileged class, must be *warranted*, that is, the distinguishing characteristics must be able to carry the moral superstructure placed upon them.

A large and exceedingly disparate collection of features has been suggested as distinguishing humans from non-humans and justifying human chauvinism. But it turns out that every one of these, on examination, either fails to pick out the desired privileged class of humans in an unequivocal fashion, that is, it applies to some non-humans or excludes some humans who should not be excluded, or, when it does select the desired class, fails on condition 3 and does not warrant the exclusive claim to moral consideration of the privileged class. Many suggested criteria in fact fail on more than one count.

The traditional distinction between humans and the rest in terms of rationality illustrates the point. Once the theological doctrines of the exclusively human soul on which the distinction once rested are abandoned, it is not so easy to see what is meant by this term. Indeed it often appears to function as little more than a self-congratulatory predicate applied exclusively to humans, with no other clear function at all. However, various clarifications are sometimes offered. For example rationality may be said to be the ability to reason, this being tested by such basically linguistic performances as the ability to do logic, to prove theorems, to draw conclusions from arguments and to engage in inductive and deductive linguistic behaviour. But such stringent and linguistically loaded criteria will eliminate far too many members of the human species who cannot perform these tasks. If, however, behavioural criteria for rationality are adopted, or the ability to solve problems and to fit action to individual goals becomes the test—that is, practical reasoning is the test—it is obvious that many non-human animals will qualify for rationality, perhaps more easily than many humans. But in either case the distinction fails on condition 3, for why must the ability to perform such tasks be *the* criterion for admission to the Moral Club rather than the ability to perform some other tasks or meet some other set of standards, such as orienteering ability, or the ability to mix concrete (the use of concrete being, after all, a far more conspicuous feature of modern human society than the use of reason)? One senses also in the appeal to such criteria (and especially to linguistic criteria) the overvaluation of the things in which the privileged class typically excels and the undervaluation of the skills—not obviously, in any non-circular way, inferior—of the non-privileged class, which is such a typical feature of chauvinism.

We list some of the suggested characteristics supposedly justifying human chauvinism and indicate in brackets after each some of the conditions they fail: using tools (fails 1, 2, 3); altering the environment (1, 2, 3); possessing intelligence (2, 3); the ability to communicate (1, 2, 3); the ability to use and learn language (1, 2, 3); the ability to use and learn English (1, 3); possession of consciousness (2, 3); self-consciousness or self-awareness (1, 2?, 3); having a conscience (1, 2?, 3); having a sense of shame (1, 2?, 3); being aware of oneself as an agent or initiator (1, 2, 3); having awareness (2, 3); being aware of one's existence (1, 2?, 3); being aware of the inevitability of one's own death (1, 2?, 3); being capable of self-deception (1, 3); being able to ask questions about moral issues such as human chauvinism (1, 3); having a mental life (2, 3); being able to play games (1, 2, 3); being able to laugh (1, 3); to laugh at oneself (1, 3); being able to make jokes (1, 3); having interests (2, 3); having projects (1, 2, 3); being able to assess some of one's performances as successful or not (1, 2, 3); enjoying freedom of action (2, 3); being able to vary one's behaviour outside a narrow range of instinctual behaviour (1, 2, 3); belonging to a social community (1, 2, 3); being morally responsible for one's actions (1); being able to love (1, 2); being capable of altruism (1, 2); being capable of being a Christian, or capable of religious faith (1, 3); being able to produce the items of (human) civilization and culture (1, 3).[7]

It appears that none of these criteria meets the conditions of adequacy; furthermore it seems most unlikely that any other characteristics or any combination of these characteristics does so. Thus we conclude that these contingent direct arguments for human chauvinism do not establish its

---

[7] This feature typifies a number of rather circular distinguishing characteristics, or at least ones which raise serious theoretical problems for human chauvinism because they attempt to explain the unique value of humans in terms of their ability to produce items which are taken to be independently valuable, thus contradicting human chauvinism. (See the discussion in V. Routley, 'Critical Notice of Passmore, *Man's Responsibility for Nature*', *Australasian Journal of Philosophy*, 53 (1975): 177.)

inevitability and that indeed the position rests on a shaky base and so far lacks a coherent theoretical justification.

Human chauvinism cannot be restored by a detour through the concept of a person, that is, by linking personhood with membership of the Moral Club and identifying the class of persons contingently with the class of humans. For then the same problem as above arises with different terminology since, even if the notion of person can be specified in such a way as to justify the restriction of moral privileges to persons, the class of persons will then not coincide (even approximately) with the way human chauvinism requires with the class of humans, but will either include a great many non-humans or exclude a good many humans normally morally considered.

Attempts to enlarge the privileged class—for example, to persons (broadly specified)—or to sentient or preference-having creatures may avoid many of the problems of arbitrariness and justification which face the strong form of human chauvinism, but, as we shall argue, it will face a set of problems of coherence and consistency common to all instrumentalist theories of value and morality.

II

There are a number of indirect arguments for human chauvinism based on features of value and morality. We turn now to consider these. One abstract argument which is supposed to establish that values are, or must be, determined through the interests of humans or persons—a central argument underlying chauvinism—takes the following form:

A Values are determined through the preference rankings of valuers (the *no detachable values assumption*).
B Valuers' preference rankings are determined through valuers' interests (the *preference reduction thesis*).
C Valuers are humans (persons) (the *species assumption*).
D Therefore, values are determined through human interests (through the interests of persons).

Hence, it is sometimes concluded, not only is it perfectly acceptable for humans to reduce matters of value and morality to matters of human interest, but moreover there is no rational or possible alternative to doing so; any alternative is simply incoherent.

Although this argument does not, so far as we are aware, appear anywhere with its premises explicitly stated, it does seem to reflect the sorts of consideration those who claim that there is no rational or coherent alternative to organizing everything in human interests usually have in mind. Of course once the premisses are exposed, it is easier to see that this initially persuasive argument, like others in the area, rests on fallacious assumptions. We shall claim that although the argument to conclusion D is formally valid—given only some quite conventional assumptions such as that the relation of determination or functionality is appropriately transitive and the principle of replacement of necessary identicals—not all the premisses should be accepted.

The argument can be treated as the major representative of a family of similar arguments. For there are many variations that can be made on the argument with a view to amending it, tightening it, varying or strengthening its conclusion, and so on. Our criticisms of the argument will, for the most part, transfer to the variations. A first group of variations replaces or qualifies the determining relation; for example, 'determined through' or 'determined by' may be replaced by 'answer back to', 'reflect', 'are a matter of', 'can be reduced to', or 'are a function of'. (The latter functional form makes it plain that 'determined' has to mean 'exactly determined', which ensures that no extraneous factors enter into the chauvinistic determination; mere partial determination would be quite compatible with the rejection of human chauvinism.) Alternatively, 'determined' may be modally upgraded to 'have to be determined', in order to reveal the sheer necessity of conclusion D. (In this case, it is essential that premiss C be of modal strength and not merely contingent, as it would be if the original form were retained; otherwise the argument would contain a modal fallacy).

Another familiar, and appealing, variation we have already bracketed into the form of the argument given; namely the replacement of humans as the base class by persons. This straight away increases the cogency of premiss C, which otherwise—while better than, say, 'Valuers are white (North American) humans'—would at best be *contingently* true (which is not good enough for the argument and in fact appears false, since some valuers may not be human; and certainly not all humans are valuers), while at worst it is simply a circular way of reintroducing the logical version of human chauvinism by restricting the class of valuers a priori to humans. That *all* valuers are persons *may* be made analytic on the sense of 'person'—given a redefinition of 'person' away from its normal English usage, which philosophical English appears almost to tolerate—thus shielding premiss C from criticism. Other base classes than persons can replace humans in premiss C—for example animals—thus leading to the conclusion, of animal chauvinism, that values are determined through the interests (considerations and concerns) of animals, sentient creatures, or whatever. In the end, of course, premiss C could be absorbed (as, for example, valuers are valuers or valuing creatures) and accordingly omitted, leaving the conclusion: values are determined in the interests of valuers. However, even the analytic form of premiss C does not, as we shall see, save the argument.

Much the same applies in the case of premiss A. The premiss is certainly not unobjectionable in the usual sense of 'determined'; but there are ways of repairing it so that the argument still works in a sufficiently damaging form, and one way goes as follows: what is true, analytically, if sufficiently many valuers are taken into account, is that values are determined through the *value* rankings of valuers. Value rankings cannot however be cashed in for preference rankings since, as is well known, preference rankings and value rankings can diverge; a valuer can prefer what has less value and can value what is not preferred.[8] Let us amend the argument then—so that we can locate the real cause of damage—by replacing premiss A by the following premiss:

A_1 Values are determined through the value rankings of (appropriate) valuers. Correspondingly, B will be adjusted to B_1 in which 'value' replaces 'preference'.

The really objectionable premiss in the central argument is neither premiss A nor premiss C, but premiss B—or, more exactly, where A is repaired, premiss B_1. Suspicion of premiss B may be aroused by noticing that it plays an exactly parallel role in the class chauvinism argument to that of the critical premiss

BE One's preferences or choices are always determined through self-interest

plays in familiar arguments for egoism, that whatever course of action one adopts, it is always really adopted in one's own selfish interest. The argument for egoism runs along the following, parallel, lines:

---

[8] There is nonetheless an esoteric, semantical, sense of 'determined' in which premiss A is demonstrably true, and so a sense in which it is analytically true that value rankings are semantically determined by the *preference* rankings of situations by a class of valuers. The details of these semantical foundations for values are set out in R. and V. Routley, 'Semantical Foundations of Value Theory', *Noûs*, 17 (1983), 441–56. But while premiss A can be corrected by replacing 'determined' by 'semantically determined' and giving this an appropriate construal, such a move would do nothing to restore the intended argument; for it would either invalidate the argument, through change in the key middle term 'determined', or, alternatively, if 'determined' is systematically replaced throughout the argument, drastically alter the intended conclusion D—so that looking at the interests that humans in fact have would no longer provide a guide to values (instead the interests of hypothetical valuers with respect to worlds that never exist would have to be gathered).

AE Individual persons (agents) always act (in freely chosen cases) in the way they prefer or choose, i.e. in accordance with their preference rankings.

BE Individual preference rankings are always determined through (reflect) self-interest.

Therefore:

DE Individual persons (agents) always act in ways determined by self-interest (that reflect their own interests).

Thereafter follows the slide from *in their own interests* to *to their own advantage* or for their own uses or purposes. The final conclusion of egoism, again paralleling the class chauvinism case, is not only that the egoistic position is perfectly in order and thoroughly rational but that there are no alternatives, that there is, or at least ought to be, no other way of acting, 'that men can only choose to do what is in their own interests or that it is only rational to do this'.[9]

Thus human chauvinism, as based on the central argument, stands revealed as a form of group selfishness, group egoism one might almost say. Likewise, the criticisms of the Group Selfishness argument, as we shall now call the central argument, parallel those of egoism; in particular premiss B (B_1) succumbs to similar objections to those that defeat premiss BE (BE_1). Group selfishness is no more acceptable than egoism, since it depends on exactly the same set of confusions between values and advantages, and slides on such terms as 'interests', as the arguments on which egoism rests. Nowell-Smith's very appealing critique of egoism[10] may, by simple paraphrase, be converted into a critique of group selfishness. This is obvious once we recast B_1 and BE_1 and set them side by side:

BE_1 Individual value rankings are determined through (individual) self-interest.

B_1 Valuers' (groups') value rankings are determined through valuers' (group) interests (joint interests of groups).

Because, however, one sets up or selects one's own preference or value rankings, it does not follow that they are set up or selected in one's own interests; similarly in group cases, because a group determines its own rankings, it does not follow that it determines them in its own interests. Just as BE_1 is, prima facie at least, refuted by a range of examples where value, and also preference, rankings run counter to self-interest, e.g. cases of altruism, so prima facie at least, B_1 is refuted by examples where value,

---

[9] P. H. Nowell-Smith, *Ethics* (London: Penguin, 1954), 140.
[10] Ibid. 140–4.

and also overall preference rankings, vary from group interests, e.g. cases of group altruism. In the case of limited groups, examples are easy to locate, e.g. resistance movements, environmental action groups, and so on; in the case, however, of the larger human group, examples are bound to be more controversial (since B_1 unlike BE_1 is a live thesis), but are still easy to find, especially if future humans are discounted; for example, it is in humans' selfish interests to have plentiful supplies of this and that, electricity from uranium, oil, whalemeat, fish, etc., right now rather than the more limited supplies which would result from restraint, but altruistic value rankings would rank the latter above the former. It is often in selfish human interests (no less selfish because pertaining to a group) to open up and develop the wilderness, strip mine the earth, exploit animals, and so on, but environmentalists who advocate not doing so, in many cases not merely because of future humans, are apparently acting not just out of their own or human group interests.

But, just as BE_1 is not demolished by such counter-examples of apparently altruistic action, neither is B_1: in each case it can be made out that further selfish interests are involved; e.g. in the case of B_1, that an agent did what he did, an altruistic action, because he *liked* doing it. As Nowell-Smith explains in the egoism case, interest is written in as an internal accusative, thereby rendering such theses as BE_1 true at the cost, however, of trivializing them. More generally, valuing something gets written in as a further sort of 'interest'; whatever valuers value that does not seem to be in their interests is said to provide a further interest, either the value itself or an invented value surrogate; for example, the environmentalist who works to retain a wilderness he never expects to see may be said to be so acting only because he has an interest in or derives benefit or advantage from just knowing it exists, just as he would be said to be acting in the egoist case. By such strategies the theses can be retained; for then a valued item really is in valuers' interests, in the extended sense, even if they are in obvious ways seriously inconvenienced by it, that is, even if it is *not* in their interests in the customary sense.[11] Thus, B_1, like BE_1, is preserved by stretching the elastic term 'interests', in a way that it too readily admits, to include values, or value surrogates, among interests. Then, however, the conclusion of the Group Selfishness argument loses its intended force and becomes the platitude that values are determined through valuers' values, just as egoism, under the extension which makes us all covert egoists, loses its sting and becomes a platitude. It can be seen that human chauvinism in

[11] The technique of rescuing philosophical theses by natural extensions and accompanying redefinitions of terms, including the thesis 'We're all selfish really,' is delightfully explained in J. Wisdom, *Other Minds* (Oxford: Blackwell, 1952), ch. 1.

this form, like egoism, derives its plausibility from vacillation in the sense of 'interests', with a resulting fluctuation between a strong false thesis—the face of human chauvinism usually presented—and a trivial analytic thesis, between paradox and platitude.

To sum up the dilemma for the argument then: when 'interest' is used in its weaker sense premiss B may be accepted but the argument does not establish its intended conclusion or in any way support human chauvinism. For the intended effect of the argument in the crude form is this: in determining values it is enough to look at human advantage; nothing else counts. If the argument were correct, then one could assess values by checking out the local (selfish) advantage of humans, or, more generally, the advantage of the base class somehow assembled. If, on the other hand, 'interest' is used in its strong sense, the conclusion would license a form of human chauvinism, but premiss B now fails.

Most philosophers think they know how to discredit the egoist arguments. It is curious indeed then, that an argument which is regarded as so unsatisfactory in the individual case—that for egoism—remains unchallenged and is still considered so convincing in a precisely parallel group case—that for human chauvinism.

III

The Group Selfishness argument is often employed in another way, as the presentation for a choice between the conclusion D, that value is determined by or reducible to a matter of human interests, and the denial of premiss A, which denial is seen as entailing a commitment to a detached, intrinsic, or naturalistic theory of value. Thus, it may be said either one accepts the conclusion, with its consequent instrumentalist account of value, or one is committed to an intrinsic or detached value theory which takes values to be completely independent of valuers, and no way determined by them. But, it is assumed, the latter theory is well known as untenable, and may even be seen as involving mysticism or as being irrational.[12] Thus, it may be concluded, there is no real coherent alternative to such an instrumental account of value, and hence no real alternative to human chauvinism.

The form of the argument then, is essentially: $\sim A \lor D$, but A, therefore D—or, if a stronger connection, of intensional disjunction, is intended: $\sim D \to \sim A$, but A, therefore D. It can be seen that the main premiss, $\sim A$

---

[12] Passmore, *Man's Responsibility for Nature*, ch. 7.

$\bigvee$ D, has resulted from the exportation and suppression of premisses B and C of the Group Selfishness argument. This suppression does nothing to improve the standing of the premisses although it does have the (possibly advantageous) effect of making it more difficult to see the fallacious assumptions on which it is based. For of course the choice presented, $\sim$A $\bigvee$ D, is a false one, and for precisely the same reasons that led us to say that premiss B was false. To reject the instrumentalist conclusion D is by no means to be committed to A, or to the view that the valuers and their preference rankings play *no* role in determining values, and that values are a further set of mysterious independent items in the world somehow perceived by valuers through a special (even mystical and non-rational) moral sense. Valuers' preference rankings may be admitted to play an important role in evaluations;[13] we are still not committed to D unless we assume—what amounts to premiss B—that these preference rankings reflect, or can be reduced to, valuers' interests.

The dichotomy frequently presented between instrumentalist accounts of value, on the one hand, and detached theories (or what are mistakenly taken to be the *same*, intrinsic theories) is, for the same reason, a false one. Instrumental theories are those which attempt to reduce value to what is instrumental to or contributes to a stated goal. Typically such theories take the goal to be the furtherance of the interest of a privileged class; for example, the goal may be taken to be determined in terms of the interests, concerns, advantage, or welfare of the class of humans, or of persons, or of sentient creatures, depending on the type of chauvinism. In particular, human chauvinist theories are, characteristically, instrumentalist theories. In contrast, an item is valued intrinsically where it is valued for its own sake, and not merely as a means to something further; and an intrinsic-

---

[13] Value rankings can be semantically analysed in terms of preference or interest rankings, as in R. and V. Routley, 'Semantical Metamorphosis of Metaphysics', *Australasian Journal of Philosophy*, 54 (1976) explains. The semantical foundations, while conceding nothing to subjectivism or instrumentalism, make it easy to concede main points of the case (attributed to Dewey) against detached values, against the view that there are values somehow out there (in Meinong's *aussersein*), purely naturalistic values completely detached from all valuers, or from all preference rankings of valuers. Put differently, there are no values that do not somehow answer back to preference rankings of valuers, and so no values that are entirely detached from valuers and valuational activity such as preference-ranking of situation. But the answering back is made explicit and precise by the semantical analysis, *not* by any syntactical reduction or translation of value statements into statements about valuers' preference or interest rankings; and the valuers of the analysis are, like the situations introduced, ideal and need in no way exist. As a result then, valuations may be independent of the aggregated preference-rankings of all actual humans or, for that matter, of all persons over all time. Thus too the semantical analysis makes it easy to navigate a course between the alternatives of two influential false dichotomies, to the effect that values are either instrumental or else detached, or that values are either subjective or else detached. For though a semantical analysis can be given, upsetting the detached value thesis, no translation or syntactical reduction of the sort subjectivism assumes is thereby effected.

value theory allows that some items are intrinsically valuable. Intrinsic theories then, contrast with instrumental theories, and what 'intrinsic' tells us is no more than that the item taken as intrinsically valuable is not valued merely as a means to some goal, i.e. is not merely instrumentally valued. Accordingly, detached value theories, since disjoint from instrumental theories, are a sub-class of intrinsic value theories; and they are a proper sub-class since intrinsic values need not be detached. Something may be valuable in itself without its value being detached from all valuing experience. It is evident, furthermore, that the identification of intrinsic and detached value theories presupposed in the argument is no more than a restatement of the false dichotomy $\sim A \lor D$, or $\sim D \rightarrow \sim A$, i.e. non-instrumental, therefore detached. The assumption that if preference or value rankings are involved at all the resulting assignments must be instrumental is either false or is a variation of the fallacious premise B which plays a crucial role in the Group Selfishness and Egoist arguments. The variation is that if value or preference rankings are involved they must reflect valuers' interests; therefore such values are instrumental because the items valued are valued according as they reflect valuers' interests; and therefore according as they are a means to the end of satisfying the valuers' interests. It follows that intrinsic value theories may allow for a third way between instrumental and detached theories because of the possibility of value rankings (and also preference rankings) which are not themselves set up in a purely instrumentalist way, that is, attributing value to an item only according as it is a means to some goal.

The argument that there is no coherent alternative to instrumentalism does not, however, rely just on misrepresenting alternative intrinsic accounts as logically incoherent by assimilating them to detached accounts. It also trades on a contemporary insensitivity to the serious logical and epistemological problems of instrumental accounts of value, problems which were well-known to classical philosophers (see e.g. Aristotle, *Metaphysics* 994^{b}9–16). It does not appear to be widely realized that the classical arguments apply not just to a few especially shaky instrumentalist theories which adopt questionable goals but to instrumentalism in general, since they assume only quite general features of the instrumentalist position.

Instrumentalist positions take as valuable (or in the moral case, as creating moral constraints) just what contributes to a stated end. An obvious example which comes to mind is utilitarianism. However, in the more general case we are concerned with, of instrumentalist forms of human chauvinism, there may be a *set* of goals, not just a single goal such as that of maximizing net happiness of humans; the human-chauvinist assumption is that the values (indeed constraints) are goal reducible, and that all goals reduce in some way to human goals, or at least can be assessed in terms of human concerns and interests. Human chauvinist positions are not necessarily instrumental, but those that are not (e.g. the position that just humans and nothing else are intrinsically valuable) tend to make the arbitrary chauvinistic nature of their assumptions unwisely explicit—most successful contemporary chauvinisms being covert ones.

Problems for instrumentalism arise (as Aristotle observed) when questions are asked about the status of the goal itself. Instrumentalism relies entirely for its plausibility upon selecting a set of goals which are widely accepted and are, in the theory, implicitly treated as valuable. It relies at bottom on an implicit valuation which cannot itself be explained in purely instrumental terms. Of course, a value assumption is not eliminated in this fashion; it is merely hidden under the general consensus that such a goal is appropriate, that such an end is valuable. But the strategy of successful instrumentalism is to avoid recognition of the fact that the goal is, and indeed *must be*, implicitly treated as valuable, by selecting a set of goals so much part of the framework of contemporary thought, so entrenched and habitual as a valued item by humans, that the value attached to the goal becomes virtually invisible, at least to those within the framework. Thus it is with the assumption of human chauvinist instrumentalism that goals are exclusively determinable in terms of human interest. The basic, convincing and self-evident character of this assumption rests on nothing more than the shared beliefs of the privileged class of humans concerning the paramount and exclusive importance of regarding their own interests and concerns, on a valuational assumption or goal which is 'self-evident' because it is advantageous and is habitual. The consensus features, of which instrumentalists make so much, are nothing more than the consensus of the privileged class about the goal of maintaining their own privilege, that is, a consensus of interests. This sort of agreement of course shows very little about the well-groundedness of the position.

Unless the goals set are widely accepted as valuable, the account will be unconvincing to those who do not share the goal and even to those who appreciate that it is possible to reject the goal. In order for instrumentalism to work logically, however, the goal must be implicitly treated within the theory as valuable, for otherwise the proposed analysis loses explanatory and justificatory power and lacks compulsion. For how can the value of an item be explained and justified in terms of its contribution to an end not itself considered valuable? Serious problems also arise about the nature of value statements under the instrumentalist analysis unless the goal is treated as valuable. For if the goals themselves are not so treated within the theory, but are taken simply as unevaluated facts, then a valuational statement 'x is valuable' becomes, under the proposed analysis, simply the statement that x tends to produce a certain result, to contribute to certain human states, a statement whose logical status, openness to verification, allowance for disagreement, and so on, does not substantially differ from the statement that x tends to produce ferric oxide, to contribute to the rusting of human products. Such an account of value statements is open to the same sort of objections as other naturalistic reductions of value, for example, Mill's account of the desirable in terms of the desired. The special logical and epistemological character of value statements then, especially with respect to verification and disagreement, must be supplied in instrumentalism, if it is to be supplied at all, by the implicit treatment of the goal itself as valuable.

The fact that the goal of an instrumental account must be taken as itself valuable gives rise to two choices. In the first, the goal is taken as itself instrumentally valuable, which creates an infinite regress. For if the end, reason, or assignment for which other items are instrumentally valuable is itself only instrumentally valuable, then there must in turn be some other end, reason, or assignment in terms of which it is valuable (by definition of instrumental). A regress is thus begun, and if this regress is not to be viciously infinite, in must terminate in some end or feature which is taken as valuable just in itself, that is, with intrinsic values.

On the alternative option, the goal is not taken to be instrumentally valuable but is admitted to be valuable in some other way. Unless an 'except' clause is added to the original instrumentalist account so that all values are held to be instrumental with the exception of the goal, the account will of course be contextually inconsistent, since it is inconsistent when contextually supplied assumptions are added. For these include the assumption that the goal itself is valuable, but not in the way that the instrumentalist thesis claims is the only way possible. Thus the goal is taken to be both valuable and not valuable.

If, on the other hand, an 'except' clause is added, this amounts to an admission that the goal is taken to be non-instrumentally valuable. Thus the account may be able to retain consistency, but does so at the expense of explicitly admitting a value, that of the goal, which cannot be accounted for in purely instrumental terms; in short, the goal is taken as intrinsically valuable.

To sum up, the dilemma for the instrumentalist can be put as follows: consider the desirability of the goal of the instrumental theory; it must implicitly be judged to be desirable, for otherwise nothing could be justified by reduction to it. Ask: is this goal also instrumentally desirable (valuable) or not? If it is, that is, it is only desirable as a means to a further goal, then either a regress is initiated or the same issue arises with respect to the new goal. But if it is not, then the instrumental theory is again refuted, since the goal is desirable though not desirable according to the test of the theory because it is not instrumental to the goal.

Whichever horn of the dilemma is taken, then, the outcome is the same: the instrumentalist must rely on treating the goal itself as implicitly valuable in a way not purely instrumental, that is, as intrinsically valuable. Thus the instrumentalist is, at bottom, guilty of precisely the same crime of which he accuses the adherent of an intrinsic account, with the added delinquency of failing to admit and face up to his basic assumptions. The logical and epistemological position of such an instrumental account is certainly no better than that of an intrinsic account, since there is logically no difference between the recognition of one intrinsic value (or one set in the case where goals are multiple) and the recognition of many of them, and the logical and epistemological status of the instrumentalist's account is no better than that of the goal to which his values are taken as instrumental. Since the instrumentalist has implicitly admitted the legitimacy of an intrinsic value assignment in setting up his account, he cannot claim any superiority over a more general intrinsic theory which allows for many intrinsic values, since what is legitimate in the case of one value assignment must be equally legitimate in the multiple case.

This abstract dilemma for human-chauvinist instrumentalism is illustrated in a concrete case by Passmore's procedure in *Man's Responsibility for Nature*; for Passmore (1) wishes to say that there is no coherent alternative to instrumental values, that an item is valuable in so far as it serves human interest, and (2) wants to explain the unique value attributed to humans in terms of their production of valuable civilized and cultural items. But (2) involves the admission of values, that of civilized items, which cannot be valuable in the way (1) states, and indeed (2) amounts to the admission of non-instrumental values. The proposed account is inconsistent because if intrinsic values are admissible in the case of civilized items, they cannot be logically incoherent in the way (1) claims.

The sort of problem faced by Passmore is, however, not a readily avoidable one for the instrumentalist; for if the charge of arbitrary and unjustifiable human chauvinism is to be avoided by those who opt for (1), and humans are not themselves to be awarded intrinsic values—thus conceding the logical legitimacy of intrinsic values generally, and hence the avoidability of human chauvinist accounts of value—some explanation must be provided for the exclusive value attributed to humans. But any explanation capable of justifying this valuation in a non-arbitrary and non-chauvinistic way would have to refer to properties of humans and would have to say something like: 'Humans are uniquely valuable because they alone have valuable properties $x, y, z, \ldots$ or produce valuable items A, B, C...'. The list of proposed distinguishing features already considered above is usually what will be employed here. But this is to admit intrinsic value for the properties which explain the exclusive value of humans. The dilemma for the human chauvinist is that he must either take the exclusive human-value assumption (the goal) as ultimate—laying him open to the charge of arbitrary chauvinism and of attributing intrinsic values to humans—or attempt to explain it—in which case he will again end by conceding non-instrumental values.

Thus the case for the inevitability of human chauvinism, that alternatives to it must be based on an incoherent and logically and epistemically defective account of values, namely a non-instrumental account, has not been established by these arguments.

IV

Egoism, not group selfishness, is one of the assumptions underlying the next series of abstract defences of chauvinism. The leading ideas of the representative argument we first consider are essentially those of social contract theories. This argument takes the following form (the bracketed parameters X and Z are filled out in the representative argument respectively by: 'justification of moral principles', and: 'enter into contracts'):

J.   The only justification of moral principles (only X) is a contractual one, i.e. the entry into contracts of agents (Zry).

K.   Agents only enter into contracts (only Z) if it serves their own interests (the *egoist assumption*).

L.   Humans (persons) are the only agents that enter into contracts (that Z).

Therefore, by K and L: M. Humans (persons) only enter into contracts (only Z) if it serves their own interest.

Therefore, from J and M: N. The only justification for moral principles (only X) is the (selfish) interests of humans (persons).[14]

---

[14] The logical transitions in the argument take on more evidently valid form upon analytic transformation of the premisses, to those now illustrated: J'. All justifications of moral principles are cases of (justified by) the entry into contracts of agents. K'. All cases of the entry into contracts are cases of self-interests of agents. And so on for L' through M'.

The argument can be varied by different choices of parameters, X and Z. For example, X could be filled out by 'determination of value judgements', and 'contractual' replaced by 'community-based' (i.e. Z is filled out by 'are community-based' or some such) yielding in place of J the familiar premiss that the only justification of value judgements is a community-based one, and leading to a conclusion, analytically linked to D above, that all value judgements are determined by human self-interest. Alternatively, just one of X or Z may be so replaced, leaving the other as in the original example. Another variation of the argument that has figured prominently in the discussion of animal rights fills out X and Z respectively by 'determination of rights' and 'belong to human society'. Under this assignment, the parametric premise J becomes essentially that commonly adopted statement[15] (already criticized above) that rights are determined solely by reference to human society.

As the arguments are in each case valid, the issue of the correctness of the conclusions devolves on that of the correctness of the premisses. In each case too, the arguments could be made rather more plausible by replacing 'humans' by 'persons' (and correspondingly 'human society' by 'society of persons', etc.); for otherwise premisses such as L and its variations are suspect, since there is nothing, legally or morally, to prevent consortia, organizations, and other non-humans from entering into contracts (and these items are appropriately counted as persons in the larger legal sense). Given that amendment to premiss L, the correctness of the arguments turns on the correctness of premisses J and K. But both these premisses are false and premiss J imports the very chauvinism that is at issue in the conclusion.

Though the representative contract argument is only one of several important variations that can be made on the general parametric argument, it is often regarded as having special appeal, because the contract model appears to explain the origin of obligation, and offer a justification for it, in a way that no other model does, and appears thus to provide a bulwark against moral, and political, scepticism. That the appearance is illusory, because the obligation to honour contracts is assumed at bottom, is well enough known and not our concern here. What is of concern is the correctness of representative premisses J and K.

The egoist assumption K is faulted on the same grounds as egoism itself. For agents sometimes enter into contracts that are not in their own interests but are in the interests of other persons or creatures, or are undertaken on behalf of, for instance to protect, other items that do not have

---

[15] See nn. 3 and 4 above.

interests at all, e.g. rivers, buildings, forests. The attempt to represent all these undertakings as in human interests, because done in the 'selfish interests' of the agents, is the same as in the egoist arguments, and the resolution of the problem is the same, namely, to distinguish acting, valuing, and so on, clearly from acting in one's own selfish (or in-group) interests. However, even if premiss K were amended to admit that agents may enter into contracts on behalf of non-human items, it would still result in a form of human chauvinism given familiar assumptions, since non-human items will still be unable to create moral obligations except through a human sponsor or patron, who will presumably be able to choose whether or not to protect them. Natural items will generate no more constraints unless humans freely choose to allow them to do so; since the obligatory features of moral obligation thus disappear, no genuine moral obligations can be created by natural items under such an amended account. Thus the amended premiss assumes the question at issue.

Premiss J, the view that moral obligations are generated solely by contracts undertaken by moral agents, is then the crucial assumption for this argument for human chauvinism. J, however, has serious difficulties, for there are many recognized moral principles which apparently cannot be explained as contractually based, at least if 'contract' is to be taken seriously. There is no actual contract underlying the principle that one ought not to be cruel to animals, children, and others not in a position to contract. Adherents of a social contract view of moral obligation are of course inclined to withhold recognition of those moral principles that cannot be contractually based so that the contract thesis becomes not so much explanatory as prescriptive. But even allowing for this, the thesis has many unacceptable consequences just concerning humans, and if the notion of contract plays a serious role, it is difficult to reconcile with the view of all humans as possessing rights.

A crucial feature of contracts is that they are freely undertaken by responsible parties. If they can be freely undertaken there must be a choice with respect to them—the choice of not so contracting. But then we are left with the conclusion that it is permissible to treat those who do choose not to contract as mere instruments of those who do, in the way that the non-human world is presently treated; these contractual dropouts, like those outside society, can have no rights and there can be no moral constraints on behaviour concerning them, whatever their capacity for suffering. A similar conclusion emerges if humans who are not morally responsible are considered, for although we are normally thought to have quite substantial obligations to such humans, e.g. babies, young children, those who are considered mentally ill or as having diminished responsibility, they cannot themselves be free and responsible parties to a contract and will, on the social contract view, presumably have to depend for their rights on others freely choosing to contract on their behalf. If, for some reason, this does not occur we will be left with a similarly unacceptable conclusion as in the case of the contractual drop-outs. Obviously then, moral obligations do not require morally equal, free, and responsible contracting parties, in the way the social contract account presupposes. Worse, the argument would appear, with but little adaptation, to justify the practices of such groups as death squads, multinational corporations, and the Mafia, or any other group that contracts to protect the interests of its own members.

If these unacceptable conclusions are to be avoided, all humans will have to be somehow, in virtue of simply being human, subject to some mysterious, fictional, social contract which they did not freely choose to enter into, cannot get out of, and which can never exclude any member of the human species. So the unacceptable consequences are avoided only if crucial features of the notion of contract such as freedom and responsibility are dropped, and the notion of contract and premise J so seriously weakened as to become virtually without conditions. For the argument to work the residue has to be mere common humanity, and the 'contract' little more than the convention of morally considering just other members of the human species. Such a convention differs little, however, from a restatement of human chauvinism; the preferred explanation is really no explanation, for such a convention can neither justify human chauvinism nor, since different conventions could be arranged, explain why it is inevitable.

The social contract account of moral obligation is defective because it implies that moral obligations can really only hold between responsible moral agents and attempts to account for *all* moral obligation as based on contract. But of course the account is correct as an account of the origin of some types of moral obligation; there are moral obligations of a type that can only hold between free and responsible agents and others which only apply within a social and political context. Yet other types of obligation, such as the obligation not to cause suffering, can arise only with respect to sentient or preference-having creatures—who are not necessarily morally responsible—and could not significantly arise with respect to a non-sentient such as a tree or a rock. What emerges is a picture of types of moral obligation as associated with a nest of rings or annular boundary classes, with the innermost class, consisting of highly intelligent, social, sentient creatures, having the full range of moral obligations applicable to them, and outer classes of such non-sentient items as trees and rocks having only a much more restricted range of moral obligations significantly applicable to them. In some cases there is no sharp division between the rings. But there is no single uniform privileged class of items, no one base class, to which all and only moral principles directly apply, and moreover, the zoological class of humans is not one of the really significant boundary classes. The recognition that some types of moral obligation only apply within the context of a particular sort of society, or through contract, does nothing to support the case of human chauvinism.

The failure of the contract theory nevertheless leaves the issue as to whether there is some logical or categorial restriction on what can be the object of moral obligations, which would reinstate human chauvinism or animal chauvinism. There is, however, no such restriction on the object place of the obligation relation to humans or sentient creatures. Even if the special locution 'Y has an obligation toward X' requires that X is at least a preference-having creature, there are other locutions which are not so restricted, and one can perfectly well speak of having duties toward land and of having obligations concerning or with respect to such items as mountains and rivers, and without necessarily implying that such moral constraints arise only in an indirect fashion. Thus neither natural language nor the logic of moral concepts rules out the possibility of non-sentient items creating direct moral constraints.

There is then, given this point and the annular model, no need to opt for the position of Leopold[16] as the only alternative to human (or animal) chauvinism, that is, for a position which simply transfers to natural items the full set of rights and obligations applicable to humans, leading to such non-significance as that rocks have obligations to mountains. Distinctions between the moral constraints appropriate to different types of items can be recognized without leading back to human chauvinism. The point is an important one since many objections to allowing moral obligations to extend beyond the sphere of humans, or in some cases the sphere of sentient creatures, depend on ignoring such distinctions, on assuming that it is a question of transferring the full set of rights and obligations appropriate to intelligent social creatures to such items as trees and rivers—that the alternative to chauvinism is therefore an irrational and mystical animism concerning nature.[17]

16 A. Leopold, *A Sand County Almanac* (New York: Ballantine, 1966).
17 See Passmore, *Man's Responsibility for Nature*, 187 ff.

V

The ecological restatement of the strong version of human chauvinism, according to which items outside the privileged human class have zero intrinsic value, is the Dominion thesis,[18] the view that the earth and all its non-human contents exist or are available for man's benefit and to serve his interests and, hence, that man is entitled to manipulate the world and its systems as he wants, that is, in his interests. The thesis indeed follows, given fairly uncontroversial, analytic assumptions, from the conclusions of the main chauvinistic arguments examined, notably D, that values are determined through human interests. The earth and all its non-human contents thus have no intrinsic value, but at best have instrumental value and so can create no direct moral constraints on human action. For what has only instrumental value is already written down, in this framework as serving human interests. And since what has no instrumental value cannot be abused or have its value diminished, it is permissible for humans to treat it as they will in accord with their interests. Therefore, the Dominion thesis. Conversely, if non-human items are available for man's use, interests, and benefits, they can have no value except in so far as they answer his interests. Otherwise there would be restrictions on his behaviour with respect to them, since not any sort of behaviour is permissible as regards independently valuable items. Accordingly, value is determined through man's interests, that is, D holds. Thus the Dominion thesis is strictly equivalent to D. It follows that the Dominion thesis, like D, strictly implies human chauvinism. Conversely, the strong version of human chauvinism strictly implies D, and so the Dominion thesis, completing the sketch of the equivalence argument. Since the positions are equivalent, what counts against one also counts against the others. In particular, then, the Dominion thesis is no more inevitable than, and just as unsatisfactory as, strong human chauvinism.

The upshot is that the dominant ethical systems of our times, those clustered as the Western ethic and other kindred human chauvinistic systems, are far less defensible, and less satisfactory, than has been commonly assumed, and lack an adequate and non-arbitrary basis. Furthermore, alternative theories are far less incoherent than is commonly claimed, especially by philosophers. Yet although there are viable alternatives to the Dominion thesis, the natural world is rapidly being pre-empted in favour of human chauvinism—and of what it ideologically underwrites, the

[18] This view encompasses what Passmore has isolated as the Western environmental ideologies, both the dominant view and the lesser traditions; see V. Routley, 'Critical Notice of Passmore, *Man's Responsibility for Nature*'.

modern economic-industrial superstructure—by the elimination or over-exploitation of those things that are not considered of sufficient instrumental value for human beings. Witness the impoverishment of the non-human world, the assaults being made on tropical rainforests, surviving temperate wildernesses, wild animals, the oceans, to list only a few of the victims of man's assault on the natural world. Observe also the associated measures to bring primitive or recalcitrant peoples into the Western consumer society and the spread of human-chauvinist value systems. The time is fast approaching when questions raised by an environmental ethic will cease to involve live options. As things stand at present, however, the ethical issues generated by the pre-emptions—especially given the weakness and inadequacy of the ideological and value-theoretical basis on which the damaging chauvinistic transformation of the world is premised and the viability of alternative environmental ethics—are not merely of theoretical interest but are among the most important and urgent questions of our times, and perhaps the most important questions that human beings, whose individual or group self-interest is the source of most environmental problems, have ever asked themselves.

VII

ATTITUDES TO NATURE

JOHN PASSMORE

The ambiguity of the word 'nature' is so remarkable that I need not remark upon it. Except perhaps to emphasize that this ambiguity—scarcely less apparent, as Aristotle long ago pointed out, in its Greek near-equivalent *physis*—is by no means a merely accidental product of etymological confusions or conflations: it faithfully reflects the hesitancies, the doubts, and the uncertainties, with which men have confronted the world around them. For my special purposes, it is enough to say, I shall be using the word 'nature' in one of its narrower senses—so as to include only that which, setting aside the supernatural, is human neither in itself nor in its origins. This is the sense in which neither Sir Christopher Wren nor St Paul's Cathedral forms part of 'nature' and it may be hard to decide whether an oddly shaped flint or a landscape where the trees are evenly spaced is or is not 'natural'. The question I am raising, then, is what our attitudes have been, and ought to be, to nature in this narrow sense of the word, in which it excludes both the human and the artificial. And more narrowly still, I shall be devoting most of my attention to our attitudes towards that part of nature which it lies within man's power to modify and, in particular, towards what Karl Barth calls 'the strange life of beasts and plants which lies around us', a life we can by our actions destroy.

In what respect is animal and plant life 'strange'? The attitudes of human beings to other human beings are themselves variable and complicated; our fellow human beings often act in ways which are, in our eyes, strange. But there are ways of dealing with human beings which fail us when we confront nature. We can argue with human beings, expostulate with them, try to alter their courses by remonstration or by entreaty. No doubt there are human beings of whom this is not true: the hopelessly

From R. S. Peters, ed., *Nature and Conduct* (New York: St Martin's Press, 1975), 251–64. Reprinted with permission.

The paper attempts to bring together and to reformulate some of the basic philosophical themes in J. Passmore, *Man's Responsibility for Nature* (Duckworth and Charles Scribner, 1974). Those who are interested will find most of the historical references fully annotated in that book.

insane. And just for that reason there has been a tendency to exclude them from humanity, in some societies as supernatural beings, in others as mere animals: old Bedlam was, indeed, a kind of zoo. The psychopath, immune to argument or entreaty, arouses in us a quite peculiar fear and horror. As for artefacts, these admittedly we cannot modify in the ways in which we modify human beings; it is pointless to entreat a building to move out of the way of our car. But we understand them as playing a designed part in a form of human behaviour which we might, in principle, attempt to modify; we look through them to their human makers. When this is not so, when we encounter what clearly seems to be an artefact but cannot guess in what way of life it played a part, we find it, like Stonehenge, 'uncanny'.

'Strange', as Karl Barth uses the word, connotes not only unfamiliar but foreign, alien. (The uneducated find any foreigner 'uncanny' because they cannot communicate with him—to get him to act they have to *push* him like a natural object rather than speak to him.) That nature is thus alien, men have, of course, by no means always recognized. During most of their history they have thought of natural processes as having intentions and as capable of being influenced exactly in the manner of human beings, by prayer and entreaty—not by way of an anthropomorphically conceived God but directly, immediately.

For the last two thousand years, however, the Graeco-Christian Western world has entirely rejected this conception of nature. At least, it has done so in its *official* science, technology, and philosophy: the ordinary country-man was harder to convince that natural processes cannot have intentions, even when they are not so much as animal. As late as the nineteenth century German foresters thought it only prudent to explain to a tree they were about to fell exactly why it had to be cut down. In Ibsen's *Wild Duck*, Old Ekdal is convinced that the forest will 'seek revenge' for having been too ruthlessly thinned; in Büchner's *Woyzeck* a countryman explains the drowning of a man in a river by telling his companion the river had been seeking a victim for a long time past. (Recall the familiar newspaper metaphor: a dangerous stretch of coast 'claims another victim'.)

Such attitudes, I believe, still exert an influence; in some of the recent ecological literature, the view that nature 'will have its revenge' on mankind for their misdeeds operates as something more than a metaphor, just as old ideas of pollution, sacrilege, hubris, are still, in such writings, potent concepts.

The fact remains that the Stoic-Christian tradition has insisted on the absolute uniqueness of man, a uniqueness particularly manifest, according to Christianity, in the fact that he alone, in Karl Barth's words, has been 'addressed by God' and can therefore be saved or damned but also, in the

Stoic-Christian tradition as a whole, apparent in his capacity for rational communication. If nature, on that view, is not wholly strange, this is only because it has been created by God for men to use. Animals and plants can for that reason be assimilated, at least in certain respects, to the class of tools, dumb beasts but none the less obedient to men's will. Peter Lombard summed up the traditional Christian view in his *Sentences*: 'As man is made for the sake of God, namely that he may serve him, so is the world made for the sake of man, that it may serve him.' So although nature is 'alien' in so far as it is not rational, it is for orthodoxy neither hostile nor indifferent, appearances to the contrary notwithstanding. Every natural process exists either as an aid to men materially or as a spiritual guide, recalling, as flood or volcano or tempest, their corrupt state.

In this doctrine, which they trace back to the Old Testament, the ecologically-minded critics of Western culture discern the roots of its destructiveness. This is a mistake on two accounts. First, that everything exists to serve man is certainly not the regular teaching of the Old Testament, which constantly insists that, in the words of the Book of Job, God 'causes it to rain on the earth, where no man is; on the wilderness, wherein there is no man; to satisfy the desolate and the waste ground; and to cause the bud of the tender herb to spring forth'. To Paul's rhetorical question: 'Doth God care for oxen?' an Old Testament Jew would have answered 'Yes, of course.' It was the Stoics who took the contrary view. And it is they, under the pretence that it was the Old Testament, who were followed by such influential Christian intellectuals as Origen. Secondly, the doctrine that 'everything is made for man' does not at once entail that man should go forth and transform the world. On the contrary, it was for centuries interpreted in a conservative fashion: God knows best what we need. To attempt to reshape what God has created is a form of presumption, of hubris. Sinful corrupt men ought not to attempt to reshape the world in their own image.

After the Crusades, Europe witnessed the development of the 'mechanical arts', as exemplified in the water-wheel, windmills, the compass, clocks. But these inventions were in many quarters condemned as diabolical. In a wonderful example of Heideggerian etymology, 'mechanical' was derived from 'moecha', an adulteress. God, so it was argued, had provided ready-made on earth all it was proper for men to desire. For them to seek to make their labours less onerous was to go directly against God's will, by attempting to construct a world which was as if Adam had never sinned.

Yet there is this much truth in the ecological diagnosis: the view that everything exists to serve man encouraged the development of a particular way of looking at nature, not as something to respect, but rather as something to utilize. Nature is in no sense sacred; this was a point on which Christian theology and Greek cosmology agreed. God, no doubt, could make particular places or objects sacred by choosing to take up residence in them, as in Roman Christianity he made sacred the sacrificial bread and wine. But no natural object was sacred in itself; there was no risk of sacrilege in felling a tree, or killing an animal. When Bacon set up as his ideal the transformation of nature—or, more accurately, the re-creation of the Garden of Eden—he had to fight the view that man was too corrupt to undertake any such task but not the view that nature was too sacred to be touched. It was man, he pointed out, whom God made in his own image, not nature.

When Christian apologists see in science and technology the product of a distinctively Christian civilization, they are so far right: Christianity taught men that there was nothing sacrilegious either in analysing or in modifying nature. But only when Christianity modified its belief in original sin, only when it became, in practice, Pelagian could it witness without disapproval, let alone positively encourage, the attempt to create on earth a new nature, more suitable to human needs. Locke's vigorous attack on original sin—explicit in his theological writings, implicit in the *Essay*—formed part of his task as an under-labourer, clearing away obstacles to the transformation of nature—and man—by man.

Associated with the Christian concept of nature was a particular ethical thesis: that no moral considerations bear upon man's relationship to natural objects, except where they happen to be someone else's property or except where to treat them cruelly or destructively might encourage corresponding attitudes towards other human beings. This thesis the Stoics had strongly maintained and it was no less warmly advocated by Augustine. Jesus, Augustine argues, drove the devils into swine—innocent though the swine were of any crime—instead of destroying them, as a lesson to men that they may do as they like with animals. Not even cruelty to animals, so Aquinas tells us, is wrong in itself. 'If any passage in Holy Scripture seems to forbid us to be cruel to brute animals that is either . . . lest through being cruel to animals one becomes cruel to human beings or because injury to animals leads to the temporal hurt of man.' In other words, cruelty to animals is wrong only in virtue of its effects on human beings, as Kant, in this same tradition, still maintained in the final decades of the eighteenth century. And what is true of cruelty to animals applies, on this view, even more obviously to our dealings with other members of the non-human world. Only in Jewish, or Jewish-inspired, speculation, was the opposite view at all widespread. The Talmud in several places advocates a more considerate attitude to nature and when Kant reaffirms the traditional position it is in opposition to Baumgarten, who had on this question followed the Talmud.

The question whether it is intrinsically wrong to be cruel to animals has an importance much greater than at first sight appears: it is precisely for that reason that philosophers like Kant, humane though they certainly were, insist that cruelty to animals is wrong only on the—in fact very dubious—empirical hypothesis that it encourages cruelty to human beings. For if cruelty to animals is intrinsically wrong, then it is *not* morally indifferent how men behave towards nature; in at least one case—and then perhaps in others—man's relationship with nature ought to be governed by moral considerations which are not reducible to a concern for purely human interests, to a duty either to others or, as Kant thought, to oneself.

There is one simple and decisive way of denying that it is wrong unnecessarily to cause suffering to animals, namely by denying that animals can in fact suffer. This is the step Descartes took. The philosophy of Descartes represents, in certain respects, the culmination of the tendency of Graeco-Christian thought to differentiate man from his fellow-animals. For Descartes denies that animals can so much as feel, let alone exercise intelligence. (One is forcibly reminded at this point of the Ciceronian dictum, to which he subscribes, that there is no doctrine so absurd but that some philosopher has held it.) All suffering, so his follower Malebranche tells us, is the result of Adam's sin: animals, as not implicated in that sin, cannot suffer. As a result of our actions animals do not *really* suffer, they only behave exactly as if they suffered—a doctrine that some of the Stoics had also managed to believe. So it is not only wrong to suppose that we can reason with animals but wrong to suppose, even, that we can sympathize with them. It is true that this conclusion was reached at the cost of placing the human body itself within nature, as something not sacred; what was left outside nature was only consciousness. Yet at the same time the human body was for Descartes unique in being in some way 'united' with consciousness; the human person, conjoining mind and body, could thus be set in total opposition to the non-human world it encounters.

So the Cartesian dualism could be used, and was used, to justify the view that, in his relationships with nature, man was not subject to any moral curbs. Yet at the same time Descartes broke this doctrine loose from its historical association with the view that everything is made for man's use— a view he characterized as 'childish and absurd'. It was, he thought, *obvious* that 'an infinitude of things exist, or did exist, which have never been beheld or comprehended by any man and which have never been of any use to him'. No doubt, man could in fact make use of what he found in nature, and he ought indeed to do so, but nature did not exist as something ready-made for him. Effectively to use it, he had first to transform it. One is not surprised, then, to find Descartes proclaiming that it is man's task 'to make himself master and possessor of nature'; the proper attitude to the world, in his eyes, is exploitative. The paradigmatic case of a material substance is, for Descartes, a piece of wax, the traditional symbol of malleability.

Like Bacon before him he also suggests a particular method of exploitation, what he calls a 'practical philosophy', what we should call a 'science-based technology'. So far as we can make natural processes less 'strange', the assumption is, this is only by first bringing them under concepts which are either inherent in or created by human reason and then using this conceptual grasp to make them work in a manner more conformable with human interests. This is the attitude to nature which has dominated Western science: understanding through laws, transformation through technology.

The philosophy of science associated with this enterprise has been, in certain important respects, Platonic. 'Understanding' has been identified with the discovery of mathematically expressible functional relationships between abstractly-conceived processes and objects. Science, so it is then said, is not about the particular things we see and attempt to cope with in the world around us, except in a rather indirect way. The physics textbook talks about everyday natural objects only in its description of experimental set-ups. And physics is presumed to be science in its ideal form. Rutherford's notorious description of science as 'physics and stamp-collecting' expresses this attitude very precisely; natural history, the direct investigation of nature in a manner which is content to describe qualitative relationships between everyday natural objects and processes, is condemned as mere 'stamp-collecting'. Only a third-rate mind, the presumption is, could devote itself to studying, let us say, the life-history of the whale. To be what Plato calls 'a lover of sights and sounds', to take delight in the flight of birds as such as distinct from the mathematical problems set by that flight, is at once to show oneself an inferior, sensual, being.

Of course, this attitude to nature has always had its critics. Poets like Blake protested against it; painting, before painters, too, were beguiled into pure geometry, drew attention, sensually, to the forms and colours in the world around us. Biologists like John Ray emphasized against Descartes the importance of the multiplicity and diversity of forms of life. But the mainstream of science has been Cartesian–Platonic.

Philosophers, however, were generally unhappy with Cartesian dualism, for reasons which practising scientists found, and still find, it difficult to understand. Descartes, so philosophers argued, had separated conscious-ness from nature so absolutely that the two could no longer be brought into any relationship with one another. In general, if in very different ways, they reacted against Descartes by trying to maintain that nature was a great deal more human-like than Descartes had been prepared to admit. But they did so, in many cases, at the cost of denying to nature a wholly independent existence, or, at best, by treating independent nature as a sort of 'thing in itself', not as the nature we encounter and try to deal with in our everyday life.

For Berkeley, indeed, the whole of nature is nothing but a vast system of signs, warning and admonishing men. In a different tradition, for Hegel, as for Marx after him, nature in itself is 'negativity'. This does not mean, of course, that it does not exist. But it exists simply in order to be overcome, to be humanized. Man offers it liberty, frees it from its fetters, only by making it human, as he does, to use a favourite example of Hegel's, when he eats plants and flesh. In one way or another, that is, post-Cartesian metaphysicians—with, of course, some notable exceptions—try to main-tain that nature is man-centred, even to the extent, in extreme instances, of denying that it so much as exists when man is not perceiving it, thus cut-ting the ground completely from beneath Descartes's argument against anthropocentrism. Nature is made less 'strange' by being converted into a tool, a language, a secret ally, an aspirant after humanity—or by being denied actuality, except in so far as man cares to bestow actuality upon it. (Remember Hume's reference, although he was not a consistent phenomenalist, to the perceptions 'we choose to dignify' with the name of reality.)

Associated with this attitude to nature is a depreciation of natural beauty as vastly inferior to works of art: the feeling one finds in classical literature and which is still enunciated by Hegel that nature deserves appreciation only when it has been transformed into a farm, a garden, and so has lost its wildness, its strangeness. It was a common theme in Christian thought that the world had been created a perfect globe; nature as we now see it with its mountains and its valleys is a dismal ruin, a melancholy reminder of Adam's sin. Malebranche regretted that nature contains shapes other than the regular solids; the seventeenth-century formal gardener, in the most Augustinian of centuries, did his best to convert nature into such shapes with his pyramidal trees and cubic hedges. The less geometrically-minded Hegelians were no less confident that nature was as it ought to be only when man had transformed it, converting wildernesses into tamed landscapes. Herbert Spencer saw the human task as the conversion of the world into one vast garden.

The two leading traditions in modern Western thought, then, can be put thus: the first, Cartesian in inspiration, that matter is inert, passive, that man's relationship to it is that of an absolute despot, reshaping, reforming, what has in it no inherent powers of resistance, any sort of agency; the second, Hegelian, that nature exists only *in potentia*, as something which it is man's task to help to actualize through art, science, philosophy, technology, converting it into something human, something in which he can feel thoroughly 'at home', in no sense strange or alien to him, a mirror in which he can see his own face. Man, on this second view, *completes* the universe not simply by living in it, as the Genesis myth suggests, but by actually helping to make it.

It is easy to see from this brief historical excursus why the ecological critics of Western civilization are now pleading for a new religion, a new ethics, a new aesthetics, a new metaphysics. One could readily imagine a sardonic history of Western philosophy which would depict it as a long attempt to allay men's fears, their insecurities, by persuading them that natural processes do not represent any real threat, either because they are completely malleable to human pressures, or because men are ultimately safe in a universe designed to secure their interests—an enterprise which issued in wilder and wilder absurdities in a desperate attempt to deny the obvious facts. This would not be a wholly accurate history of philosophy; even phenomenalism has its merits as the *reductio ad absurdum* of the plausible-looking theory of perception. Philosophy, as we have already suggested, had good reasons for rejecting the Cartesian dualism even if its reasons are less good for replacing it with a new version of anthropocentrism. At the same time, to think of philosophy thus is not an entirely monstrous interpretation; it is quite understandable that philosophy should look like an apologia for anthropocentrism to those who now so urgently emphasize man's responsibility for nature. Western metaphysics and Western ethics have certainly done nothing to discourage, have gone a great deal to encourage, the ruthless exploitation of nature, whether they have seen in that exploitation the rightful manipulation of a nature which is wax in man's hands or the humanizing of it in a manner which somehow accords with nature's real interests.

As philosophers, of course, we cannot merely acquiesce in the demand for a new metaphysics or a new ethics on the simple ground that the widespread acceptance of the older metaphysics, the older ethics, has encouraged the exploitation of nature—any more than a biologist would acquiesce in the demand for a new biology if that demand were grounded merely on the fact, or alleged fact, that men would be less inclined to act in ecologically destructive ways if they were persuaded that all living things possessed a developed brain. The philosopher is unlikely to be at all satisfied, in particular, with the demand of the primitivist wing of the ecological movement that he should encourage man to revert to the belief that nature is sacred. We are in fact *right* in condemning as superstitious the belief that trees, rivers, volcanoes, can be swayed by arguments; we are *right* in believing that we have found in science ways of understanding their behaviour; we are *right* in regarding civilization as important and thus far in attempting to transform nature. It is not by abandoning our hard-won tradition of rationality that we shall save ourselves.

We can, however, properly ask ourselves what general conditions any philosophy of nature must fulfil if it is to do justice to the scientific themes of the ecological movement, as distinct from its reactionary, mystical overtones. Any satisfactory philosophy of nature, we can then say, must recognize:

1. That natural processes go on in their own way, in a manner indifferent to human interests and by no means incompatible with man's total disappearance from the face of the earth.

2. When men act on nature, they do not simply modify a particular quality of a particular substance. What they do, rather, is to interact with a system of interactions, setting in process new interactions. Just for that reason, there is always a risk that their actions will have consequences which they did not predict.

3. In our attempt to understand nature the discovery of physics-type general laws is often of very limited importance. The complaint that biology and sociology are inferior because they know no such laws can be reversed, formulated as an argument against an undue emphasis on a Platonic-Cartesian analysis of 'understanding'. When it comes to understanding either biological or social structures, we can then say, what is important is a detailed understanding of very specific circumstances rather than a knowledge of high-level functional relationships. The 'laws' involved are often trite and ill-formulated, serving only as boundaries to what is possible. Whales, to revert to my previous example, must, like every other animal, eat and breed; we can describe it, if we like, as a 'biological law' that every animal must ingest food and must have a way of reproducing itself. But these 'laws' leave almost everything of interest about whales still to be discovered.

One could put the general conditions I have laid down by saying that in an important sense the philosopher has to learn to live with the 'strangeness' of nature, with the fact that natural processes are entirely indifferent to our existence and welfare—not *positively* indifferent, of course, but *incapable* of caring about us—and are complex in a way that rules out the possibility of our wholly mastering and transforming them. So expressed, these conclusions sound so trite and obvious that one is almost ashamed to set them out. But, from what has already been said, it will be obvious that they have not been satisfied in most of the traditional philosophies of nature. To that degree it is true, I think, that we do need a 'new metaphysics' which is genuinely not anthropocentric and which takes change and complexity with the seriousness they deserve. It must certainly not think of natural processes either as being dependent upon man for their existence, as infinitely malleable, or as being so constructed as to guarantee the continued survival of human beings and their civilization.

Such a philosophy of nature, of course, would be by no means entirely new. Its foundations have been laid in the various forms of naturalism. Naturalistic philosophies, however, like the Darwinian biology which lends them support, often attempt to reduce the 'strangeness' of nature—even if they do this by naturalizing man rather than by spiritualizing nature. That way of using the word 'nature' which I have so far employed is, so many naturalistic philosophers would say, wholly misleading; we should think of 'nature' only as something of which man forms part, not alien to him because he is a full member of it. And, of course, I should agree with the naturalistic philosophers that, in a very important sense of the word 'nature', both man and human artefacts form part of nature: they are subject to natural laws. Nature does not have that *metaphysical* 'strangeness' which Descartes ascribed to it. Both senses of 'nature', however, have a particular role to play; they are important in different types of discussion. Naturalistic philosophers are sometimes tempted into reductionism, tempted into denying that our dealings with our fellow-men differ in any important respect from our dealings with other things, that nature is any 'stranger' than those of our fellow human beings with whom we are not fully acquainted. This is a temptation which has to be resisted. It is not anthropocentric to think of human beings and what they create as having a peculiar value and importance, or to suggest that human beings have unique ways of relating to one another—most notably through their capacity for asserting and denying, but also because, as the existentialists argue, they are unique in their concern for, and about, the future. For many purposes, it is not arbitrary, but essential, to contrast the human with what is not human—with the 'natural' in the limited special sense of the word.

So it will not do to argue, for example, that what has happened in the world is just that man as the dominant species is destroying, in normal biological competition, competitive species, and that to repine at the disappearance of these species is as absurd as it would be to complain that the world no longer contains dinosaurs. It is perfectly true that like any other species men can survive only at the cost of other species. But men can see what is happening: they can observe the disappearance of competing species; they can consider what the effects of that disappearance will be; they can—at least in principle—preserve a species and modify their own behaviour so that it will be less destructive. That in many ways, fundamental ways, men are *not* unique is the starting-point for any satisfactory metaphysics. But in other ways they are. A 'new metaphysics', if it is not to falsify the facts, will have to be naturalistic, but not reductionist. The working out of such a metaphysics is, in my judgement, the most important task which lies ahead of philosophy.

What of the contention that the West now needs a new ethics, with responsibility for nature lying at its centre? This, too, is often carried further than I am prepared to follow it. Men need to recognize, it is then suggested, that they 'form a community' with plants, animals, the biosphere, and that every member of that community has rights—including the right to live and the right to be treated with respect. In opposition to any such doctrine, the Stoics long ago argued that civilization would be quite impossible, that indeed human beings could not even survive, if men were bound to act justly in relation to nature. Primitivists would reverse this argument; since civilization depends upon men acting unjustly towards nature, civilization ought, they would argue, to be abandoned. Men, so Porphyry for one maintained, ought to reduce their claims to the barest minimum, surviving, under these minimal circumstances, on nothing but the fruits which plants do not need for *their* survival.

Even the fruits a plant does not need, however, may be needed by a variety of micro-organisms; men cannot survive, as I have already suggested, except by being in some degree a predator. As Hume said, it is one thing to maintain that men ought to act *humanely* towards animals, quite another to maintain that they ought to act *justly* towards them. The first of these doctrines rests on no more elaborate assumption than that animals suffer; the second doctrine rests on the much less plausible assumption that animals have claims or interests in a sense which makes the notion of justice applicable to them. Some moral philosophers—Leonard Nelson for one—have taken this view. But I am not convinced that it is appropriate to speak of animals as having 'interests' unless 'interests' are identified with *needs*—and to have needs, as a plant, too, has needs, is by no means the same thing as to have rights. It is one thing to say that it is wrong to treat plants and animals in a certain manner, quite another thing to say that they have a *right* to be treated differently.

No doubt, men, plants, animals, the biosphere form parts of a single community in the ecological sense of the word; each is dependent upon the others for its continued existence. But this is not the sense of community which generates rights, duties, obligations; men and animals are not involved in a network of responsibilities or a network of mutual concessions. That is why nature, even within a naturalistic philosophy, is still 'strange', alien.

To a not inconsiderable degree, it can be added, very familiar ethical principles are quite strong enough to justify action against ecological despoilers. We do not need the help of a 'new ethics' in order to justify our blaming those who make our rivers into sewers and our air unbreathable, who give birth to children in an over-populated world or—this is a little more disputable—who waste resources which posterity will need. Only where specifically human interests are not so obviously involved does the question of a 'new ethics' so much as arise. Even the preservation of wild species and of wildernesses can largely be defended in a familiar utilitarian fashion.

What has certainly to be dropped, nevertheless, is the Augustinian doctrine that in his dealings with nature man is simply not subject to moral censure, except where specifically human interests arise. Few moral philosophers would now accept that view in its original unrestricted form. It is, indeed, very striking with what unanimity they condemn the older doctrine that cruelty to animals is morally wrong only when it does direct harm to human beings. Their predecessors, they say, were guilty of moral blindness, a blindness with theological origins, in not seeing that it was wrong to cause animals unnecessarily to suffer. The question remains, however, whether moral philosophers are not still to some extent 'morally blind' in their attitudes to nature and especially to those parts of nature which are not sentient and therefore do not suffer.

Certainly, they—and we—have a tendency to restrict such condemnatory moral epithets as vandalism and philistinism to the destruction of property and indifference to works of art. On the face of it, however, the condemnation of vandalism is as applicable to those who damage or destroy the natural as it is to those who damage or destroy artefacts. When, for example, Baumgarten condemns what he calls 'the spirit of destruction' this has as much application to the wilful destruction of natural objects as it does to the wilful destruction of property, or of things likely to be useful to our fellow human beings. The last man on earth would for that reason be blameable were he to end his days in an orgy of destruction, even though his actions could not adversely affect any other human being.

Similarly, a failure to appreciate the natural scene is as serious a human weakness as a failure to appreciate works of art. Once we fully free ourselves from the Augustinian doctrine that nature exists only as something to be used, not enjoyed, the extension of such moral notions as vandalism and philistinism to man's relationship with trees and landscapes will seem as obvious as the extension of the idea of cruelty of man's relationships with animals. It is the great importance of Romanticism that it partly saw this and encouraged us to *look* at nature, to see it otherwise than as a mere instrument. But we do not need to accept the Romantic identification of God with nature in order to accept this way of looking at the world. Indeed, the divinization of nature, even apart from the philosophical problems it raises, dangerously underestimates the *fragility* of so many natural processes and relationships, a fragility to which the ecological movement has drawn such forcible attention.

In general, if we can bring ourselves fully to admit the independence of nature, the fact that things go on in their own complex ways, we are likely to feel more respect for the ways in which they go on. We are prepared to contemplate them with admiration, to enjoy them sensuously, to study them in their complexity as distinct from looking for simple methods of manipulating them. The suggestion that we *cannot* do this, that, inevitably, so long as we think of nature as 'strange', we cannot, as Hegel thought, take any interest in it or feel any concern for it underestimates the degree to which we can overcome egoism and achieve disinterestedness. The emergence of new moral attitudes to nature is bound up, then, with the emergence of a more realistic philosophy of nature. That is the only adequate foundation for effective ecological concern.

VIII

VALUE IN NATURE AND MEANING IN LIFE

FREYA MATHEWS

The thesis that we, as human selves, stand in a holistic relation—a relation of 'oneness'—with the cosmos itself, promises more than a list of ethical prescriptions. It promises a key to the perennial questions of who we are, why we are born, what is our reason for living, etc. In short it promises to throw light on the *meaning* of life.

Deep ecology approaches this question of meaningfulness too. For in deep ecology the main emphasis is not only on the thesis of intrinsic value, but on that of a form of human 'self-realization' which springs out of 'ecological consciousness'. Naess invokes the *Bhagavadgita* to explain his concept of self-realization: 'He whose self is harmonized by yoga seeth the Self abiding in all beings and all beings in Self; everywhere he sees the same.'[1] He goes on to explain:

Through identification, higher level unity is experienced: from identifying with 'one's nearest', higher unities are created through circles of friends, local communities, tribes, compatriots, races, humanity, life, and, ultimately, as articulated by religious and philosophic leaders, unity with the supreme whole, the 'world' in a broader and deeper sense than the usual...

This way of thinking and feeling at its maximum corresponds to that of the enlightened, or yogi, who sees 'the same', the atman, and who is not alienated from anything. The process of identification is sometimes expressed in terms of loss of self and gain of Self through 'self-less' action. Each new sort of identification corresponds to a widening of the self, and strengthens the urge to further widening. This urge is in the system of Spinoza called *Conatus in sui perseverare*, striving to persevere in oneself or one's being.... It is not a mere urge to survive, but to increase the level of acting out... one's own nature or essence, and is not different from the urge toward higher levels of 'freedom' (*libertas*). Under favourable circumstances, this involves wide identification.[2]

Extr. from Ch. 4 of *The Ecological Self* (London: Routledge, 1991), 147–63. Reprinted by permission.

[1] Arne Naess, 'Identification as a Source of Deep Ecological Attitudes', in Tobias, ed., *Deep Ecology* (San Diego: Avant Books, 1985), 260.
[2] Ibid. 363.

Clearly for Naess *Self-realization* (which I italicize henceforth to distinguish it from the self-realization which here is taken to qualify systems for the status of selfhood[3]) involves the identification of the small human self—the personal ego—with ever wider wholes, up to the level of the cosmos as a whole. This identification is not, for Naess, a purely psychological affair, but is grounded in a recognition of the metaphysical fact of interconnectedness. The biological fact of ecological interconnectedness is taken to be a model of a deeper kind of interconnectedness which permeates the entire physical realm, from micro- to cosmo-levels. Naess appeals to Spinoza, and other writers appeal to eastern worldviews, such as those of Buddhism or Taoism, to vindicate their metaphysical preferences. But it has not been part of the programme of deep ecology to undertake any kind of thoroughgoing justification for such a metaphysic of interconnectedness.[4] Given such a metaphysic as a base however, the 'identity' of the human self with the cosmos is in some sense an ontological given, and the recognition of this identity, which Naess takes to be a good in its own right, is constitutive of *Self-realization*.

I want to explore the relation between the human self and the cosmos in the context of a particular metaphysic of interconnectedness.[5] I also want to throw light on *why* recognition of this relationship of 'oneness' should confer meaning on life. In the particular metaphysic of interconnectedness in question—which involves the concept of what I have called the ecocosm—there are two ways of viewing the universe: under the aspect of substance, and under the aspect of self. When the universe is viewed under the aspect of substance, the relation in which it stands to me, when I am viewed as an extended region of space-time, is the holistic one of geometro-dynamical interconnectedness: I am topologically conditioned by the universe, and it is topologically conditioned by me. When the universe is viewed under the aspect of self-realizing system, then the relation in which it stands to me, when I am viewed as a self, is the equally holistic one of ecological interconnectedness: its selfhood conditions mine, my selfhood conditions its.

[3] 'Selfhood' is here used in a specialized, systems-theoretic sense, explained in *The Ecological Self*, ch. 3. A system is there defined as a 'self' if it is self-maintaining or self-realizing, and accordingly possessed of *conatus*.

[4] Naess, of course, in his article 'The Shallow and the Deep, Long-Range Ecology Movement: A Summary', *Inquiry*, 16 (1973), 95–100, adumbrates a field-theoretical metaphysic of interconnectedness. Warwick Fox reveals the parallels between deep ecology and the new physics in 'Deep Ecology: A New Philosophy of Our Time?', *Ecologist*, 14 (1984). J. Baird Callicott has explored the metaphysical implications of ecology in 'The Metaphysical Implications of Ecology', *Environmental Ethics*, 8/4 (1986).

[5] This metaphysic—based on systems theory and a geometro-dynamic cosmology—is developed in *The Ecological Self*, chs. 2, 3.

Let us look first at the significance of my geometro-dynamical interconnectedness with the universe viewed as a seamless substantival unity. Certainly it implies that I am 'one with' that universe, in the sense that I am structurally and substantively shaped by its geometry, as it is, in a small way, by mine. But in this respect I am no different from any other physical thing, indeed any other region of space-time, occupied or unoccupied. Does my oneness with the universe retain its meaningfulness in light of this? When we ask for the meaning of life, do we expect an answer that will apply just as well to amoebas and rocks and gases and unoccupied regions of space-time? If meaningfulness hinges on special-ness, then our substantival unity with the geometro-dynamical world appears to offer little antidote to futility.

However this conclusion may be too hasty. Being human is different from being amoebic, or being a rock or a gas or a region of space-time, in so far as we alone amongst these entities can *grasp* our unity with the greater whole. There is nothing unique in our relation to the universe, but it makes a difference to us, to our experience, if we are *aware* of this relation—and it may be this difference that makes the difference, that invests our lives with a greater meaning. Why does awareness of our unity with the cosmos make a difference to our experience? As human beings we are endowed with self-interest, self-concern, self-love. When we recognize the involvement of wider wholes in our identity, an expansion in the scope of our identity and hence in the scope of our self-love occurs. This appears to be the meaning of *Self-realization*, according to Naess's account of it, and it leads as he indicates, to a loving and protective attitude to the world—an extension of our loving and protective attitude to our own bodies. Naess points out the preferability of such conservationist protec-tiveness springing from the heart, as it does in this case, rather than from an intellectual apprehension of the intrinsic value of nature and a rational appreciation of its consequent entitlement to moral consideration. This attitude of protectiveness, based on identification with nature, marks the shift from an ethics of duty, grounded in the recognition of the intrinsic value of selves, to an ethics of care.[6]

The benefits of this transition from self-love to *Self-love* are consider-able. It offers a conclusive cure for alienation, replacing alienation with an ineffable sense of at-homeness in nature, and a disposition to live in harmony with it. It relieves the mind of the tyranny of personal desires, and allows one to cultivate the peace and joy of 'unattachment' in something

[6] The care perspective in ethics, resting on moral sentiment, has been contrasted by feminist authors with the justice perspective, based on reason. The seminal work in this connection is Carol Gilligan, *In a Different Voice* (Cambridge, Mass.: Harvard University Press, 1982).

like the Buddhist sense of that term. Understanding our involvement in the grand scheme of nature, our whole perception of ourselves and our role in the world is transformed. We experience life differently, and the love that was narrowly beamed inwards onto our personal egos is beamed outward, illuminating everything around us, drawing it into the circle of our own concern, our own being. This loving of the world is a blissful state which warms and animates everything around us. It spills over into a real and robust love of people in their full emotional and physical richness, of other beings, of lands, and skies, and the furthest reaches of the night. It bursts the bars of the personal heart, and vastly expands our sense of self. To whoever can achieve such a whole love it is, as Naess claims, joy.

Self-realization as Naess describes it, then, would appear to correspond, in the ecocosmic framework, to a recognition of our geometro-dynamic interconnectedness with the universal substance, and a consequent expansion of our self-love to embrace it.

However, in deep-ecology identification with the universe—sustaining the widest possible identification—is taken as a sufficient end-in-itself, with little regard for the nature of that universe beyond the fact of its internal interconnectedness. There seems to be an assumption in the air that the universe is a great and magnificent thing, worthy of being identified with, but any explanation of its nature or any justification of this assumption is hard to find. No secular reason is given for supposing that the universe is in any sense alive, or that it promotes life within it, or that life dances to the tune of any particular purpose or telos; indeed no indication is given of what any of these ideas would mean in a secular context. For all that Naess or any other deep ecologists, so far as I am aware, have shown, the universe could be, like the geometro-static universe, internally interconnected but nevertheless quite meaningless, devoid of *telos* or intrinsic worth. The reason given for loving it is just, at bottom, that it is an extension of ourselves.

Various arguments can be brought against this position, and in order to have more than merely intuitive force the doctrine of *Self-realization* really has to rest on a more positive and articulated view of the universe, a view which provides independent grounds for loving the universe. If the universe were in fact a blind and neutral entity, like the geometro-static world, or worse, a self-destructive one, then identification with it may actually weaken our self-love by revealing us as less meaningful than we thought we were.

Let us concentrate for the moment however on the deep-ecological notion of *Self-realization*. If the universe with which the personal self is to identify is not shown to be a self-realizing system, then the following objection may be levelled at the claim that identification with nature will produce a spontaneously loving and protective attitude to the environment. Nature in itself, the objection runs, is not only creative but destructive. New life arises from the often violent destruction and deterioration of the old. Planets are born out of the shattered remains of blown-out stars. Elementary particles are constantly created and annihilated in the endless dance of energy at the micro-level. This is the nature of our larger Self, the 'law' of its being. To love oneself is to attempt to realize one's true nature, the 'law' of one's being. To love the greater Self then, to give expression to its presence in us, will be to do as it does, that is, to destroy as well as to create. Humanity the exploder and wrecker will in this case be seen to be expressing its interconnectedness with nature just as legitimately as humanity the worshipful or loving conserver.

This objection can be pushed even further, as we shall soon see. Before we pass on, however, there is another, even deeper objection which may be brought against the doctrine of *Self-realization* when that doctrine is not tied to the view of the universe as a self, a being possessed of its own *conatus*. According to this objection, if the universe is viewed as an internally differentiated, internally dynamic universal substance, then the destruction of particulars (particular objects, organisms, ecosystems, planets) is of no consequence to it. Change—the Buddhist *anicca*—is the underlying principle of such a reality: everything comes into being and passes away. For a particular to be destroyed is just for it to be reabsorbed into the universal flux, of which it is in any case just a momentary manifestation. If this universal flux constitutes our larger Self, then these particular comings-into-being and passings-away are of no concern to us, for the identity of our Self remains constant throughout. Indeed this Self may be relied on to give rise to new particulars, new manifestations: it is the ever-self-renewing fountain-head of all wonders and beauties. If we lose a species or two, a forest, a dune field, even Gaia itself, there is no reason for grief, for we are at one with the inexhaustible source of such forms-of-being, and are therefore not diminished. Indeed we might even point out that those who struggle to preserve the particulars are acting precisely from an un-*Self-realized* point of view, for they are seeing the objects of destruction as discrete entities, logically unconnected with the whole and for this reason irreplaceable. Conservationists are, from the point of view of this objection, acting from atomist premises.

There is something that rings true in these objections. The same chest-beating self-importance often lies behind the urge to conserve, protect, tend, look after things as lies behind the urge to blow everything sky high. There is nothing in our Western mind-set that is prepared just to leave things—including our own aggressive tendencies—alone, let things arise and pass away in their own time. There is no acceptance of ourselves as a natural phenomenon—or a natural disaster, perhaps—on a par with ice-ages and interplanetary collisions. But this zen-like surrender to our own natural tendencies turns the whole argument for *Self-realization* on its head.

To avoid these objections we have to view the universe with which we are to be identified not only under the aspect of substance, but under the aspect of self. We have to consider the implications not only of our sub-stantival but of our ecological interconnectedness with the ecocosm. Availing ourselves of the full extent of our theory of the ecocosm supplies immediate replies to the above objections.

To the first objection, that if the universe is not a self, then identifying with it might actually weaken our self-love by diminishing our sense of the worthiness of what we are, the reply is now clear-cut: the universe is itself a self, possessed of its own grand telos and immeasurable intrinsic value. There is no risk that identifying with it will diminish us, or cause our self-love to dwindle.

To the second objection—that creativity and destructiveness are symmetric principles of the universe, equal 'laws of its being', so that being true to the universe as our greater Self involves giving expression to both these tendencies—we may reply as follows. In the context of the ecocosm, creation and destruction are not symmetric principles. Selves exhibit an asymmetric will-to-exist. This is their *conatus*, their determination actively to resist destruction and to expand their being. Since the ecocosm is a self, its essential principle is the *conatus*. As vehicles of the *conatus*, selves are anti-entropic, where this must ultimately be as true of the cosmic self as of others. Positive and negative forces do not balance out in a self-realizing world: positive forces prevail. Thus in attempting to realize our greater Self—the ecocosm—we should attempt to do what it does, that is we should do our utmost to preserve and enrich, rather than to destroy, our environment.

However, this way of putting the objection, and the reply, is relatively superficial. Really to follow through on the argument would be to demon-strate that unless we allow that the universe is itself a self, it would be self-defeating for me to attempt to identify with it: the whole project of *Self-realization* would be incoherent. For suppose that the universe with which we proposed to identify was not a self, but that the 'law of its being', or underlying principle, was one of random flux, or even self-erosion. Then, since as a self the law of my own being is self-realization, my impulse will be to realize the potentialities of whatever I identify with. In other words, when my self-love is extended to things with which I have reason to identify, it will incline me to try to realize the 'law of their being'. If the law of their being happens to be, say, self-erosion, then my love of the thing in question will incline me to promote its erosion. In this way self-love, or the will-to-self-realization, can come to entail self-destruction, which is self-defeating. It therefore follows that a self may only consistently identify with beings which are also selves. Naess's doctrine of *Self-realization*, on this reasoning then, actually requires that the universe be a self. As soon as it is admitted that the universe is a self, the second objection to the doctrine of *Self-realization* dissolves.

The third objection—that the arisings and passings-away of particulars are of no concern to my larger Self because its continued existence is consistent with, indeed entails, this internal flux—cannot be dealt with until we have examined the way in which I, as a self, am related to the ecocosm.

It was pointed out earlier that when the universe is viewed only under the aspect of substance, and I am identified merely as a particular region within its universal extension, then my relation to the universe is no different from that of a rock. But as a self, my relation to the universe viewed as an ecocosm is entirely different from that of a rock. I am related as subsystem to a nested series of parent-systems, up to the level of cosmic self. I stand in the relation of ecological part to whole. The rock, not being a self-realizing system, is not a part of the ecological order, and hence does not stand in the relation of ecological part to cosmic whole. This is not of course to say that rocks do not contribute to ecosystems. They do, but as their nature is given independently of the ecosystem to which they may contribute, it cannot be claimed of a rock that it is a holistic part of the ecosystem, that is that it is ecologically interconnected with it. For in order for this to be true, the rock would not only have to help shape the ecosystem, but would have itself to be shaped by it, and this is not the case. As a holistic part of the universal substance, a rock topologically shapes and is shaped by the whole in this way. But as the rock does not influence, and is not influenced by, the *selfhood* of the universe (except in so far as without the property of selfhood the universal substance, and hence the rock, would not exist), it cannot be seen as a holistic part of the order of selves, that is the ecological order. I, as self, in contrast, reflect and am reflected in the higher order self-realizing systems.

But in which way do I reflect the higher-order selves in which I am nested? The general characteristic which distinguishes a self is of course its *conatus*, its power of self-realization, the will-to-exist. So the way in which any self reflects the dynamics of a wider self at the most general level is through its *conatus*. The *conatus* of the individual, by helping to shape the wider system, helps to sustain the *conatus* of that system, and the *conatus* of the system, by maintaining that specialized environment in existence, provides the conditions for the emergence of self-realizing forms. It is the dynamics of the *conatus* which is reflected up through the levels of systems.

As ecological part then it is through my *conatus* that I mirror, and am mirrored in, the wider systems of nature. It is through my *conatus* that I, and other selves, achieve oneness with the ecocosm. Recognition of the fact that my *conatus* unites me with the ecocosm, which is thus seen to be my greater Self, in itself expands the scope of my *conatus*: my will-to-exist now encompasses the wider systems of nature. The expanded self-love that I experience in this case is not a passive contemplative matter, as is Spinoza's intellectual love of God. Since I am ontologically at one with nature, my *conatus* actually feeds the cosmic *conatus*, actually helps to maintain the ecocosm in existence! It is in this human participation in the cosmic process that the meaningfulness of our relation to nature may be found: through our awareness of our interconnectedness with it we experience a love for this great self, a love which is actually constitutive of, or a tributary to, its own *conatus*, its own will-to-exist.

But how does this work? Animals and plants are holistic parts of the ecocosmic order too, so their self-love, their will-to-self-realization, must reinforce the cosmic *conatus* in the same way that ours does. Each organism, in fulfilling its *conatus* and achieving a state of flourishing, is helping to maintain the ecosystems further up the line, and each system, by maintaining itself in place, is preserving the conditions in which the organism can achieve self-realization. So if animals can contribute to the self-maintenance of the ecocosm without being aware of their unity with it, and acting only out of their own narrow self-interest, why can't we? Why can we not fulfil our cosmic role just by looking out for ourselves, following the path of egoism, and through our own flourishing helping to secure the self-realization of the wider systems?

Why? Because following the path of egoism does *not* lead to flourishing, and hence does not help to sustain the ecosystems in which we are embedded. A viable human being is, for reasons explained elsewhere,[7] one who is informed with a viable culture. A viable culture is, for reasons also explained elsewhere,[8] an eco-sensitive culture. Human beings who are products of non-viable cultures are not viable individuals, and non-viable individuals cannot be described as flourishing.

---

[7] See discussion of culture in *The Ecological Self*, ch. 4, §IV.
[8] Ibid.

But how are these statements to be justified? Many people who live in cultures which are not eco-sensitive, and are therefore presumably non-viable, give every appearance of flourishing. They appear to live long, healthy, successful, productive lives. Indeed has not our non-viable Western culture, with its unprecedentedly high standards of living, produced more flourishing individuals than any other culture in history?

Since human beings are *essentially* and not just contingently enculturated, any criterion of human flourishing will have to include a cultural dimension. A person will count as flourishing only if she is culturally as well as physically and materially well-off. She is culturally well-off if she is richly fulfilled in her emotional, imaginative, artistic, intellectual, and spiritual life. How many Western commuters on the morning freeway would claim to be this?

The kind of culture that enables us to fulfil our *conatus* and hence to flourish as human beings is precisely the culture that understands and represents our interconnectedness with nature. The reason for this is simply that, on the present view, *this is the way we are*. To represent us as anything less than this is in fact to *misrepresent* us to ourselves, and hence to interfere with our possibilities of self-realization. A central function of culture is, as we have seen, to provide a symbolic representation of the world. This representation may be more or less figurative, more or less universal, but if it is misleading or false in its presentation of the way things are, then neither society nor individual can flourish. Sooner or later they will stub their toe on reality, their predictions and expectations will be disappointed. The reason that we, unlike non-human animals, depend on a culture—an abstract representation of reality—to help us to negotiate the world, is that our actions are not narrowly programmed by instinct. This is not to say that the disposition to create a culture is not itself a programmed, naturally selected device. But it is one which is especially susceptible to error. If our world and our relation to it are not adequately represented in our culture, then our action will not be appropriate to the ontological facts. If the ontological facts are that we are cosmic beings, selves within wider selves, then our *conatus* can only be fulfilled—and we can only realize our true possibilities—if our culture represents this truth to us.

Non-human animals, being selves within wider selves, are cosmic beings in exactly the same sense that we are. They do not need to be aware of this metaphysical fact in order to act in ways appropriate to it however, because they do not depend on abstract representations of reality to guide their actions—their actions are more or less narrowly programmed. But that those actions do testify to the ontological facts is beyond doubt.

Animals do not follow the so-called law of 'dog eat dog', in the manner of the human egoist. They do indeed cherish their physical integrity and resist disintegration when they can—they would not qualify as selves if they did not. But this is consistent with their behaving in ways which benefit the species or the ecosystem more directly than they benefit their physical selves: they are unswerving if unwitting servants of the ecosystem. If there were thinking behind their behaviour, it would not be the thinking of the egoist, but it would rather be the kind of thinking that would affirm perfectly the view that their identity is simultaneously a unity yet a function of greater wholes. Egoism is the province of the free-rider, the one who takes, accumulates, consumes without returning, who abdicates roles of responsibility to family and society, and whose actions spring from the belief that his interests are defined in opposition to those of others and should prevail over them. If animals acted in accordance with this kind of 'thinking', they would not work indefatigably and tediously to nourish and defend their (totally 'ungrateful') young, they would not share food (as many do) but would try to accumulate it instead, they would bury their dead in an attempt to cheat the food chain, they would expand their territories and colonize, they would 'overgraze the commons', and engage in intra-species conflict for reasons additional to those of territorial and sexual need. Animals generally act exactly as if the interests they serve are those of the self-in-environment; and the flourishing of the self-in-environment is self-perpetuating up through the levels of system.

For human beings to flourish then, on this view, requires that we be represented within our culture as selves-within-wider-selves, and that our actions be generated in the light of this awareness of our role in the scheme of things.

Each viable self does its best, within the terms of its own particular faculties, to further the interests both of itself and of the ecosystem through which it is defined. The faculties of human beings are not restricted to the physical and behavioural, but include the psychological. As self-conscious beings our *conatus* has psychological as well as physical and behavioural dimensions. We experience the *conatus* psychologically as self-love, as an intense emotional investment in everything that we see as falling within the circle of our being. When this self-love is expanded—by our awareness of our unity with nature—to encompass the wider systems of nature, then we experience the kind of joy in existence to which Spinoza was pointing.

Is this love, this will-to-exist, this ardent affirmation which takes the cosmos-as-a-whole as its object, merely a shadow cast in the mind, a kind of after-image of the physical impact of the *conatus*, an epiphenomenon of ecological dynamics, or does it also have an active function, contributing in its own way to the self-realization of the ecocosm? Let us put the question another way. Would it matter to nature if, while acting in ecologically optimal ways, we did so from motives other than those of love—if we acted in the service of the ecocosm, yet without loyalty to it, without joy in it? It cannot be said that this is the way that animals act, because since they lack the faculty for such conscious affirmation they cannot be capable of withholding it either. Does the love itself then, the affirmation, help to keep the fabric of the world intact?

This is perhaps the hardest of all these hard questions to answer. Yet I think we must say yes to it. For the *conatus* that animates the ecocosmic self is an emergent will, or 'spirit', which may be reinforced by us in 'spiritual' ways. But how is 'spiritual' to be understood here? Does it necessarily connote the self-conscious and the psychological? Is the ecocosmic will-to-exist transparent to itself, is it experienced, felt, as our will-to-exist is experienced, felt, as interest, expansiveness, energy, love? Or is this cosmic *conatus* unconscious of itself, animating physical reality but without an inner awareness of itself doing so? I do not think it is really necessary to decide whether or not the cosmic *conatus* is conscious of itself in order to resolve the question whether or not we can reinforce it through consciousness. The cosmic *conatus* is not *constituted* through our feelings of love of and joy in Nature, anymore than it is constituted by our ecological actions; it is *expressed* through both feelings and actions. What is expressed is an impulse which in itself is neither purely physiological nor emotional nor behavioural, but is in us accompanied by sensations, feelings, and actions. Perhaps the closest we can come to pinning down the quality of the *conatus* in itself is through the notion of unqualified affirmation. Such affirmation is not in itself emotional, although it may be accompanied by overwhelming feelings of joy and love. Nor is it in itself purely physiological, though it may be accompanied by overwhelming sensations of fullness, overflowing and bodily expansion. And it is not merely behavioural, though it will typically give rise to ecological actions. An act of affirmation, if it is not accompanied by any particular propositional content, is an expression of the 'inner' life of beings, an expression which is not essentially self-conscious, nor essentially unconscious, but may be expressed on conscious and unconscious levels. Perhaps this is what marks the quality of an assertion of the 'spirit'.

On this view then, the feeling that we call love is perhaps the faint psychological shadow in us of that inner spiritual impulse of which our universe is the external manifestation. The universe may be conceived as a gigantic act of self-affirmation. It is the inner affirmation which is the *sine qua non* of the outer reality.

Since our human *conatus* participates in the *conatus* of the ecocosm, our affirmation of our larger Self is a force for the *Self-realization* of the universe. Indeed this inner attitude of affirmation may ultimately be more important than the outer, ecologically beneficial actions which help to perpetuate selves up through the levels of system, precisely because it is this impulse to affirm which is, as I have said, the *sine qua non* of the external systems. This may be, if you like, the real work of conservation—cultivating in ourselves the unrestricted will-to-exist, the spirit of pure affirmation, the well-spring of 'love', that creates and perpetuates the ecocosm. In this lies the key to the third objection, which was left un-answered many pages ago. The objection was that the arisings and passings-away of particular life-forms are of no concern to the cosmic Self, since the cosmic Self persists perfectly unscathed through these comings and goings and is indeed the inexhaustible fountain-head of all beauties and wonders. This was a serious objection for anyone who takes identifica-tion with the cosmos (Naess's *Self-Realization*) to be a motive for the con-servation of nature. But if my identification with ever-wider self-systems right up to the ecocosm has this essentially affirmative character, then it follows that I cannot be indifferent to the particular life-forms that my world presents. To participate in their *conatus*, as the identification thesis requires, involves for me, as a human self, a sense of love for them. I cannot help, in light of this, wanting to prevent any harmful interference with them, and so the outer work of conservation is assured.

Meaningfulness, then, enters our life not merely through a passive, Spinoza-style contemplation of sublime nature, and a joyful basking in our unity with it, nor even through our attempts to preserve its particular external manifestations—battling to save forests, ban bombs, to phase out the ever-proliferating forms of wanton exploitation. Meaningfulness is to be found in our *spiritual* capacity to keep the ecocosm on course, by teaching our hearts to practise affirmation, and by awakening our faculty of active, out-reaching, world-directed love. Though a tendency to 'tread lightly' on the earth, and to take practical steps to safeguard the particular manifestations of nature, will flow inevitably from such an attitude, the crucial contribution will be the attitude itself, a contribution of the heart and spirit.

This way of thinking may be deeply foreign—and objectionable—to the Western intellect, but it has been central to the cosmologies of many primal peoples, who saw their vocation, executed in ceremony and ritual, as helping to sustain the order of things, helping to keep the fabric of the world well-knit.

It is perhaps the fact that we are implicated in the cosmic *conatus* that is the well-spring of spiritual feelings in cultures everywhere. For spiritual feeling involves, above all, faith—trust in the order of things, an affirmation and surrender of the ego to a wider reality. Such faith and affirmation necessarily lie beyond knowledge and reason, as spokespersons for religions invariably attest. If faith were merely a substitute for knowledge—an interim measure enabling us to lay claim to a belief while we wait for validation, or an abdication of our own reason in deference to the reason of higher authorities, higher intelligences, who *know* the laws that are beyond our knowing—then it would not be an authentic instance of spirituality. For when the knowledge for which faith was the substitute was, by whatever means, attained, the need for affirmation would vanish. Besides, I can be as indifferent to the 'facts' of karma and reincarnation, or whatever other esoteric matters, as I can to the facts of over-population and pollution. Knowledge of a reality can never logically compel an affirmation: we have not only to understand that reality, but to want it to exist. In the same way, knowledge of the facts of my own personal future— however rosy—could not compel my affirmation: I would have furthermore to *want* to experience them, to want myself to exist. Nor perhaps could a set of co-instantiable possibilities impart actuality to a merely abstract world. To exist, whether as an individual or as a world, requires a leap into existence that is in itself a declaration of trust, an act of affirmation, an instance of *conatus*. This leap, whether from knowledge or ignorance, into existence, is the locus of spirituality.

Happily, as self-realizing beings, this leap-inducing affirmativeness, which in its wider dimensions constitutes our spirituality, is innate to us. But although rational understanding of a reality cannot compel our allegiance or our readiness to affirm it, a misrepresentation of the world can rationally discourage us. When our culturally-endorsed cosmology represents the world as inert, blind, bereft of worth or purpose, indifferent to our attitudes towards it, then our natural urge to celebrate nature may be thwarted. To yield to this natural urge may seem, in this case, to be succumbing to irrationality, and the impulse may be displaced or suppressed in favour of an altogether more constricted—egoistic—self affirmation. It is therefore in the interests of both our greater and our lesser selves to remove such falsifying obstacles to our self-fulfilment.

IX

NATURE, SELF, AND GENDER: FEMINISM, ENVIRONMENTAL PHILOSOPHY, AND THE CRITIQUE OF RATIONALISM

VAL PLUMWOOD

Most mainstream environmental philosophers continue to view environmental philosophy as mainly concerned with ethics. For example, instrumentalism is generally viewed by mainstream environmental philosophers as a problem in ethics, and its solution is seen as setting up some sort of theory of intrinsic value. This neglects a key aspect of the overall problem that is concerned with the definition of the human self as separate from nature, the location of this self in reason, the connection between this and the instrumental view of nature, and broader *political* aspects of the critique of instrumentalism.

One key aspect of the Western view of nature, which the ethical stance neglects completely, is the view of nature as sharply discontinuous or ontologically divided from the human sphere of reason. This leads to a view of humans as apart from or 'outside of' nature, usually as masters or external controllers of it. Attempts to reject this view often speak alternatively of humans as 'part of nature' but rarely distinguish this position from the obvious claim that human fate is interconnected with that of the biosphere, that humans are subject to natural laws. But on the divided-self theory it is reason, the essentially or authentically human part of the self, and in that sense the human realm proper, that is outside nature, not the human as a physical phenomenon. The view of humans as outside of and alien to nature seems to be especially strongly a Western one, although not confined to the West. There are many other cultures which do not hold it, which stress what connects us to nature as genuinely human virtues, which emphasize continuity and not dissimilarity.[1]

[1] e.g. Bill Neidjie's words 'This ground and this earth/like brother and mother' (B. Neidjie with S. Davis and A. Fox, *Kakadu Man* (Canberra: Mybrood P/L, 1985), 46) may be interpreted

As ecofeminism points out, Western thought has given us a strong human–nature dualism that is part of the set of interrelated dualisms of mind–body, reason–nature, reason–emotion, masculine–feminine and has important interconnected features with these other dualisms.[2] This dualism has been especially stressed in the rationalist tradition. In this dualism what is characteristically and authentically human is defined against or in opposition to what is taken to be natural, nature, or the physical or biological realm. This takes various forms. For example, the characterization of the genuinely, properly, characteristically, or authentically human, or of human virtue, in polarized terms to exclude what is taken to be characteristic of the natural is what John Rodman[3] has called 'the Differential Imperative' in which what is virtuous in the human is taken to be what maximizes distance from the merely natural. The maintenance of sharp dichotomy and polarization is achieved by the rejection and denial of what links humans to the animal. What is taken to be authentically and characteristically human, defining of the human, as well as the ideal for which humans should strive, is *not* to be found in what is shared with the natural and animal (e.g. the body, sexuality, reproduction, emotionality, the senses, agency) but in what is thought to separate and distinguish them—especially reason and its offshoots. Hence humanity is defined not as part of nature (perhaps a special part) but as separate from and in opposition to it. Thus the relation of humans to nature is treated as an oppositional and value dualism.

The process closely parallels the formation of other dualisms, such as masculine–feminine, reason–emotion, and spirit–body criticized in feminist thought,[4] but this parallel logic is not the only connection between

as an affirmation of such kinship or continuity. (See also Neidjie, *Kakadu Man*, 53, 61–2, 77, 81–2, 88.)

[2] The logic of dualism and the masculinity of the concept of humanity are discussed in Val Plumwood, 'Ecofeminism: An Overview and Discussion of Positions and Arguments', *Women and Philosophy*, Supplement to *Australasian Journal of Philosophy*, 64 (June 1986), 120–38; and 'Women, Humanity and Nature', *Radical Philosophy*, 48 (1988), 6–24. See also Karen J. Warren, 'Feminism and Ecology: Making Connections', *Environmental Ethics*, 9 (1987), 17–18; and 'The Power and Promise of Ecological Feminism', *Environmental Ethics*, 12/2 (1990), 121–46.

[3] John Rodman, 'Paradigm Change in Political Science', *American Behavioural Scientist*, 24/1 (1980), 54–5.

[4] See e.g. Rosemary Radford Ruether, *New Woman New Earth* (Minneapolis: Seabury Press, 1975); Susan Griffin, *Woman and Nature: The Roaring Inside Her* (New York: Harper and Row, 1978); Joan L. Griscom, 'On Healing the Nature/History Split in Feminist Thought', *Heresies*, 4/1 (1981), 4–9; Ynestra King, 'Feminism and Revolt', *Heresies*, 4/1 (1981), 12–16; Genevieve Lloyd, 'Public Reason and Private Passion', *Metaphilosophy*, 14 (1983), 308–26; and 'Reason, Gender, and Morality in the History of Philosophy', *Social Research*, 50/3 (1983), 490–513; Alison Jaggar, *Feminist Politics and Human Nature* (Totowa, NJ: Rowman & Allenheld; Brighton: Harvester, 1983).

human–nature dualism and masculine–feminine dualism. Moreover, this exclusion of the natural from the concept of the properly human is not the only dualism involved, because what is involved in the construction of this dualistic conception of the human is the rejection of those parts of the human character identified as feminine—also identified as less than fully human—giving the masculine conception of what it is to be human. Masculinity can be linked to this exclusionary and polarized conception of the human, via the desire to exclude and distance from the feminine and the non-human. The features that are taken as characteristic of humankind and as where its special virtues lie, are those such as rationality, freedom, and transcendence of nature (all traditionally viewed as masculine), which are viewed as not shared with nature. Humanity is defined oppositionally to both nature and the feminine.

The upshot is a deeply entrenched view of the genuine or ideal human self as not including features shared with nature, and as defined *against* or in *opposition to* the non-human realm, so that the human sphere and that of nature cannot significantly overlap. Nature is sharply divided off from the human, is alien and usually hostile and inferior. Furthermore, this kind of human self can only have certain kinds of accidental or contingent connections to the realm of nature. I shall call this the discontinuity problem or thesis and I argue later that it plays a key role with respect to other elements of the problem.

Although the discontinuity problem is generally neglected by the ethical stance, a significant exception to its neglect within environmental philosophy seems to be found in deep ecology, which is also critical of the location of the problem within ethics.[5] Furthermore, deep ecology also seems initially to be more likely to be compatible with a feminist philosophical framework, emphasizing as it does connections with the self, connectedness, and merger. Nevertheless, there are severe tensions between deep ecology and a feminist perspective. Deep ecology has not

---

[5] Nonetheless, deep ecology's approach to ethics is, like much else, doubtfully consistent, variable, and shifting. Thus although Arne Naess calls for recognition of the intrinsic value of nature, he also tends to treat 'the maxim of self-realization' as *substituting for* and obviating an ethical account of care and respect for nature (Arne Naess, *Ecology, Community, and Lifestyle* (Cambridge: Cambridge University Press, 1988), 20, 86) placing the entire emphasis on phenomenology (see also his 'The Shallow and the Deep, Long-Range Ecology Movement: A Summary', *Inquiry*, 16 (1973), 95–100; and 'Intrinsic Value: Will the Defenders of Nature Please Rise', in M. Soule, ed., *Conservation Biology* (Sunderland Mass.: Sinauer Associates, 1986). In more recent work, however, the emphasis seems to have quietly shifted back again from holistic intuition to a broad and extremely vague 'biocentric egalitarianism' which places the centre once again in ethics and enjoins an ethic of maximum expansion of Self (see Warwick Fox, *Towards a Transpersonal Ecology: Developing New Foundations for Environmentalism* (Boston: Shambala, 1990)).

satisfactorily identified the key elements in the traditional framework or observed their connections to rationalism. As a result, it fails to reject adequately rationalist assumptions and indeed often seems to provide its own versions of universalization, the discarding of particular connections, and rationalist accounts of self.

Deep ecology locates the key problem area in human-nature relations in the separation of humans and nature, and it provides a solution for this in terms of the 'identification' of self with nature. 'Identification' is usually left deliberately vague, and corresponding accounts of self are various and shifting and not always compatible.[6] There seem to be at least three different accounts of self involved—indistinguishability, expansion of self, and transcendence of self—and deep ecologists appear to feel free to move among them at will. As I shall show, all are unsatisfactory from both a feminist perspective and from that of obtaining a satisfactory environmental philosophy, and the appeal of deep ecology rests largely on the failure to distinguish them.

A. THE INDISTINGUISHABILITY ACCOUNT

The indistinguishability account rejects boundaries between self and nature. Humans are said to be just one strand in the biotic web, not the source and ground of all value and the discontinuity thesis is, it seems, firmly rejected. Warwick Fox describes the central intuition of deep ecology as follows: 'We can make no firm ontological divide in the field of existence . . . there is no bifurcation in reality between the human and non-human realms . . . to the extent that we perceive boundaries, we fall short of deep ecological consciousness.'[7] But much more is involved here than the rejection of discontinuity, for deep ecology goes on to replace the human-in-environment image by a holistic or gestalt view that 'dissolves not only the human-in-environment concept, but every compact-thing-in-milieu concept'—except when talking at a superficial level of communication.[8] Deep ecology involves a cosmology of 'unbroken wholeness which

---

[6] Other critics of deep ecology, such as Richard Sylvan ('A Critique of Deep Ecology', *Radical Philosophy*, 40–1 (1985)) and Jim Cheney ('Ecofeminism and Deep Ecology', *Environmental Ethics*, 9 (1987), 115–45) have also suggested that it shifts between different and incompatible versions. Ecofeminist critics of deep ecology have included Ariel Salleh ('Deeper than Deep Ecology', *Environmental Ethics*, 6 (1984), 339–45); Marti Kheel ('The Liberation of Nature: A Circular Affair', *Environmental Ethics*, 7 (1985), 139–49); Janet Biehl ('It's Deep, But is it Broad? An Ecofeminist Looks at Deep Ecology', *Kick It Over*, Special Supplement (Winter 1987)); and Warren ('The Power and Promise of Ecological Feminism').

[7] Warwick Fox, 'Deep Ecology: A New Philosophy of Our Time?', *Ecologist*, 14 (1984), 7.

[8] Ibid. 1.

denies the classical idea of the analysability of the world into separately and independently existing parts'.[9] It is strongly attracted to a variety of mystical traditions and to the Perennial Philosophy, in which the self is merged with the other—'the other is none other than yourself.' As John Seed puts it: 'I am protecting the rainforest' develops into 'I am part of the rainforest protecting myself. I am that part of the rainforest recently emerged into thinking.'[10]

There are severe problems with these claims, arising not so much from the orientation to the concept of self (which seems to me important and correct) or from the mystical character of the insights themselves as from the indistinguishability metaphysics which is proposed as their basis. It is not merely that the identification process of which deep ecologists speak seems to stand in need of much more clarification, but that it does the wrong thing. The problem, in the sort of account I have given, is the discontinuity between humans and nature that emerges as part of the overall set of Western dualisms. Deep ecology proposes to heal this division by a 'unifying process', a metaphysics that insists that everything is really part of and indistinguishable from everything else. This is not only to employ overly powerful tools but ones that do the wrong job, for the origins of the particular opposition involved in the human–nature dualism remain unaddressed and unanalysed. The real basis of the discontinuity lies in the concept of an authentic human being, in what is taken to be valuable in human character, society, and culture, as what is distinct from what is taken to be natural. The sources of and remedies for this remain unaddressed in deep ecology. Deep ecology has confused dualism and atomism and then mistakenly taken indistinguishability to follow from the rejection of atomism. The confusion is clear in Fox, who proceeds immediately from the ambiguous claim that there is no 'bifurcation in reality between the human and non-human realms' (which could be taken as a rejection of human discontinuity from nature) to the conclusion that what is needed is that we embrace an indistinguishability metaphysics of unbroken wholeness in the whole of reality. But the problem must be addressed in terms of this specific dualism and its connections. Instead, deep ecology proposes the obliteration of all distinction.

Thus deep ecology's solution to removing this discontinuity by obliterating *all* division is far too powerful. In its over-generality it fails to provide a genuine basis for an environmental ethics of the kind sought, for the view of humans as metaphysically unified with the cosmic whole will be equally true whatever relation humans stand in with nature—the situation of

[9] Naess, quoted Ibid. 3, 10.
[10] John Seed, Joanna Macey, Pat Fleming, and Arne Naess, *Thinking Like a Mountain: Towards a Council of All Beings* (Philadelphia and Santa Cruz: New Society Publishers, 1988).

exploitation of nature exemplifies such unity equally as well as a conserver situation and the human self is just as indistinguishable from the bulldozer and Coca-Cola bottle as the rocks or the rainforest. What John Seed seems to have in mind here is that once one has realized that one is indistinguishable from the rainforest, its needs would become one's own. But there is nothing to guarantee this—one could equally well take one's own needs for its.

This points to a further problem with the indistinguishability thesis, that we need to recognize not only our human continuity with the natural world but also its distinctness and independence from us and the distinctness of the needs of things in nature from ours. The indistinguishability account does not allow for this, although it is a very important part of respect for nature and of conservation strategy.

The dangers of accounts of the self that involve self-merger appear in feminist contexts as well, where they are sometimes appealed to as the alternative to masculine-defined autonomy as disconnection from others. As Jean Grimshaw writes of the related thesis of the indistinctness of persons (the acceptance of the loss of self-boundaries as a feminine ideal): 'It is important not merely because certain forms of symbiosis or "connection" with others can lead to damaging failures of personal development, but because care for others, understanding of them, are only possible if one can adequately distinguish oneself *from* others. If I see myself as "indistinct" from you, or you as not having your own being that is not merged with mine, then I cannot preserve a real sense of your well-being as opposed to mine. Care and understanding require the sort of distance that is needed in order not to see the other as a projection of self, or self as a continuation of the other.'[11]

These points seem to me to apply to caring for other species and for the natural world as much as they do to caring for our own species. But just as dualism is confused with atomism, so holistic self-merger is taken to be the only alternative to egoistic accounts of the self as without essential connection to others or to nature. Fortunately, this is a false choice;[12] as I argue below, non-holistic but relational accounts of the self, as developed

---

[11] Jean Grimshaw, *Philosophy and Feminist Thinking* (Minneapolis: University of Minnesota Press, 1986), 182–3. Also published as *Feminist Philosophers* (Brighton: Wheatsheaf, 1986).

[12] This is argued in R. Routley and V. Routley, 'Social Theories, Self-Management and Environmental Problems', in D. Mannison, M. McRobbie, and R. Routley, eds., *Environmental Philosophy* (Canberra: ANU Department of Philosophy Monograph Series RSSS, 1980), 217–332), where a relational account of self developed in the context of an anarchist theory is applied to relations with nature. Part of the problem lies in the terminology of 'holism' itself, which is used in highly variable and ambiguous ways, sometimes carrying commitment to indistinguishability and sometimes meaning only 'non-atomistic'.

in some feminist and social philosophy, enable a rejection of dualism, including human–nature dualism, without denying the independence or distinguishability of the other. To the extent that deep ecology is identified with the indistinguishability thesis, it does not provide an adequate basis for a philosophy of nature.

B. THE EXPANDED SELF

In fairness to deep ecology it should be noted that it tends to vacillate between mystical indistinguishability and the other accounts of self, between the holistic self and the expanded self. Vacillation occurs often by way of slipperiness as to what is meant by identification of self with the other, a key notion in deep ecology. This slipperiness reflects the confusion of dualism and atomism previously noted but also seems to reflect a desire to retain the mystical appeal of indistinguishability while avoiding its many difficulties. Where 'identification' means not 'identity' but something more like 'empathy', identification with other beings can lead to an expanded self. According to Arne Naess, 'The self is as comprehensive as the totality of our identifications. . . . Our Self is that with which we identify.'[13] This larger self (or Self, to deep ecologists) is something for which we should strive 'in so far as it is in our power to do so',[14] and according to Fox we should also strive to make it as large as possible. But this expanded self is not the result of a critique of egoism; rather, it is an enlargement and an extension of egoism.[15] It does not question the structures of possessive egoism and self-interest; rather, it tries to allow for a wider set of interests by an expansion of self. The motivation for the expansion of self is to allow for a wider set of concerns while continuing to allow the self to operate on the fuel of self-interest (or Self-interest). This is apparent from the claim that 'in this light . . . ecological resistance is simply another name for self defense'.[16] Fox quotes with approval John Livingstone's statement: 'When I say that the fate of the sea turtle or the tiger or the gibbon is mine, I mean it. All that is in my universe is not merely mine; it is *me*. And I shall defend myself. I shall defend myself not only against overt aggression but also against gratuitous insult.'[17]

[13] Naess, quoted in Warwick Fox, *Approaching Deep Ecology: A Response to Richard Sylvan's Critique of Deep Ecology*, Environmental Studies Occasional Paper 20 (Hobart: University of Tasmania Centre for Environmental Studies, 1986), 54.
[14] Fox, *Approaching Deep Ecology*, 13–19.   [15] As noted by Cheney.
[16] Fox, *Approaching Deep Ecology*, 60.   [17] Ibid. 60.

Deep ecology does not question the structures of rational egoism and continues to subscribe to two of the main tenets of the egoist framework—that human nature is egoistic and that the alternative to egoism is self-sacrifice.[18] Given these assumptions about egoism, the obvious way to obtain some sort of human interest in defending nature is through the expanded Self operating in the interests of nature but also along the familiar lines of self-interest.[19] The expanded-self strategy might initially seem to be just another pretentious and obscure way of saying that humans empathize with nature. But the strategy of transferring the structures of egoism is highly problematic, for the widening of interest is obtained at the expense of failing to recognize unambiguously the distinctness and independence of the other.[20] Others are recognized morally only to the extent that they are incorporated into the self, and their difference denied.[21] And the failure to critique egoism and the disembedded, non-relational self means a failure to draw connections with other contemporary critiques.

C. THE TRANSCENDED OR TRANSPERSONAL SELF

To the extent that the expanded Self requires that we detach from the particular concerns of the self (a relinquishment that[22] despite its natural difficulty we should struggle to attain), expansion of self to Self also tends

[18] Thus John Seed says: 'Naess wrote that when most people think about conservation, they think about sacrifice. This is a treacherous basis for conservation, because most people aren't capable of working for anything except their own self-interest . . . Naess argued that we need to find ways to extend our identity into nature. Once that happens, being out in front of bulldozers or whatever becomes no more of a sacrifice than moving your foot if you notice that someone's just about to strike it with an axe.' (John Seed, interviewed by Pat Stone, *Mother Earth News* (May/June 1989).)

[19] This denial of the alterity of the other is also the route taken by J. Baird Callicot, who indeed asserts that 'The principle of axiological complementarity posits an essential unity between self and world and establishes the problematic intrinsic value of nature in relation to the axiologically privileged value of self.' (J. Baird Callicot, 'Intrinsic Value, Quantum Theory, and Environmental Ethics', *Environmental Ethics*, 7 (1985), 275.) Given the impoverishment of Humean theory in the area of relations (and hence its inability to conceive a self-in-relationship whose connections to others are not merely contingent but essential), Callicot has little alternative to this direction of development.

[20] Grimshaw, *Philosophy and Feminist Thinking*, 182. See also the excellent discussion in Warren, 'The Power and Promise of Ecological Feminism', 136–8, of the importance of recognition and respect for the other's difference; Lawrence A. Blum, *Friendship, Atruism, and Morality* (Boston and London: Routledge & Kegan Paul, 1980), 75; and Seyla Benhabib, 'The Generalized and the Concrete Other', in E. Kittay and D. Meyers, eds., *Women and Moral Theory* (Totowa, NJ: Rowman and Allenheld, 1987), 166.

[21] Warren, 'The Power and Promise of Ecological Feminism'.

[22] According to Fox, *Towards a Transpersonal Ecology*, 12.

to lead into the third position, the transcendence or overcoming of self. Thus Fox urges us to strive for *impartial* identification with *all* particulars, the cosmos, discarding our identifications with our own particular concerns, personal emotions, and attachments. Fox presents here the deep ecology version of universalization, with the familiar emphasis on the personal and the particular as corrupting and self-interested—'the cause of possessiveness, war, and ecological destruction'.

This treatment of particularity, the devaluation of an identity tied to particular parts of the natural world as opposed to an abstractly conceived whole, the cosmos, reflects the rationalistic preoccupation with the universal and its account of ethical life as oppositional to the particular. The analogy in human terms of impersonal love of the cosmos is the view of morality as based on universal principles or the impersonal and abstract 'love of man'. Thus Fox reiterates (as if it were unproblematic) the view of particular attachments as ethically suspect and as oppositional to genuine, impartial 'identification', which necessarily falls short with all particulars.

Because this 'transpersonal' identification is so indiscriminate and intent on denying particular meanings, it cannot allow for the deep and highly particularistic attachment to place that has motivated both the passion of many modern conservationists and the love of many indigenous peoples for their land (which deep ecology inconsistently tries to treat as a model). This is based not on a vague, bloodless, and abstract cosmological concern but on the formation of identity, social and personal, in relation to particular areas of land, yielding ties often as special and powerful as those to kin, and which are equally expressed in very specific and local responsibilities of care.[23] This emerges clearly in the statements of many indigenous peoples, such as in the moving words of Cecilia Blacktooth explaining why her people would not surrender their land:

You ask us to think what place we like next best to this place where we always lived. You see the graveyard there? There are our fathers and our grandfathers. You see that Eagle-nest mountain and that Rabbit-hole mountain? When God made them, He gave us this place. We have always been here. We do not care for any other place. . . . We have always lived here. We would rather die here. Our fathers did. We cannot leave them. Our children were born here—how can we go away? If you give us the best place in the world, it is not so good as this. . . . This is our home. . . . We

---

[23] This traditional model of land relationship is closely linked to that of bioregionalism, whose strategy is to engage people in greater knowledge and care for the local areas that have meaning for them and where they can most easily evolve a caring and responsible lifestyle. The feat of 'impartial identification with all particulars' is, beyond the seeking of individual enlightenment, strategically empty. Because it cares 'impartially' for everything it can, in practice, care for nothing.

cannot live anywhere else. We were born here and our fathers are buried here. . . . We want this place and no other. . . .[24]

In inferiorizing such particular, emotional, and kinship-based attachments, deep ecology gives us another variant on the superiority of reason and the inferiority of its contrasts, failing to grasp yet again the role of reason and incompletely critiquing its influence. To obtain a more adequate account than that offered by mainstream ethics and deep ecology it seems that we must move toward the sort of ethics feminist theory has suggested, which can allow for both continuity and difference and for ties to nature which are expressive of the rich, caring relationships of kinship and friendship rather than increasing abstraction and detachment from relationship.[25]

[24] T. C. McLuhan, ed., *Touch the Earth* (London: Abacus, 1973), 28.

[25] Thus some ecofeminists, such as Cheney (see Cheney, 'Ecofeminism and Deep Ecology'; his 'The Neo-Stoicism of Radical Environmentalism', *Environmental Ethics*, 11 (1989), 293–325); and Warren (see Warren, 'The Power and Promise of Ecological Feminism'), have been led to the development of alternative accounts of ethics and ethical theory building and the development of distinctively ecofeminist ethics.

X

CAN ENVIRONMENTALISTS BE LIBERALS?

MARK SAGOFF

Classical liberalism, as Brian Barry notes, comprises many ideas, but one is 'certainly the idea that the state is an instrument for satisfying the wants that men happen to have rather than a means of making good men (e.g. cultivating desirable wants or dispositions in its citizens)'. [1] The state, on this view, seeks to ensure that all its citizens will be able to pursue personal interests and private preferences under conditions that are convenient and equitable to all. 'The state, on the liberal view,' Barry summarizes, 'must be capable of fulfilling the same self-effacing function as a policeman on point duty, who facilitates the motorists' getting to their several destinations without bumping into one another but does not have any power to influence those destinations.' [2]

Once liberalism is defined in this way, as an individualism, it merges easily with the value premise on which many economists base the cost-benefit or efficiency criterion in public policy. 'The value premise', as Kneese and Bower state it, 'is that the personal wants of the individuals in the society should guide the use of resources in production, distribution, and exchange, and that these personal wants can most efficiently be met through the seeking of maximum profits by all producers.' [3]

Liberal political theory, likewise, may construe values as 'personal wants of the individuals in the society'; thus it may regard public values as a peculiar kind of personal desire. In that case, political theory may dismiss idealistic, impersonal, or community values as illegitimate meddling in other people's affairs, or it may treat them as a weird sort of 'intangible' that deserves a surrogate market price. 'What underlies this view,' as Brian Barry explains, 'is a rejection of any suggestion that an ideal-regarding

Reprinted by permission from *The Economy of the Earth* (Cambridge: Cambridge University Press, 1988), 146–70.

[1] Brian Barry, *Political Argument* (London: Routledge & Kegan Paul, 1965), 66.
[2] Ibid. 74.
[3] Allen Kneese and Blair Bower, *Environmental Quality and Residuals Management* (Baltimore: Johns Hopkins University Press, 1979), 4–5.

judgement should be treated as anything other than a peculiar kind of want.'[4]

Those who support a cost-benefit approach to social regulation, as we have seen, consider the welfare of the individual to be the major desideratum of public policy. They often appeal for support to individualistic concepts that are central to the institutions of a liberal society, such as private property, personal freedom, and individual choice. Environmentalists, as I have argued, would base social regulation largely on shared or public values, which may express not our wants and preferences as individuals but our identity, character, and aspirations as a community. Environmentalism may seem, then, to involve a sort of communitarianism that is inconsistent with principles traditionally associated with a liberal state.

On the one hand, environmentalists (e.g. the Greens in Germany) apparently belong to the political left. On the other hand, they cannot (as I have argued) derive their policies simply from considerations of efficiency or equality, interests or rights. Where, then, do environmentalists fit into the political spectrum? Are the policies they propose consistent with the concepts and principles on which the institutions of a liberal society are based?

TWO KINDS OF ENVIRONMENTALISM

'Conservation', Aldo Leopold wrote, 'is a state of harmony between men and land.'[5] Leopold supposed that natural communities possess an order, integrity, and life that command our love and admiration and which, therefore, we should seek to protect for their sake and not simply to increase our own welfare. The National Environmental Policy Act of 1969 (NEPA) echoes Leopold's concern with the ethical and aesthetic relations between man and nature. The statute seeks to encourage a 'productive and enjoyable harmony between man and his environment'.[6] According to one observer, 'NEPA incorporates the basic principle of the Leopoldian ethic.'[7]

This 'ethic' contrasts with the economic approach to environmental policy advocated by early conservationists like Gifford Pinchot. 'The first great fact about conservation', Pinchot wrote, 'is that it stands for develop-

---

    [4] Barry, *Political Argument*, 71.
    [5] Aldo Leopold, 'The Land Ethic', in *A Sand County Almanac* (New York: Oxford University Press, 1966), 222.
    [6] NEPA s. 2, 42 USC. s. 4321.
    [7] George S. Sessions, 'Anthrocentrism and the Environmental Crisis', *Humboldt Journal of Social Relations* (Fall–Winter, 1974): 80.

ment.[8] He added, 'Conservation demands the welfare of this generation first, and afterward the welfare of the generations to follow.'[9]

The difference between the positions of Leopold and Pinchot may be summarized as follows. Both recognize that only human beings (so far as we know) have values; in other words, only human beings make judge-·ments of the kind: 'This is valuable' or 'This is good.' Leopold and Pinchot agree, then, that human values and only human values count in resource policy. They disagree, however, over which values are important. In that sense, they disagree about *what is valuable*.

Leopold argued that land use and environmental policy ought to respond to the love, admiration, and respect many of us feel for the natural world. Love, admiration, and respect are human values, of course, but they do not necessarily involve human welfare. Rather, these values (although they arise in human beings) may be directed to the well-being and integrity of the rest of nature. Values such as these engender a widely shared attitude of aesthetic contemplation and moral altruism, for example, toward other species, for love typically seeks benefits not for itself only but also for its object.[10] Thus, the values Leopold emphasized, although they are human values, are directed toward the good of nature, not toward Leopold's own good or the good of humanity.

Pinchot, on the other hand, apparently believed that resource policy should serve the good of humanity and therefore should attempt to maximize social welfare as this is understood in economic theory. Pinchot assumed that only human welfare—and therefore nothing else in nature—can be valued for its own sake or have intrinsic worth. On this view, the reverence and respect people feel for nature do not endow it with intrinsic value; rather, these attitudes simply represent preferences the satisfaction of which will contribute to human 'satisfaction'.

Thus, Leopold and Pinchot agree that only human beings have values; only humans, so far as we know, value things. Those in the tradition of Pinchot, however, assert that the only object that can have intrinsic value or worth—the only goal that can be considered an end in itself—is human welfare. This differs from the view of Leopold and his followers, who assert that nature, as an object of reverence, love, and respect, itself has a moral worth and therefore should be protected for its own sake and not simply for the 'satisfactions' or 'benefits' it offers human beings.

I shall be concerned in this chapter with environmentalism as a movement that follows Leopold in espousing on ethical grounds the political

---

[8] Gifford Pinchot, *The Fight for Conservation* (Seattle: University of Wahington Press, 1910), 42.

[9] Ibid. 43.   [10] Aristotle, *Nichomachean Ethics*, 1115ᵃ–1157ᵇ.

goal of maintaining harmony between people and their environment. This movement asserts the importance of the cultural, historical, aesthetic, and religious values I described in the preceding chapter; it attempts—at times successfully—to embody these values in legislation. This sort of environmentalism rejects the individualistic view that society is essentially an 'assemblage associated by a common acknowledgement of right and community of interest'.[11] Instead, it visualizes society as a nation or people, which is, in Augustine's phrase, 'an assemblage of reasonable beings bound together by the objects of their love'.[12]

The tradition of classical liberalism, in emphasizing the importance of the individual, may support Pinchot's view that individual welfare is what matters in policy choices. It is easy, for example, to show how Locke's conception of property might justify the idea that perfectly competitive markets define the best or most valuable uses of land. In the next chapter, I shall discuss this use of Locke's theory. Here, I need only refer to the kinship many commentators have noted between traditional statements of liberal political theory, for example, in John Locke and Adam Smith, and classical economic theory. 'The classical liberal view of individuality merged easily with economic rationality, and together these two ideologies spoke against any intervention' by the government except to ensure the fair and efficient functioning of markets.[13]

Today, many liberal political theorists emphasize the importance of state neutrality among the competing goals, values, or ends individuals may seek to achieve.[14] Bruce Ackerman, for example, argues for a 'neutrality principle' according to which no one can argue for a social arrangement by claiming 'that his conception of the good is better than that asserted by any . . . of his fellow citizens'.[15] Likewise, Ronald Dworkin contends that the liberal state 'must be neutral on what might be called the question of the good life' and that 'political decisions must be, so far as possible, independent of any particular conception of the good life, or of what gives value to life'.[16]

---

[11] Saint Augustine ascribes this view to Cicero. See Saint Augustine, *The City of God*, tr. Marcus Dods (New York: Random House, Modern Library, 1950), 61–2.

[12] Ibid. 706.

[13] Andred Dobelstein, *Politics, Economics, and Public Welfare* (Englewood Cliffs, NJ: Prentice-Hall, 1980), 109.

[14] John Rawls summarizes: 'Systems of ends are not ranked in value.' *A Theory of Justice* (Cambridge, Mass.: Harvard University Press, 1971), 19.

[15] Bruce Ackerman, *Social Justice in the Liberal State* (New Haven, Conn.: Yale University Press, 1980), 11.

[16] Ronald Dworkin, 'Liberalism', in Stuart Hampshire, ed., *Public and Private Morality* (Cambridge: Cambridge University Press, 1978), 127.

Liberals strive to prevent 'moral' majorities from imposing ethical views and religious beliefs on minorities, for example, with respect to abortion, homosexuality, and school prayer. Environmentalists, however, may be said to constitute a moral lobby, if not a moral majority, of a sort, in so far as they advocate laws that embody ethical and perhaps even religious ideals concerning the way we ought to treat our natural surroundings.[17] If the laws and policies supported by the environmental lobby are not neutral among ethical, aesthetic, and religious ideals but express a moral conception of people's appropriate relation to nature, can environmentalists be liberals? May liberals support environmental laws even when these conflict with the utilitarian and egalitarian goals we usually associate with liberalism?

TWO KINDS OF LIBERALISM

Let me begin to answer these questions by presenting a view of what liberalism is. Liberalism is the political theory that holds that many conflicting and even incommensurable conceptions of the good may be fully compatible with free, autonomous, and rational action. Liberals contend, therefore, that political and social institutions should be structured to allow free and equal individuals the widest opportunities, consistent with the like opportunities of others, to plan their own lives and to live the lives they plan.

Liberals differ in this respect from conservatives, who believe that social institutions should reward virtue and punish vice, as these are conceived within a particular cultural or religious tradition, and that these institutions therefore should not be neutral among the ways people may choose to live.[18] The conservative will favour the conception of the good life associ-

---

[17] For a statement of these ideals, see e.g. John Muir, *The Wilderness World of John Muir* (Boston: Houghton Mifflin, 1976). Muir writes (317), 'Why should man value himself as more than a small part of the one great unit of creation? And what creature of all the Lord has taken the pains to make is not essential to the completeness of that unit—the cosmos? The universe would be incomplete without the smallest trans-microscopic creature that dwells beyond our conceitful eyes and knowledge.'

For further development of similar themes, see Leopold, *A Sand County Almanac*; Marjorie Hope Nicolson, *Mountain Gloom and Mountain Glory: The Development of the Aesthetic of the Infinite* (New York: Norton, 1963); John Passmore, *Man's Responsibility for Nature: Ecological Problems and Western Traditions* (New York: Scribner, 1974); and Joseph Sax, *Mountains Without Handrails: Reflections on the National Parks* (Ann Arbor: University of Michigan Press, 1980).

[18] See e.g. Patrick Devlin, *The Enforcement of Morals* (New York: Oxford University Press, 1965). Devlin writes (13–14), 'Society is justified in taking the same steps to preserve its moral

ated with the religion and culture of his or her community, for example, with respect to prayer, pornography, and sexual behaviour, and he or she may wish to enforce that conception with the steel of the law.

Socialists differ from liberals because they, like conservatives, subscribe to a conception of virtue they would oblige citizens to practice. Socialists would officially discourage a hedonic or bourgeois lifestyle, for example, in the classless society they expect to flourish after the Marxist revolution. The socialist derives his or her conception of virtue and vice, however, from a priori arguments and philosophical theories, of the sort known to a political vanguard. In this the socialist differs greatly from the conservative, whose view of the good life is much less esoteric and rests in familiar religious and cultural traditions.[19]

Liberalism has been understood historically in terms of a distinction between two imaginary entities: civil society and the state.[20] According to this picture, individuals are joined in civil society to pursue their own interests, whatever they may be, by co-operating and, if necessary, by competing with one another within a system of rights that is fair to all. Individuals are joined as citizens in the state strictly for the purpose of enforcing those rights. The liberal state does not dictate the moral goals its citizens are to achieve; it simply referees the means they use to satisfy their own preferences. It respects the right of each person to pursue his or her own conception of the good life as long as his or her actions do not infringe on the same right of others.

It is common nowadays to sort liberal political theories under two headings: deontological (or 'Kantian') and utilitarian. These theories differ essentially in the way they construe the relationship between the *right* and

code as it does to preserve its government and other essential institutions. The suppression of vice is as much the law's business as the suppression of subversive activities; it is no more possible to define a sphere of private morality than it is to define a sphere of private subversive activity. It is wrong to talk of private morality or of the law not being concerned with immorality as such or to try to set rigid bounds to the part which the law may play in the suppression of vice.'

For a subtle defence of Devlin's general position, see Roger Scruton, *The Meaning of Conservatism* (Totowa, NJ: Barnes & Noble, 1980), esp. 71–93. For a liberal reply, see Ronald Dworkin, *Taking Rights Seriously* (Cambridge, Mass.: Harvard University Press, 1977), ch. 10, and H. L. A. Hart, *Law, Liberty, and Morality* (New York: Random House, Vintage Books, 1966).

[19] Ronald Dworkin characterizes conservatism and various forms of socialism or Marxism as adopting the thesis 'that the treatment government owes its citizens is at least partly determined by some conception of the good life'. Marxism and conservatism differ, of course, in the conception of the good life they endorse. Dworkin, 'Liberalism', in Stuart Hampshire, ed., *Public and Private Morality*, 113–43; quotation on p. 128.

[20] The distinction between civil society and the state is defined by Hegel in T. M. Knox, ed., *Hegel's Philosophy of Right* (New York: Oxford University Press, 1952), esp. s. 258, 156. For discussion of the distinction, see Shlomo Avineri, *Hegel's Theory of the Modern State* (Cambridge: Cambridge University Press, 1972), 141–54.

the *good*. *Rightness* is a quality that attaches to actions, for example, in so far as those actions are just or meet some other ethical criterion. *Goodness* attaches primarily to the consequences of actions, for example, in so far as these consequences increase happiness, satisfy preferences, or achieve some other goal assumed to be worth while.

Deontological approaches to liberalism, which I shall discuss presently, hold that a legal or political decision is right in so far as it is just and fair and respects the fundamental equality of persons. For the deontological liberal the principles of justice are established independently of social interests and preferences, and 'against these principles neither the intensity of feeling nor its being shared by the majority counts for anything.'[21] Deontological liberals argue, therefore, that policies that advance justice, fairness, and social equality 'trump' claims that may be made on behalf of the general welfare.[22]

Utilitarian political theories argue, on the contrary, that a policy or decision is right not independently of its effect on social welfare but precisely because of it. The utilitarian liberal may argue, indeed, that rights themselves are justified only because they maximize overall welfare when consistently enforced over the long run. A utilitarian may concede, then, that the rights secured by a theory of justice 'trump' the claims of social welfare in specific cases. Nevertheless, the utilitarian will argue that, at a higher level of analysis, the principles of justice are themselves to be justified in relation to their consequences for social welfare.[23]

Utilitarian liberalism differs from deontological liberalism, then, primarily because it takes the right to be subservient to the good. By this I mean that utilitarians consider an action or a decision to have the moral quality of rightness to the extent that it leads to (or is derived from rules that lead to) the maximization of good consequences, conceived in terms of social welfare or utility, over the long run.

Deontological liberals may agree with a conception of the good that ties it to social welfare, wealth maximization, or utility, in so far as such a conception remains arguably neutral among the values that preferences, desires, or satisfactions express. The deontological liberal insists, however, that the rightness, fairness, or justice of decisions cannot be analysed at any level in terms of the satisfaction of preferences or the maximization of utility. In that sense the deontological liberal takes the right to be prior to the good.

---

[21] Rawls, *A Theory of Justice*, 450.   [22] Dworkin, 'Liberalism', 136.
[23] For discussion, see Dworkin, *Taking Rights Seriously*, 94–100.

We are now in a position to understand more clearly the logic of the conflict or 'trade-off', which we discussed elsewhere,[24] between efficiency and equality as criteria for social choice. It is a thesis of deontological liberalism that no such trade-off makes conceptual sense. Those who take the deontological position hold that since the rights secured by justice and equality are prior to goals like preference satisfaction and efficiency, they cannot be balanced against them. As John Rawls puts this point:

Each person possesses an inviolability founded on justice that even the welfare of society as a whole cannot override.... Therefore in a just society the liberties of equal citizenship are taken as settled; the rights secured by justice are not subject to political bargaining or to the calculus of social interests.[25]

Liberals argue for this lexical priority of the right over the good on various grounds. Charles Fried, for example, asserts that concepts of right and wrong 'establish our basic position as freely choosing entities'.[26] The norms that ensure the equality, freedom, and inviolability of persons are thus 'absolute in respect to the various ends we choose to pursue'.[27] The goal of social equality, because it ensures the integrity or autonomy of the person who forms preferences, must be prior to the goal of social efficiency, which concerns only the extent to which those preferences are satisfied. This is the fundamental reason that a trade-off between efficiency and equality—roughly a trade-off between preferences and the persons who have them—is conceptually not in the cards.

Earlier this century, utilitarian liberals joined conservationist movements to advocate the prudent use and wise exploitation of natural resources. As one commentator observes, conservationist movements

were mostly concerned with making sure that natural resources and environments were used in a fashion that reflected their true worth to man. This resulted in a utilitarian conception of environments and in the adoption of means to partially preserve them—for example, cost-benefit analysis and policies of multiple use on federal lands.[28]

The environmental, or 'ecology', movement that arose in the 1960s and 1970s differs from conservationism in defending a non-utilitarian conception of man's relationship to nature. Environmentalists often refer to a dictum of Aldo Leopold's to describe this relationship. 'A thing is right when it tends to preserve the integrity, stability, and beauty of the biotic

[24] Sagoff, *The Economy of the Earth*, ch. 3.   [25] Rawls, *A Theory of Justice*, 3–4.

[26] Charles Fried, *Right and Wrong* (Cambridge, Mass.: Harvard University Press, 1978), 8–9.

[27] Ibid. 29. See also Ackerman, *Social Justice*, 48–9, and Robert Nozick, *Anarchy, State, and Utopia* (New York: Basic, 1974), 30–3.

[28] Martin Krieger, 'What's Wrong with Plastic Trees?', *Science*, 179 (1973): 446–80; quotation on p. 446.

community. It is wrong otherwise.'[29] Speaking of actions in so far as they affect the environment, commentators add that 'the good of the biotic *community* is the ultimate measure of the moral value, the rightness or wrongness, of actions,'[30] and that 'the effect on ecological systems is the decisive factor in the determination of the ethical quality of actions.'[31]

If environmentalists take a moral position about environmental policy, as they seem to do, and if, therefore, they would not regard preference satisfaction or welfare as the desideratum of social choice, can they be liberals? To answer this question, we shall next consider deontological liberalism and its relation to environmentalism.

We shall find in the course of this discussion that the deepest questions are not those that concern the relation between liberalism and any particular ideological cause, such as environmentalism. They concern, rather, the perplexing relations among political theory, public policy, and law.

DEONTOLOGICAL LIBERALISM AND ENVIRONMENTALISM

Deontological, or 'Kantian', liberalism may best be understood as a reaction to liberal political theories associated with utilitarianism.[32] Deontological liberals typically argue that utilitarianism fails to respect the boundaries between individuals and the fact of their separate existences; they claim that utilitarianism replaces persons with their pleasures or preferences, all of which it then combines, in a fungible way, into a single social aggregate.[33] Utilitarians treat persons with equal respect and concern, so this criticism goes, by treating them with no respect or concern but only as locations where pleasures may be produced and preferences may be found.[34]

---

[29] Leopold, 'The Land Ethic', 240.   [30] See Essay II.

[31] Ibid. See also Don Marietta, Jnr., 'The Interrelationship of Ecological Science and Environmental Ethics', *Environmental Ethics*, 1 (1979): 195–207. 'The basic concept behind an ecological ethic is that morally acceptable treatment of the environment is that which does not upset the integrity of the ecosystem as it is seen in a diversity of life forms existing in a dynamic and complex but stable interdependency' (197).

[32] For a critical study of deontological liberalism and its relation to Kantian moral theory, see Michael J. Sandel, *Liberalism and the Limits of Justice* (Cambridge: Cambridge University Press, 1982), esp. 1–14.

[33] See Amartya Sen and Bernard Williams, 'Introduction', in *Utilitarianism and Beyond* (Cambridge: Cambridge University Press, 1982), 4: 'Essentially, utilitarianism sees persons as locations of their respective utilities—as the sites at which such activities as desiring and having pleasure and pain take place. . . . Utilitarianism is the combination . . . of welfarism, sum ranking and consequentialism, and each of these components contribute to this narrow view of a person.'

[34] For discussion, see H. L. A. Hart, 'Between Utility and Rights,' in A. Ryan, ed., *The Idea of Freedom* (New York: Oxford University Press, 1979), 77–98.

The deontological approach, on the contrary, recognizes that justice, equality, and autonomy are the irreducible conditions under which freedom is possible, and persons may be said to choose and not merely to channel their preferences and desires.[35] A utilitarian state, its critics further contend, fails to treat its citizens as ends in themselves but regards them merely as means to be dedicated to the maximization of social welfare or utility. And thus a utilitarian government will sacrifice the interests of some individuals unfairly in order to confer greater benefits on others or on society as a whole.[36]

Utilitarian liberals are by now familiar with this criticism, and many respond that intuitions about justice and equality are, indeed, important; therefore, a trade-off or balance must be struck between equity and efficiency.[37] As deontological liberals are quick to argue, however, goals like 'allocatory efficiency', 'preference satisfaction', and 'wealth maximization' are not to be considered as independent ideals, to be weighed or balanced against other ideals, namely, distributional justice and equality, which unfortunately conflict with them.[38] Rather, an efficient allocation of resources, in so far as it differs from an equitable one, has no value to begin with and therefore has no moral claim against which to balance the claims of equity.[39]

This argument goes back to Kant, who considered wants, desires, and preferences to be mere 'inclinations', which may be arbitrary or contingent from a moral point of view, and thus the satisfaction of which *per se* has no value or moral significance.[40] As John Rawls puts this point: 'The satisfaction of these feelings has no value that can be put in the scales against the claims of equal liberty.'[41]

Many environmentalists, agreeing with this critique of utilitarianism, have tried to make common cause with deontological liberalism. They have attempted to do this in two ways. First, environmentalists have appealed to the rights of future generations as reasons to protect wilderness and other natural areas.[42] This appeal fails, however, because it

---

[35] Fried, *Right and Wrong*, 7–17.   [36] Nozick, *Anarchy, State, and Utopia*, 71–84.

[37] Arthur Okun, *Equality and Efficiency: The Big Tradeoff* (Washington, DC: Brookings Institution, 1975).

[38] Ronald Dworkin, 'Why Efficiency?', *Hofstra Law Review*, 8 (1980): 563–90.

[39] Rawls, *A Theory of Justice*, 31.

[40] Immanuel Kant, *Critique of Practical Reason*, tr. L. W. Beck (Indianapolis: Bobbs-Merrill, 1956), esp. 18–20.

[41] Rawls, *A Theory of Justice*, 450.

[42] See e.g. Bryan Norton, 'Environmental Ethics and the Rights of Future Generations', *Environmental Ethics*, 4 (1982): 319–37. For good anthologies collecting relevant essays, see Douglas MacLean and Peter Brown, eds., *Energy and the Future* (Totowa, NJ: Rowman & Littlefield, 1983); Ernest Partridge, ed., *Responsibilities to Future Generations* (Buffalo:

amounts to no more than the conservationist principle that we should exploit environmental resources wisely to maximize the long-run benefits nature offers humankind. Utilitarianism itself may treat present and future interests, pleasures, and preferences on an equitable basis, moreover, by insisting that cost-benefit analyses employ a social discount rate that balances the welfare of future individuals fairly with our own.[43]

Second, some environmentalists, seeking deontological arguments for preserving the natural environment, have appealed to the rights and interests of animals and other natural things. Indeed, a few scholars have explored the possibility that natural objects, like animals and trees, might have rights of the sort that give them legal standing or, failing that, interests that might be entered into the cost-benefit analyses on which social regulations may be based.[44]

These suggestions proved futile, however, in part because only individuals, that is, particular plants or animals, could possess rights or interests, but it is collections, such as species, communities, and ecosystems, that environmentalists are concerned to protect. As Joel Feinberg observes, species cannot be a proper object of moral concern in the context of a theory of rights, fairness, or justice. 'A whole collection, as such, cannot have beliefs, expectations, wants or desires. . . . Individual elephants can have interest, but the species elephant cannot.'[45]

To protect a few members of one species, it may be necessary to seal the fate of many more of another, for example, the millions of krill eaten by a single whale. To preserve the healthy functioning and integrity of an ecosystem, it might be necessary again to let many individual creatures perish—deer, for example—that might easily be saved from starvation by human intervention or might even prosper in a managed environment.

Although the animal rights movement correctly emphasizes the important truth that man ought not to be cruel to animals and thus has insisted,

Prometheus Press, 1980); and Richard Sikora and Brian Barry, eds., *Obligations to Future Generations* (Philadelphia: Temple University Press, 1978). For an excellent review of the issues, see Annette Baier, 'For the Sake of Future Generations', in Tom Regan, ed., *Earthbound: New Introductory Essays in Environmental Ethics* (New York: Random House, 1984).

[43] For discussion of the social discount rate, see Talbot Page, 'Intergenerational Justice as Opportunity', in MacLean and Brown, *Energy and the Future*, 38–58, and sources cited therein.

[44] See e.g. Christopher Stone, *Should Trees Have Standing? Toward Legal Rights for Natural Objects* (Los Altos, Calif.: Kaufmann, 1974), and Laurence Tribe, 'Ways Not to Think About Plastic Trees: New Foundations for Environmental Law', *Yale Law Journal*, 83 (1974): 1315–48. I have commented on this literature most recently in Mark Sagoff, 'Animal Liberation and Environmental Ethics: Bad Marriage, Quick Divorce', *Osgoode Hall Law Journal*, 22 (1984): 297–307.

[45] Joel Feinberg, 'The Rights of Animals and Unborn Generations', in William T. Blackstone, ed., *Philosophy and Environmental Crisis* (Athens: University of Georgia Press, 1974), 55–6.

quite properly, on humane conditions for pets and livestock, it is unclear how the rights or interests of animals and other natural objects can be systematically connected with the goals and values of environmentalism. Accordingly, the rights and interests of animals, although important in the domestic context, will not allow environmentalism to hitch its wagon to the star of either deontological or utilitarian liberalism.[46]

From the point of view of the environmentalist, indeed, there may be little to choose between utilitarian and deontological liberalism, for all the controversy between them. The controversy comes down to this: the utilitarian allows certain trade-offs the deontological liberal refuses to permit. As Brian Barry observes:

On the surface, rights theories stand in opposition to utilitarianism, for rights, whatever their foundation (or lack thereof), are supposed to trump claims that might be made on behalf of the general welfare. The point here is, however, that the whole notion of rights is simply a variation on utilitarianism in that it accepts the definition of the ethical problem as conterminous with the problem of conflicting interests, and replaces the felicific calculus (in which the interests are simply added) with one which does not permit certain interests to be traded off against others.[47]

The environmentalist does not define the ethical problem as 'conterminous' with the problem of conflicting interests. The environmentalist analyses the ethical problem, in so far as it concerns our relation to the natural environment, in terms of cultural, aesthetic, and moral responsibilities or in terms of national ideology, character, and pride. This is not the same thing as asserting an interest; rather, it is to assert a conception of the good that is not based on a calculus of interest. Nor is it to affirm a right that 'trumps' conceptions of the good, for it is itself a conception of the good. The trade-offs environmentalists would prohibit are not the same as those deontological liberals are concerned to prevent.

POLITICAL THEORY AS A POLICY SCIENCE

More than a century ago, Christopher Columbus Langdell, then dean of the Harvard Law School, wrote that it 'was indispensable to establish at

[46] In reaching this conclusion, I have drawn upon a large literature, including Essay II; Bryan Norton, 'Environmental Ethics and Non-human Rights', *Environmental Ethics*, 4 (1982): 17–36; Eric Katz, 'Is There a Place for Animals in the Moral Consideration of Nature?', *Ethics and Animals*, 4 (1983): 74–85. For arguments for an opposing conclusion, see Tom Regan, *The Case for Animal Rights* (Berkeley: University of California Press, 1983), 361–3; and Edward Johnson, 'Treating the Dirt: Environmental Ethics and Moral Theory', in Regan, ed., *Earthbound*, 336–65, esp. 351–4.

[47] Brian Barry, 'Self-Government Revisited', in David Miller and Larry Siedentrop, eds., *The Nature of Political Theory* (New York: Oxford University Press, 1983), 121–54; quotation on p. 125.

least two things: first, that law is a science; secondly, that all the available materials of the science are contained in printed books (of judicial opinions)'.[48] The task of the legal scholar, according to Langdell, is to unify the data found in judicial decisions by discovering the few underlying principles by means of which these opinions may be explained and predicted and aberrant decisions may be criticized and overturned.

Now, more than a century later, the search for a 'Comprehensive View' of the law continues as a primary task of legal philosophy and scholarship. Bruce Ackerman describes a 'Comprehensive View' as 'a relatively small number of principles describing the general abstract ideals which the legal system is understood to further'.[49] Ackerman proposes that judges, in adjudicating cases brought before them, act either as 'Ordinary Observers', by grounding their decisions on precedents and other institutionally based norms and expectations, or as 'Scientific Policy-makers', by deriving decisions from a Comprehensive View. The function of a Comprehensive View, Ackerman adds, 'is to provide a set of standards by which policy-makers may determine the proper legal content of legal rules and evaluate the performance of the legal system as a whole'.[50]

The distinction Ackerman draws between 'Ordinary Observers' and 'Scientific Policy-makers' parallels the distinction I have drawn between two conceptions of rationality. The Ordinary Observer would base decisions on deliberation constrained by various intellectual virtues, like open-mindedness, clarity, publicity, and attention to detail. The Observer does not rely on esoteric theories or on terms of art; rather, he or she appeals to precedents and to commonplace ideas that are based on the good sense and reasonable expectations of the general public.

The Scientific Policy-maker, on the contrary, construes rationality to require a Comprehensive View, replete with principles, criteria, and definitions laid down in advance. The policy-maker reaches decisions by applying these principles and criteria to data, which is to say, the circumstances of a given case. Ideally, the policy-maker should have a methodology that deduces the policy solution from the data mechanically, which is to say, simply by applying formal rules to the relevant phenomena. Apparently this was Langdell's view of how judges in an ideal legal order would behave.[51]

---

[48] Christopher Columbus Langdell, 'Record of the Commemoration, November Fifth to Eighth, 1886, of the Two Hundred and Fiftieth Anniversary of the Founding of Harvard College (1887)', 96, excerpted in Arthur E. Sutherland, *The Law at Harvard* (Cambridge, Mass.: Harvard University Press, 1967), 175.

[49] Bruce Ackerman, *Private Property and the Constitution* (New Haven, Conn.: Yale University Press, 1977), 11 (footnote omitted).   [50] Ibid.

[51] Duncan Kennedy identifies and criticizes this kind of legal formalism in 'Legal Formality', *Journal of Legal Studies*, 2 (1973): 351–98.

Bruce Ackerman, in discussing Scientific Policy-making, describes two Comprehensive Views on which social policy may be based.[52] The first makes efficiency or the maximization of wealth the criterion for social regulation; the second bases political decisions on a conception of rights, justice, and the equality of persons instead. Such criteria correspond roughly to the principles of utilitarian and deontological liberalism. These two forms of liberalism, then, would have an important characteristic in common. They each would require public officials to deduce the right answer or the correct decision by applying the standards and criteria contained in the Comprehensive View to the circumstances involved in any particular policy or legal question. They would therefore not allow citizens or their representatives, who may have their own moral views and ethical agendas, to work out policy through political deliberation.

Democracy, therefore, would be a problem for each of these forms of liberalism—as it would likewise be a problem for socialism or conservatism, in so far as these set out standards and criteria on which they would base policy decisions. The problem for all Scientific Policy-making is that legislatures are full of Ordinary Observers, which is to say, people who either do not understand or are perversely opposed to the true criteria, methodologies, and principles of collective choice. Accordingly, both utilitarian and deontological liberalism must explain away, reverse, or somehow account for a lot of statutes that have no apparent connection with the Comprehensive View on which public policy, if it is Scientific, must be based.

Utilitarian legal theorists are aware of the importance of public or statutory law, which since the New Deal has increasingly pre-empted private or common law adjudication. A 'Scientific Policy-maker' might square this orgy of statute-making (as Grant Gilmore calls it)[53] with utilitarianism, however, in one of two ways. First, contemporary utilitarians, following in the tradition of such political scientists as Truman[54] and Bentley,[55] may regard the legislative process as a method by which competing interest groups work out compromises by bargaining for votes. Statutory bargains of this sort, to be sure, would soon become obsolete, and

---

[52] Ackerman, *Private Property*, 11.

[53] Grant Gilmore, *The Ages of American Law* (New Haven, Conn.: Yale University Press, 1977), 95.

[54] David Truman, *The Governmental Process* (New York: Knopf, 1951).

[55] Arthur Bentley, *The Process of Government* (1908; Bloomington: Indiana University Press, 1949). For recent literature modelling the democratic processes by analogy with markets, see James Buchanan and Gordon Tullock, *The Calculus of Consent: Logical Foundations of Constitutional Democracy* (Ann Arbor: University of Michigan Press, 1962); and Anthony Downs, *An Economic Theory of Democracy* (New York: Harper, 1957).

after a few years, a more efficient compromise might better be struck by the courts.

Second, a utilitarian may argue that Congress attempts or should attempt to judge what an efficient or a wealth-maximizing policy would be. Congress would not itself be a market, then, but it would attempt to correct the failure of markets.[56] Either way, judges could legitimately review legislation on utilitarian or cost-benefit grounds, since, on the utilitarian view, courts and legislatures would engage in essentially the same business, namely, the socially necessary task of balancing interests, allocating resources efficiently, and maximizing social wealth.

Deontological liberals also believe that the courts should play an active role in reviewing legislation. They assert, however, that judges should enforce the principles of fairness, equality, and justice in so far as these conflict with the principles of welfare economics. Ronald Dworkin goes farther: He argues that the Bill of Rights 'must be understood as appealing to moral concepts'.[57] He therefore calls for a 'fusion of constitutional law and moral theory'.[58] To apply constitutional law, a court must 'decide where moral progress lies'.[59] It must be an activist court, 'in the sense that it must be prepared to frame and answer questions of political morality'.[60]

Dworkin means that judges should frame and answer questions of political morality not the way a utilitarian, a socialist, or a fundamentalist Christian or Muslim would but the way a philosopher schooled in the Kantian tradition, particularly one who has read *Taking Rights Seriously*, would frame and answer them. Just as utilitarian liberalism apparently makes the judicial decision an exercise in economic theorizing, so deontological liberalism may make it an exercise in moral theorizing. Is this what Langdell intended? In order to make law 'scientific', would he close the law schools and instruct lawyers to study economics and philosophy instead?[61]

---

[56] 'In the economic vision, it is only the prospect of overcoming the market's failure to capture gains from trade that can justify, from the individual's standpoint, the risks of exploitation inherent in majoritarian political institutions. Would it not, then, make economic sense to include in the constitution a direction to courts to nullify any majoritarian intervention which plainly cannot even make a pretence of being a solution to a market-failure problem?' In Frank Michelman, 'Politics and Values or What's Really Wrong with Rationality Review', *Creighton Law Review*, 13 (1979): 487–507; the quoted passage, on 498–9, does not necessarily reflect Michelman's own position.

[57] Dworkin, *Taking Rights Seriously*, 147.   [58] Ibid. 149.

[59] Ibid. 147.   [60] Ibid.

[61] For an excellent analysis of the relation (or non-relation) between philosophy and law, see Charles Fried, 'The Artificial Reason of the Law or: What Lawyers Know', *Texas Law Review*, 60 (1981): 35–58. See also Michael Walzer, 'Philosophy and Democracy', *Political Theory*, 9 (1981): 379–99. Walzer writes (ibid. 391): 'So the philosopher asks judges to recapitulate in their chambers the argument he has already worked out in solitary retreat . . . by deciding cases in its

In an important book, *A Common Law for the Age of Statutes*,[62] Guido Calabresi observes the difficulty democratic legislatures pose to those who would have the courts base their decisions on a Comprehensive View of public policy. The problem is that a legislature may fail to adopt a Comprehensive View, it may adopt one that is incorrect, or it may express conflicting Views in different statutes. What is more, even if the legislature recognizes the efficiency criterion, social welfare, or some other acceptable 'scientific' rationale, the statutes it enacts may soon become obsolete and may therefore inhibit rather than advance the purposes they are intended to serve. Accordingly, Calabresi argues that the courts should have the power to review on subconstitutional (e.g. efficiency) grounds statutes they 'deem out of phase'.[63] At times this doctrine would approach granting to courts the authority to treat statutes as if they were no more and no less than part of the common law.[64]

Can environmentalists be liberals? To ask this question is to ask whether the constitutive political philosophy of liberalism is tied to a Comprehensive View and to making all policy decisions conform to 'scientific' principles and criteria laid down in advance. It is to ask whether liberalism must regard every value that is not a *right* as an *interest* or a *preference* and therefore a mere feeling or inclination, utterly arbitrary and contingent from a moral point of view. If so, then we may conclude that liberalism defines every policy question as one of maximizing utility or enforcing rights. If liberalism makes these assumptions—which, perhaps, it need not—then it is plainly incompatible with environmentalism. And it appears to be incompatible with democracy as well.

DEONTOLOGY AND DEMOCRACY

'The essential normative principle of democracy', Charles Fried writes, 'requires that the democratic process be seized of moral questions as readily as that process is seized of political questions; the democratic citizenry has the *moral* right to seek to understand and implement moral arguments.'[65] Environmentalists, peace advocates, feminists, welfare

---

terms. When necessary, the judges must preempt or overrule legislative decisions. This is the crucial point, for it is here that the tension between philosophy and democracy takes on material form.'

[62] Guido Calabresi, *A Common Law for the Age of Statutes* (Cambridge, Mass.: Harvard University Press, 1982).

[63] Ibid. 15.   [64] Ibid. 2.

[65] Fried, 'What Lawyers Know', 38 (describing Walzer's view).

activists, veterans, and many other citizens' groups all give moral reasons why society should adopt the policies they support. A democratic society has the right to reject these policies in favour of ones that maximize utility, or it may reject policies that maximize utility in order to benefit the poor, protect the environment, reward veterans, or whatever it finds a moral reason to do. Liberal political theory cannot commit a democracy beforehand to adopt any general rule or principle that answers the moral questions that confront it; if political theory could do this, it would become autocratic and inconsistent with democracy.

Comprehensive moral views, even those associated with Kant and Mill, therefore, do not provide an appropriate foundation for liberalism as a democratic political philosophy. This is true, in part, because public agreement on these views and all they entail about the nature of the good could not be achieved without the autocratic use of state power. That is the reason, as John Rawls says, no such conception can provide the basis for political judgement in a modern democratic state.[66] Political philosophy must rely on a concept of justice that makes legitimate political judgement possible without the autocratic use of state power. It may not prescribe, then, what public choices should be; it may only describe the basic structure of social institutions in which free and equal individuals may make those choices.

If liberalism insists on a utilitarian conception of the good in social policy, it is not only inconsistent with democracy, but it undermines its own neutrality and credibility as well. Michael Sandel observes, 'If the good is nothing more than the indiscriminate satisfaction of arbitrarily given preferences regardless of worth, it is not difficult to imagine that the right . . . must outweigh it.'[67] The morally diminished status of the good, Sandel argues, calls into question the status of rights, in so far as these are defined simply in opposition to it. 'Given a conception of the good that is diminished in this way, the priority of the right would seem an unexceptionable claim indeed.'[68] When deontological liberalism accepts a utilitarian conception of the good, it invites the question whether the right could sustain its priority over a less impoverished conception. Would the rights of individuals still 'trump' legislation intended to reflect a fuller, richer, more plausible conception of human striving and achievement?

[66] John Rawls, 'Justice as Fairness: Political, Not Metaphysical', *Philosophy and Public Affairs*, 14 (1985): 225.
[67] Michael J. Sandel, *Liberalism and the Limits of Justice*, 168.
[68] Ibid. 174. Sandel adds that 'utilitarianism gave the good a bad name, and in adopting it uncritically, justice as fairness wins for deontology a false victory.' Ibid.

Deontological liberalism has a reply to this question that at once disengages its death grip on utilitarianism and shows it to be consistent with democracy as well. Liberalism as a political philosophy may concern itself simply with the problem John Rawls, among others, has addressed. This is the problem of structuring social institutions so that individuals and groups, likely to differ fundamentally in their moral beliefs and commitments, can nevertheless live peacefully together and secure the benefits of social co-operation. The fundamental problem for a liberal theory of justice, then, would be that of defining the basic structure of political institutions in a modern democratic state.

The rights secured by such a conception of justice do not take their status from their opposition to a utilitarian or any other particular conception of the good. Rather, respect for these rights would provide the basic structure in which free and equal individuals may join in diverse groups and communities, each with its own full, moral, and constitutive conception of the good, and still co-operate with one another to make collective decisions under arrangements that are fair to all.

We are now in a position to distinguish two different questions. We may ask, first, how liberalism would determine the basic structure of social and political institutions. Because society is likely to contain many communities, each with its own full, constitutive conception of the good, this structure must allow for their peaceful and harmonious coexistence. Such a structure will allow individuals of all persuasions to participate as free and equal citizens in the democratic process. The rights this social structure guarantees, then, must be preserved, for example, because they are constitutive of the democratic decision-making process itself. Rights that preserve the integrity of structures—the processes of a free market and of a representative legislature—must 'trump' any conception of the public interest that emerges from those structures.

Second, we may ask what particular conceptions of the good liberals will advocate not in their political theory, which must be neutral among all such conceptions, but in their social policy. We may ask, in other words, about the political programme rather than the political philosophy of liberalism. We know that liberals cannot deduce their programme from their philosophy, for otherwise their political philosophy would fail to maintain neutrality among many incompatible and incommensurable conceptions of the good. On the other hand, the programme should be close enough to the philosophy so that we can understand why it should be called 'liberal'.

I cannot describe in any detail here the political programme of liberalism or its relation to the constitutive political theory of liberalism. In the next sections, however, I shall try to characterize this programme well enough to explain, in so far as I can, its relation to the moral principles of environmentalism.

LIBERALISM AND PUBLIC POLICY

Liberalism, as I understand it, relies on two distinctions, the first of which, as I have said, divides the state from civil society. We need not interpret this distinction as drawing a sharp division, however, between rights and preferences or between the rules that govern competition and the interests that motivate it. We might better understand the distinction in relation to its provenance in the separation between secular and religious authority—*imperium* and *sacerdotium*—and the attendant difference between matters of legitimate public concern and matters to be left to the conscience of the individual.

It is essential to liberalism that the state not try to improve upon, or even influence, the intimate, personal, or religious activities of its citizens, provided that the freedom of conscience of one person does not infringe on the like freedom of another. In this respect—in matters of personal morality and private conscience—the state must strive for strict neutrality, and its decisions, in so far as possible, should be independent of any particular conception of the good life. The reason for this neutrality, incidentally, need not depend on a metaphysical thesis about the separateness and inviolability of persons. It may rely instead on the pragmatic lesson of history: when a government tries to establish a religion in a heterogeneous society, it is likely to produce civil insurrection instead.

This tells us nothing, of course, about the relation between liberalism and environmentalism. Environmental decisions, by and large, have to do with what goes on out of doors not indoors; they concern the character and quality of the public household not of the private home. Environmental policies, in general, restrict what corporations and municipalities may do with their investments and effluents—not what individuals may do with their lovers, co-worshippers, or friends. Thus the content of environmental policy rarely becomes relevant to the kind of neutrality essential to liberalism.

Accordingly, the distinction between civil society and the state, at least as I interpret it, need not prevent environmentalists from being liberals. This distinction, moreover, need not prevent liberals from endorsing even those environmental policies that are based on particular ethical, cultural, or aesthetic convictions. These convictions must not infringe on the right of every citizen to make his or her own intimate decisions, for example, with respect to choices of friends, religion, and sexual relationships. I cannot think of any environmental statute that restricts these personal choices and beliefs.

The second distinction on which an understanding of liberalism depends divides between the basic structure of institutions and the social policies that emerge from those institutions. Liberal political theory concerns only the former, that is, the basic structure of social arrangements. At this level, liberals insist on structures that are fair among the individuals who participate in them. These arrangements must be neutral among conceptions of the good and treat individuals as equals independently of their race, sex, colour, preferences, principles, or beliefs. Thus, liberal theory as a Comprehensive View applies at the level of social structure, not at the level of social policy.

This is not to say that liberals, as liberals, have no view of the good society and no particular conception of what social policy should be. What I suggest is simply that liberal social policy cannot be inferred from liberal political theory. Instead, liberals endorse, for a variety of reasons, social policies that provide a lively, diverse, and hospitable environment in which people can develop their own values and exercise their talent and imagination. No theory, of course, tells liberals what kind of environment this is. Liberals depend, at the level of policy, not on a Comprehensive View about neutrality and equality but on aesthetic judgement, moral intuition, human compassion, honesty, intelligence, and common sense.

What distinguishes liberalism at the level of social policy is not the absence of a particular conception of the good society but an openness to a variety of such conceptions and a willingness to experiment with and judge each on its merits with respect to particular issues. What distinguishes liberalism at the policy level, then, is its freedom from the toils of ideology, policy science, and political philosophy. This tolerance for competing views makes liberalism particularly compatible with democratic institutions, in which individuals and groups may argue for the policies they favour and may advocate various conceptions of the good. Because liberalism is liberal in this way, it is open-minded; it attends to the views individuals express, and not simply to their rights and their wants.

ENVIRONMENTALISM, LIBERALISM, AND THE NATIONAL IDEA

The word 'liberal' rarely appeared in political discussion in America before the New Deal; when it was used politically, it was usually used pejoratively, to refer to free-thinking secularism and an irresponsible attitude toward time-tested ideas and traditions. Then, when Franklin Roosevelt became president, his administration pre-empted its critics by proudly describing itself as liberal. Writers, politicians, and the general public quickly followed in using the term 'liberal' to describe the outlook and policies of the New Deal.[69]

What was essential to the outlook of the New Deal, as Samuel Beer has argued, was not just its progressive economic policy; it was also a *national idea.* Beer explains:

The national idea is not only a view of American Federalism, but also a principle of public policy. As a principle of public policy, it is a doctrine of what is commonly called 'nation-building'. Its imperative is to use the power of the nation as a whole not only to promote social improvement and individual excellence, but also to make the nation more solidary, more cohesive, more interdependent in its growing diversity; in short, to make the nation more of a nation.[70]

In order to make the nation 'more of a nation', New Deal liberals supported a nationalism of shared ideals and aspirations. For New Deal liberals—one would include, for example, Hubert Humphrey—the Democratic party was the nationalistic party, the party of Hamilton not Jefferson, in so far as it opposed regionalism and the competition of special interests. Yet the common purposes New Deal Democrats sought to achieve were those of a peace-loving society and had nothing to do with the militarism that dominated the nationalistic movements in Europe.

Among the unifying goals and aspirations that New Deal Democrats emphasized, environmental protection was prominent. 'When Franklin Roosevelt became President,' as Stephen Fox points out, 'the organized conservation movement was controlled by members of the opposition party.'[71] After the New Deal, 'most conservationists were democrats'.[72] Under the leadership of Harold Ickes, Roosevelt's secretary of the interior, moreover, conservationism began to merge with environmentalism. 'I do not happen to favor the scarring of a wonderful mountainside,' Ickes said after two years in office, 'just so we can say we have a skyline drive.'[73]

After the New Deal, the Democratic party continued to indentify itself with nationwide as opposed to special and regional interests; it became the party of a strong central government as distinct from what it once was, the

---

[69] Ronald Rotunda, *The Emergence of Liberalism in the United States,* BA thesis, Harvard University, 1967. See also Samuel Beer, 'Liberalism and the National Idea', *The Public Interest,* 5 (1966): 70–82.

[70] Beer, 'Liberalism and the National Idea', 71.

[71] Stephen Fox, *John Muir and His Legacy* (Boston: Little, Brown, 1981), 187.

[72] Ibid. 217.

[73] Ibid. 200; quoting Ickes in *Living Wilderness Magazine,* Sept. 1935.

party of states' rights. The goals of the Democratic party comprised progress in civil rights, entitlement programmes, full employment, support of the sciences and arts, and environmental protection. These goals are consistent with an emphasis on the welfare of the individual, but they are also 'nationalizing' in that they provide a cultural, economic, and political basis on which groups that had been excluded from the national community have been integrated into it. In the goals and doctrines of New Deal liberalism, as Sam Beer observes, 'the national idea worked to integrate the pluralism of the twentieth century.'[74]

For a more recent example of the importance of the environment in the 'national idea', one may read the farewell address of President Carter. The president began this address by describing the national idea:

Today, as people have become ever more doubtful of the ability of the Government to deal with our problems, we are increasingly drawn to single-issue groups and special interest organizations to ensure that whatever else happens, our own personal views and our own private interests are protected. This is a disturbing factor in American political life. It tends to distort our purposes, because the national interest is not always the sum of all our single or special interests. We are all Americans together, and we must not forget that the common good is our common interest and our individual responsibility.[75]

President Carter then spoke of the three issues that he thought most concerned our common good or common interest. He included 'the threat of nuclear destruction, our stewardship of the physical resources of our planet, and the pre-eminence of the basic rights of human beings'. He spoke of 'the destruction of beauty, the blight of pollution' and of 'our most precious possessions: the air we breathe, the water we drink, and the land which sustains us'. In discussing the nuclear threat, the importance of human rights, and the protection of the environment, President Carter emphasized that these issues were not just national but international concerns. He urged the country to forgo its national regionalism to identify its common interest with that of the rest of the world.

'What the Western world has stood for—and by this I mean the terms to which it has attributed sanctity,' T. S. Eliot writes, 'is "Liberalism" and "Democracy."'[76] Eliot observes that these concepts are neither identical nor inseparable. If we think of liberalism as a kind of individualism, then we may surely think of it not only as distinct from, but also as opposed to, social integration and, therefore, environmentalism and democracy.

---

[74] Beer, 'Liberalism and the National Idea', 76.
[75] *Public Papers of the President of the United States: Jimmy Carter*, 1980–81; bk 3, 29 Sept. 1980–20 Jan. 1981 (Washington, DC: Government Printing Office, 1982), 2890.
[76] T. S. Eliot, *Christianity and Culture* (New York: Harcourt Brace, 1949), 11.

Yet we need not believe that liberalism must insist on a granular conception of society or an atomic conception of the person: It need not push pluralism into individualism. Rather, by balancing pluralism with integration, individuality with community, liberalism makes itself consistent with democracy. If either is to have any value for us, we must have both.

XI

ECOLOGICAL THEORY AND VALUE IN NATURE

ANDREW A. BRENNAN

Introduction: Ethics and Ecology

In recent years, a certain kind of position has captured the attention of philosophers and people outside the discipline. Following Naess, we can speak of this position as occupied by the *deep ecology movement*.[1] For short, I will refer to this position as the one held by the 'deep ecologist', or, sometimes, simply as 'the deep position'. This stance differs from what may be called the *shallow* style of ecological thinking in a number of ways. For example, both positions show concern for the consequences of pollution, whether on a local or global scale, and about resource depletion. On the deep position, but not the shallow, we have to take account of the relatedness of organisms to each other and to the rest of their shared environment. Since we are largely ignorant of the effects of disturbances on the other knots in the net of life, the deep ecologist urges decentralized economies, 'soft' research, the use of 'soft' energy pathways, and so on, all of which are strategies that minimize disturbances to both local and terrestrial systems. A further underpinning for the 'soft' approach comes from the notion that the right to live and flourish is distributed more or less equally throughout the biosphere; and so the deep position opposes human chauvinism, imperialism, domination, and exploitation whether directed to other human beings or towards nature, and favours the sustaining of diversity among all forms of life.

One of the interesting features of the deep position is the way it combines a view of the world influenced by scientific findings on ecology with a set of norms for reforming our relationship with nature. In this paper I will be looking at the problems faced by those who are attracted to

Reprinted by permission from *Philosophical Inquiry*, 8 (1986), 66–96.

[1] A. Naess, 'The Shallow and the Deep, Long-Range Ecology Movement: A Summary', *Inquiry*, 16 (1973), 95–100.

this position in some form or another. In particular, there are several versions of it which seem to draw some support from the study of ecology itself. On each version, there is an attempt to broaden the scope of our moral concerns so that we come to recognize various natural things as proper objects of moral concern and possessors of moral value. What I want to do is follow through this extension of ethical concern, drawing attention to some aspects of ecological science which are taken to support the extension. The result of the investigation is twofold. First, it turns out that we need more conceptual clarification in some areas before we can assess the theoretical and empirical underpinnings of the deep position. The deep ecologist has a number of options available, not just one narrowly circumscribed stance. Secondly, where we do have some clear results in ecological theory, these fail to support at least one interesting version of the deep position.

Problems for the Land Ethic

The Extension of Ethical Concern

Most theories of morality focus on sane, adult human beings as the standard example of rights-holders, or items to which we can conceivably have moral obligations. Although the cynic may point out that this simply reflects the fact that most influential speculation on morality has been conducted by adult and usually sane human beings, most of us recognize the pressure to extend the class of those to whom we can have obligations beyond these limits. Even the social contract theorist, at least any who might be regarded as an ideal contractarian, these days will try to extend moral considerability to children, the elderly and even, perhaps, the insane.

However, as Mary Midgley has pointed out, in reviewing the list of items that are candidates for our moral consideration, that is, items that might involve us in non-contractarian duties, we encounter a vast range of things. Her examples include the dead, the senile, the temporarily or permanently insane, defective humans, embryos, sentient animals, non-sentient animals, artefacts, groups, villages, landscapes, countries, and God. As she pointedly observes: 'As far as sheer numbers go, this is no minority of the beings with whom we have to deal. We are a small minority of them.'[2]

Of course, we might argue about the possibility of having duties of any sort to some of the things on her list, but even a subset leaves us with a

---

[2] See Essay V.

range of items that social contract theorists can only write off at the risk of saying nothing of any substance about large areas of morality.[3]

Passmore's Challenge and the Social Contract

By contrast with most contractarians, the defender of the deep position tends to support what Leopold calls *the land ethic*. In Leopold's words, 'a thing is right when it tends to preserve the integrity, stability and beauty of the biotic community'.[4] So let us grant, then, that there are pressures on us to extend our moral concern to items that are non-human, indeed to things that are not even animals, such as plants, works of art, forests, villages, families, and ecosystems. The problem that now confronts us is: what rationale could there be for making such an extension? We can approach this problem by way of facing a challenge which I will call Passmore's Challenge. This issue is raised by Passmore in the context of talking about rights. But we can easily generalize it to talk about the moral standing of other things, where the recognition of items as having moral standing may stop short of declaring them to have rights against us.

In his original statement of the challenge, Passmore writes:

Bacteria and men do not recognise mutual obligations nor do they have common interests. In the only sense in which belonging to a community generates ethical obligations, they do not belong to the same community. To suggest then as Fraser Darling does that animals, plants, landscapes have a 'right to exist' is to create confusion.[5]

Of course, this looks very much like contractarian thinking. Passmore apologizes in a footnote to this passage for taking perhaps too dogmatic a stance by using legal rights as paradigmatic for all talk about rights. We can, however, let the remark—if not its author—focus our attention on the contractarian view. The contractarian moral theorist starts from the assumption that self-seeking, independent individuals live less than perfect lives. They thus bond together for mutual support and protection from each other by entering into a social agreement. This agreement, or contract, puts certain limits on the selfish pursuits of any individual's needs and desires; for it is argued that each person's self-interest can be more

---

[3] It might be objected that contractarians are the first to point out that 'it is wrong to be cruel to animals and the destruction of a whole species can be a great evil' (J. Rawls, *A Theory of Justice* (Cambridge Mass.: Harvard University Press, 1971). But, as Midgley notes in Essay V, Rawls's own concentration on justice to the exclusion of all other virtues makes the cases of animals, the mentally impaired, trees, and so forth appear to be morally marginal.

[4] A. Leopold, *A Sand County Almanac* (Oxford: Oxford University Press, 1949), 224.

[5] J. Passmore, *Man's Responsibility for Nature* (London: Duckworth, 1974), 116.

effectively pursued within, and under the protection of, society. Society then functions in such a way as to maximize the self-interest of each person bound by the contract, or at least to maximize each person's chances of maximizing their self-interest. If it did not do so, there would be little point in entering into the contract in the first place.

Although social contract theory originated as an attempt to explain certain political facts, it has become extended—in some recent theories—to give an account of morality.[6] Notice how such a theorist can give an apparently persuasive answer to Passmore's challenge. The community that generates ethical obligations is precisely that formed by the parties to the contract. They have mutual obligations in virtue of having subscribed to the contract and they have common interests, namely in pursuing each their own ends, these being interests that the contract both recognizes and protects. As Hobbes concisely remarked: 'The final cause, end, or design of men, who naturally love liberty and dominion over others, in the intro-duction of that restraint upon themselves . . . [namely, the contract] . . . is the foresight of their own preservation and of a more contented life thereby . . .'[7]

One advantage that might be claimed for contractarian theories of morality is that we need not go into questions concerning human good. Each person can be allowed to have her or his own needs, wants, and desires. Within society we can permit citizens to pursue their individual goods provided due regard for the rights of other citizens is maintained. In modern versions of social moral thinking there is thus the possibility of powerful union between contract theory and what we might call *liberal individualism*.

Ethics and Community

Although the social moralist can in this way meet Passmore's challenge, we can reinterpret the challenge so that critical issues remain. For we can discern in the challenge a suggestion that goes beyond any contractarian point about rights that Passmore may be making. It is entirely natural, if an individual is to be conceived as owing duties or obligations to other things, that these things be conceived as belonging in some sense to one community along with the individual concerned. The community itself

---

[6] This may be thought a controversial claim. But see the remarks by Midgley on Rawls's and Hume's trivialization of the other virtues by their concentration on a special notion of justice (Essay V). See also R. B. Brandt, *A Theory of the Good and the Right* (Oxford: Oxford University Press, 1979).

[7] Thomas Hobbes, *Leviathan* (London, 1651), II. xvii.

provides the locus of value; the fact that the individual recognizes others as belonging to that community involves the recognition on the part of the individual of some morally significant relationship between the obliged and that to which the obligation is owed.

Passmore's challenge, therefore, can be seen as posing a location problem for the value theorist. It is relatively easy to see how some communities of individuals form loci of value. The family, the village, even the society, are all communities within which it is easy for the agent to recognize moral claims from other members of the group. If we want to urge that our moral duties extend to all human beings, then we may do so by suggesting that we all form one global family. To the extent that we form relationships with animals, then we share in communities with them within which it is not hard to speak of duties owed, even when those to whom we owe the duties cannot claim these for themselves.

Communities and Interests

There is a natural connection between this location problem and the notion of *interests*. It has seemed to many theorists, for example Feinberg, that we cannot speak of the rights of items unless it makes sense to count such items as having interests.[8] These interests can then be represented, either by the items themselves, or by others acting on their behalf. Once we locate ourselves in the right communities, we then know which interests to reckon into our moral dealings. Suppose there are beings on remote planets who are rational, sentient, and possessors of emotions. Until they enter into certain relations with us, until we can recognize ourselves as forming some kind of community of mutual interests with them, there is no way that we can count their interests when deciding what to do.

By contrast, if we take the term 'community' in a non-contractarian sense, we can argue that we already do belong to such communities involving non-human creatures and other objects around us, although we often act as if we were unaware of this fact. For humans belong to larger, biotic communities and do enter into significant relations with the other members of these communities. Passmore's challenge, viewed this way, is underpinned by a piece of insight congenial to the deep ecologist: he has noted the point that humans are not isolated individuals whose practical lives occur in independence of the activity of things around them. Rather, our practical activity not only defines, as Dewey would have it, our indi-

---

[8] J. Feinberg, 'The Rights of Animals and Unborn Generations', in W. T. Blackstone, ed., *Philosophy and Environmental Crisis* (Athens: University of Georgia Press, 1974).

viduality but involves behaviour that engages with the items around us.[9] Sartre, of course, emphasized how even the look of the other could affect us and alter our perception of ourselves.[10] But ecology is able to describe many interrelations of more substantial kinds between us and our fellow sharers of the planet.

Ecological Communities

So let us consider how the defender of the deep position might respond to Passmore's challenge by appeal to ecological insights:

1. The larger, biotic community to which any individual belongs consists of plants and animals in genuine interrelationship (for example, passage of matter and energy through the system, involvement in food webs, and so on).

2. Any biotic community is inevitably in some relationship to other communities. Indeed, we can extend the notion of community without much difficulty to embrace the entire terrestrial biosphere.

3. Within each community, there are trends, let us suppose, towards end states, states of stable self-sustaining diversity. This successional phenomenon can also be perceived in the behaviour of the entire biosphere.

4. Any biotic community would be unsustainable without the abiotic resources which some of its members process into organic compounds, available for use by other members of the community. The ecosystem, conceived as a combination of biotic community and abiotic surroundings can itself become a proper locus of value.

5. The entire global ecosystem, Margulis and Lovelock's *Gaia*, can be regarded as a system within which we are but small parts.[11]

6. Just as biotic communities, and the whole biosphere, show evolutionary trends towards stable diversity, so does the terrestrial ecosystem as a whole. As Stephen Clark has further suggested, the pattern may even be one of movement towards an Aristotelian final cause, a state of self-sustaining diversity and stability.[12]

---

[9] 'The moment children act they individualize themselves; they cease to be a mass and become the intensely distinctive beings that we are acquainted with out of school . . .' (J. Dewey, *The School and Society* (Chicago: University of Chicago Press, 1915), 33).

[10] For a detailed treatment of this topic see pt. III of J. P. Sartre, *Being and Nothingness*, tr. H. E. Barnes (London: Methuen, 1969).

[11] See J. E. Lovelock, *Gaia: A New Look at the Earth* (Oxford University Press, 1974).

[12] S. R. L. Clark, 'Gaia and the Forms of Life', in R. Elliot and A. Gare, eds., *Environmental Philosophy* (Milton Keynes: Open University Press, 1983).

It should be clear from these responses that Passmore's challenge can be met in more or less grandiose ways. We seem to have grounds for locating humans within all sorts of communities of differing size and of different kinds. If we keep the community within which value has a place to relatively local dimensions, then we run the risk of being accused of something akin to selfishness—a kind of local-interest that is cousin to self-interest. But only the most shallow of ecological thinkers would suggest that so long as we treat the immediate community with respect, and take care to dump our toxic waste and pollution outside it, we have acted with due regard to our extended awareness of community.

On the grander responses to Passmore's challenge which ascend to the deeper perspective, self-interest and local-interest no longer loom so large.[13] If the community within which value is to be located becomes as large as the global ecosystem, then we need some special argument to show that our right to live and flourish is more significant than that of any other species.[14] However, our flourishing—like the flourishing of other living things—is not something that can be discerned from inspection of individual human beings on their own. On this perspective the claim that 'No man is an island' expresses a basic truth, provided the term 'man' is interpreted without regard to sex. Our potential to do harm to the system overall is, however, significantly greater than that of any other species. Our ability to contribute anything of value to the global system is considerably less than our potential for damage; perhaps, then, one of the most valuable things we can do is to refrain from spoiling the system. As Stephen Clark has put it:

... this making real to oneself that we exist and can only exist as elements within modes of a continuing community (not an aggregate or socially contracting multitude of separable individuals) is the realistic analogue of the Kantian 'kingdom of

---

[13] There is one response to Passmore's challenge that seems to combine both extended awareness and local interest. *Local ecological thinking*—if I can use such a phrase—would show the sort of concern for local (or relatively local) biotic communities that the contractarian shows for the society or state. Although no theorist to my knowledge advocates this position, it might be said to be implicit in some of our practices—for example, building high chimneys to ensure our SO_2 emissions affect only suitably distant ecosystems. Such a stance should be distinguished from one in which supporting local ecosystems is held to be of instrumental value in promoting human good (that is, the good of humans in the immediate neighbourhood, the country, the province, the state . . .). This latter position involves straightforward human chauvinism again. For comments on *egoism* and *ecoism*, see H. Rolston III, 'Is There an Ecological Ethic?', *Ethics*, 85 (1975), 93–109.

[14] Henryk Skolimowski, for one, supplies just such an argument, basing it on the claim that 'the more highly developed the organism, the greater is its complexity and sensitivity and the more reason to treat it as more valuable and precious than others' (H. Skolimowski, *Eco-Philosophy* (London: Marion Boyars, 1981), 83).

ends'. Its ethical imperative might be represented as follows: 'So act as if your maxims had to serve at the same time as universal law for all the entities that make up the world.' Its immediate corollary: 'Take no more than your share; no more than what you must to sustain the particular value that you carry for the whole.'[15]

Problems for Deep Ecology

In an impressionistic sketch of positions such as this, I have not been able to give time to an important issue, namely, how the perception of ourselves as no more than knots in a vast biospherical net is able to carry the burden of the moral shift from self-interest to ecological egalitarianism. As I am not the first to point out, the recognition of interdependence need not carry with it recognition of any kind of moral relationship.[16] Moreover, even on a global perspective, it is never clear that our dependence on other things ever amounts to a relationship carrying a moral burden. Thus all planetary life currently depends on the sun. It is prudent—to say the least—that we therefore do nothing to damage, let alone destroy, the sun. But, it might be said, our duties *regarding* the sun are owed *to* other things—humans included—but not *to* the sun itself. Although this objection does create a general difficulty for the deep ecologist, it would take me too far from the concerns of the current paper to deal with it here.

A further problem is that our recognition of others as worthy of moral consideration does not always seem to result from our recognizing any shared community with them. Thus, it can be argued, our response to victims of famine in Ethiopia clearly shows our recognition of a claim they have on us without any corresponding recognition of existing political, economic, or other significant relationships.[17] To take an even more extreme case, the discovery that a distant planet shelters a species very like our own who are dying from an infection that we—but not they—can easily cure would no doubt move us to intervene to save their lives. Here the very fact of our practical intervention would seem to establish the relationship between us and them; the community within which value has a place would be formed consequent upon our recognition of them as having moral standing.

In response to both of these objections, the defender of the deep position has a number of options. Clearly, there is still room for the weak claim

---

[15] Clark, 'Gaia and the Forms of Life', 195.

[16] J. Benson, 'Duty and the Beast', *Philosophy*, 53 (1978), 529–49.

[17] Of course, I do not mean to imply here that there are in fact no economic or political relations between the affluent and the poor nations. Nor do I deny that the global economic system is responsible, in part, for the disparity between the overnourished and the starving. Rather, the point in the text is that it is not *recognition* of any of this that motivates the humanitarian response in question.

that recognition of our forming a certain kind of community with items of a certain sort involves the recognition of such items as having moral standing and moral value. Alternatively, it would be possible to give up the concern with moral considerability and concentrate instead on an account of what is a worthwhile and good life for human beings. Such an account may deliver the result that a worthwhile life involves refraining from lording it over nature, while not going so far as assigning moral value to other natural things. To develop this position, we might want to say something about the conditions for human flourishing and perhaps return to those questions that so exercised the ancient philosophers (by looking— for example—at the connection between the good person and those things that are good for persons).

Although these are interesting matters, it is time now to turn to a scrutiny of the problems faced by the deep position when it attempts to draw support from theoretical and experimental work in ecology itself. By looking at two central areas of ecological investigation, we should become clearer about some of the things ecologists do, and what is to be discovered about the objects of their study. This will lead us to appreciate why ecological insights have informed the thinking of deep theorists and have seemed to commend an overhaul of our moral thinking. The two cases I will take are the theory of succession and the theory of tropho-dynamics.

The Theory of Succession

Biologists have often argued that the study of succession shows, among other things, exactly how the influence of individual populations on their environment can give rise to consequential changes as a result of which new populations, of a different character from the original ones, become established. At the same time, we become aware of what Haskell calls the 'counter-entropic force of life' whereby systems of increasing complexity and order succeed each other in apparent defiance of the second law of thermodynamics.[18]

Here is a simple example of what succession might involve. We imagine a lake with water plants growing at the margin. The silt and soil trapped by the roots of the marginal plants, aided by their own detritus, gradually build up over time so that the edges of the lake move inwards. The water-

---

[18] E. F. Haskell, 'Mathematical Systemization of "Environment", "Organism", and "Habitat"', *Ecology*, 21 (1940), 1–16. The increase of complexity, of course, only appears to be in defiance of the second law. Since ecosystems are neither closed nor isolated, their decreasing entropy is fuelled by the energy input from the sun.

loving plants still inhabit the margin of the now diminishing lake, while new species occupy the very ground they have been instrumental in reclaiming. The latter, marsh-loving, species will include trees like hazel and alder. With the trees come big root systems which hold the soil more firmly and have larger water needs, so that more water is drawn from the marsh. Thus, the very modification engendered by the trees creates the conditions that are suitable for further new species such as ash and birch. If the successional process continues, the lake will disappear and the area will become cloaked in broad leaved woodland. The pioneer species which started the whole process will themselves disappear in the course of the various phases of succession.

This idealization accords to some extent with many observed real life situations.[19] What it draws attention to is the fact that many communities go through phases that are far from fixed or stable. Moreover, the transformation of their environment brought about by pioneer species seems positively suicidal. As Clements observed in a 1905 text: 'Each stage reacts upon the habitat in such a way as to produce physical conditions more or less unfavourable to its permanence, but advantageous to the invaders of the next stage.'[20]

This law of reaction, as he calls it, is one of the many principles Clements cites as among the general laws of succession. Clements also suggests that succession tends to lead to few outcomes. 'Grassland or forest', he writes, 'is the usual terminus of a succession; they predominate in lands physiographically mature.'[21] Even now, eighty years later, standard textbooks describe terminal, or climax, communities—in much the way Clements did—as mature, fairly diverse, and relatively stable (sometimes noting counter-examples in the phenomena of arrested and cyclic succession).

The kind of succession described by Clements is of the type we might call 'obligatory'.[22] One simple model for succession of this sort would be to imagine the success of a number of subordinate species being closely linked to the success of the species dominant at a given time. The pattern of succession for a given place would then show different assemblages of species present at different times. Each such assemblage constitutes one

---

[19] See e.g. E. P. Odum, 'The Strategy of Ecosystem Development', *Science*, 164 (1969), 262–70. Horn warns that textbook examples of succession may often be very simply explained: 'differences between communities are due largely to secular changes in the level of the water table' (H. S. Horn, 'Succession', in R. M. May, ed., *Theoretical Ecology* (Oxford: Blackwell, 1976), 193; further references to the literature given there).

[20] F. E. Clements, *Research Methods in Ecology* (Lincoln, Nebr.: University Publishing Company, 1905), 265.

[21] Ibid. 266.   [22] See Horn, 'Succession'.

phase of the sere (or chain of successive communities), the whole process terminating with the stable climax assemblage.[23] Such a model as this suggests that a study of populations at a time can give us some means for establishing how mature the community in question is. If, for example, we find biomass accumulation on a scale that far outstrips community respiratory needs, then we predict that the community is probably far from its successional climax. The accumulation of biomass in the community would not itself be a matter of note if we were not aware of succession as a biological phenomenon in the first place. However, the study of successional communities since Clements's day suggests that we need to distinguish between the obligatory succession just described and the sort of succession that results from periodic disruption (for example by fire or predator attack).

Tropho-dynamics

In traditional treatments of ecology, the theory of succession teams up in a remarkably synergistic way with the theory of *tropho-dynamics*. In a classic paper published in 1942, Raymond Lindeman produced a systematic defence of the view that the ecosystem is a unit of study in its own right, and that the passage of energy through the ecosystem gives rise to significant relationships among the system's inhabitants. As he put it:

analyses of food-cycle relationships indicate that a biotic community cannot be clearly differentiated from its abiotic environment; the *ecosystem* is hence regarded as the mere fundamental ecological unit.[24]

At the heart of any ecosystem are the *autotrophs*, organisms that are capable of transforming inorganic material into organic compounds. Without them, and the decomposers who recycle material within the system, solar energy could not be used in any way to support life, let alone be shuffled around in all the complex ways described by Lindeman and subsequent biologists. Heterotrophic organisms rely for their energy needs on either the autotrophs or on each other. The decomposers recycle dead and decaying matter whether produced by the autotrophs or the heterotrophs.

We can thus start to think about organisms in an ecosystem in terms of what Lindeman called their trophic level. The primary producers, the autotrophs, occupy a lower trophic level than large heterotrophic predators (see Fig. 1).

[23] See R. J. Putman, ed., and S. D. Wratten, *Principles of Ecology* (London: Croom Helm, 1984), ch. 3, for alternative patterns.

[24] R. L. Lindeman, 'The Trophic-Dynamic Aspect of Ecology', *Ecology*, 23 (1942), 399–418.

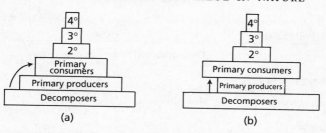

FIG. 1. Trophic pyramids. (a) Stylized Pyramid of Numbers/Biomass in a Terrestrial Community. The area of each bar in the diagram is related to the number or biomass of organisms in that particular trophic level. (b) Trophic Pyramid for a Detritus-based Aquatic Community.
Source: R. J. Putman, ed., and S. D. Wratten, *Principles of Ecology* (London: Croom Helm, 1984).

But how far up a food-chain an organism is located will be something we can associate with other factors, for example loss of energy due to respiration or efficiency in use of the food supply available. As Lindeman argues, these two factors are apparently correlated in an interesting way: the higher the level of a consumer, the greater its efficiency in the use of food available, while the greater its loss of energy through respiration. This respiratory loss, he suggested, may even be a factor that puts an upper limit on the number of levels in an ecosystem.[25]

Systems over Time

Now although modern ecologists would tend to use the metaphor of a food *web* and would accuse Lindeman's model of over-simplification, the idea of the ecosystem as an energy shunting device rich in networks for transporting the available energy and able to use alternative networks when one network breaks down is itself richly suggestive. Moreover, description in terms of tropho-dynamics is intimately linked to traditional theories of succession. What happens in obligatory succession on this view is that in each seral phase the ratio of gross community production to respiratory loss changes. When pioneer species are busy colonizing new terrain, they build up excess biomass and nutrient conservation is generally poor. There is little symbiosis, and entropy is high (see Table 1).

[25] Lindeman is here following the suggestion of C. Elton, *Animal Ecology* (New York: Macmillan, 1927).

TABLE 1. *A Tabular Model of Ecological Succession: Trends to be Expected in the Development of Ecosystems*

Ecosystem attributes	Developmental stages	Mature stages
Community structure		
Total organic matter	Small	Large
Inorganic nutrients	Extrabiotic	Intrabiotic
Species diversity—variety component	Low	High
Species diversity—equitability component	Low	High
Biochemical diversity	Low	High
Stratification and spatial heterogeneity (pattern diversity)	Poorly organized	Well organized
Nutrient cycling		
Mineral cycles	Open	Closed
Nutrient exchange rate, between organisms and environment	Rapid	Slow
Role of detritus in nutrient regeneration	Unimportant	Important
Community energetics		
Gross production/community respiration (P/R ratio)	Greater or less than 1	Approaches 1
Gross production/standing crop biomass (P/B ratio)	High	Low
Biomass supported/unit energy flow (B/E ratio)	Low	High
Net community production (yield)	High	Low
Food-chains	Linear, predominantly grazing	Web-like, predominantly detritus
Overall homoeostasis		
Internal symbiosis	Undeveloped	Developed
Nutrient conservation	Poor	Good
Stability (resistance to external perturbations)	Poor	Good
Entropy	High	Low
Information	Low	High

Source: E. P. Odum, 'The Strategy of Ecosystem Development', *Science*, 164 (1969), 262–70.

As phases succeed each other, production starts to match respiration, there is less excess biomass, conservation of biomass, increasing diversity of species, and reduction in entropy. Viewed as a dynamic system, the ecosystem seems to move towards a position of balance, or stability, in which it becomes less prone to disturbance from outside and rich in internal pathways for energy circulation. The system itself can seem to possess feedback mechanisms which protect it from destruction, damp down dangerous oscillations, and cope with the constant comings and goings of species within it. The combination of tropho-dynamics with succession theory thus starts to make plausible the view of the ecosystem as a kind of superorganism, developing like some gigantic scattered individual towards its mature, climax phase of stable diversity.

THE SUPERORGANISM

Communities as Organisms

Just as an animal's body is composed of well-regulated individual organs composed in turn of tissue, composed in its turn of individual cells, and so on, we can come to think of the ecosystem as a single organism whose functional parts are the various populations of which it is composed. The conception of the biotic community as such a superorganism is not new, and receives a typically lucid statement in Clements:

The plant formation is an organic unit.... According to this point of view, the formation is a complex organism, which possesses functions and structures, and passes through a cycle of development similar to that of a plant.... Since the formation, like the plant, is subject to changes caused by the habitat, and since these changes are recorded in its structure, it is evident that the terms, function and structure, are as applicable to the one as to the other.[26]

Gleason's assessment of this view in correspondence with Muller is as follows:

There is nothing comparable to reproduction in any assemblage of plants.... Far from being an organism, an association is merely the fortuitous juxtaposition of plants. What plants? Those that can live together under the physical environment and under their interlocking spheres of influence and which are already located within migrating distance.[27]

---

[26] Clements, *Research Methods in Ecology*, 199.
[27] H. A. Gleason, 'Delving into the History of American Ecology', *Bulletin of the Ecology Society of America*, 56 (1952), 8–10.

Does anything of moral significance hang on this disagreement? The answer is that there are at least some conceptions of ecosystem, or of community, that would exclude them from moral consideration.

One such conception would be taking them as set theoretic entities. Now, the devices of set theory are useful in all sorts of analytic situations, but we must not forget the costs incurred by using them. For example, communities can change; in fact, they suffer almost continual loss and gain of individuals and species, no matter how stable they may be. But if a community is a set of individuals, or even a set of populations, then this kind of change is just not possible for it. Sets cannot stay the same while changing their members, nor can sets even be candidates for participating in successional processes. Sets cannot be destroyed, either, whether by disruption of energy pathways or by bulldozers, but ecosystems can. So the identification of sets with ecosystems is not, to my mind, plausible. And this is just as well for deep ecology, for it is hard to see how sets could be objects of veneration, respect, or even mere consideration.

We might wonder if Clements's idea of the superorganism is all that far removed from the modern systematists' notion of the *species* as a super-individual.[28] The heart of Gleason's objection is that a plant community cannot in any real sense reproduce. No doubt, he would make this point even more forcibly about the attempt to count in the abiotic environment as part of some super-individual, the ecosystem. However, the problem that an ecosystem cannot in any literal sense be said to reproduce is not the greatest of the problems standing in the way of counting it as a unified individual. The difficulty here is in finding any structural properties that would enable us to set the individuals composing some ecosystem aside from all other individuals. Those who argue that species are unitary individuals can point, for example, to the fact that interfertilization is accompanied by morphological and genetic similarity among the items belonging to a species.[29] But unlike the parts of biological species, the parts

[28] See e.g. K. Holsinger, 'The Nature of Biological Species', *Philosophy of Science*, 51 (1984), 293–307. Of course, not all individuals are organisms. My understanding of Clark's position in Clark, 'Gaia and the Forms of Life', is that what matters for Gaia is not so much that 'she' be an organism, but that she be unitary in the way an individual is. Further, this individual displays some organism-like feature.

[29] See Holsinger, 'The Nature of Biological Species'. The conception of species as individuals can be seen as a natural outcome of arguments due to M. Ghiselin ('A Radical Solution to the Species Problem', *Systematic Zoology*, 23 (1974), 536–44) and D. Hull ('Are Species Really Individuals?', *Systematic Zoology*, 25 (1976), 174–91) that species are not natural kinds. As Sober puts it, the case for taking species as breeding populations is informed by the insight that such populations are not structured by 'laws of form' but are large individuals integrated and shaped by 'the fortuitous whims of natural selection' (E. Sober, 'Sets, Species and Evolution', *Philosophy of Science*, 51 (1984), 336. The unitariness of such large individuals means that they are more than simply the scattered individuals of Goodman (N. Goodman, *Fact, Fiction and*

of an ecosystem do not share structure in obvious ways. Nor—like the admittedly diverse parts of the body—do they share cells whose chromosomal codings are identical. If neither of these analogies work, then, although we may be reluctant to count ecosystems as sets, we still face a difficulty about claiming any sort of unified individuality for ecosystems.

Cities and Corporations

One further case, however, may seem to provide the right analogy. Cities and corporations seem to have a certain unity, are good candidates for not being sets, and yet contain diverse parts of structurally various kinds.[30] Cities, like ecosystems, have a physical extent at any given time, are subject to complex dynamic relationships among their parts and even command certain degrees of affection and respect from some of those who visit or live in them. Corporations show growth patterns that are strikingly similar to those evinced in the biological cases. For example, many now diversified and self-sustaining multinational corporations started from smaller, more uniform, pioneer beginnings. Nor are corporations mere artefacts controlled by us; as Galbraith has argued forcibly, they seem to have a life of their own, a life that needs to be regulated in order to preserve us from their worst excesses.[31]

I hope that it has now become clear why results from ecology might be thought to support certain extensions of moral consideration. We can see that, in crude terms, there are at least two versions of deep ecology's position that draw support from ecological theory. One version builds on the ecological insight associated with Passmore's original challenge. We find that study of tropho-dynamics and succession theory can support the intuition that a biotic community, or even an ecosystem, is an appropriate

---

Forecast (Indianapolis: Bobbs Merrill, 1965), pt. II) or Quine (W. V. Quine, 'Identity, Ostension, and Hypostasis', in *From a Logical Point of View* (New York: Harper and Row, 1963)). Recently, Niven has tried to give set-theoretic definitions of the basic terms of animal ecology, though—using the resources of the calculus of individuals—it may be possible to translate these into individualistic terms (see B. S. Niven, 'Formalisation of the Basic Concepts of Animal Ecology', *Erkenntnis*, 17 (1982), 306–20; N. Goodman, *The Structure of Appearance* (Indianapolis: Bobbs Merrill, 1966).

[30] I am silent here on complex issues of identity. For example, the city of New York is, for legal and political purposes, a fairly well-defined entity. Of course, it is not always that entity to which people are referring when they use the name 'New York'. In the light of problems to be raised later in the paper, it may be that the sceptic will be able to point to the evolution of corporations as simply a case of Markovian processes at work.

[31] In J. K. Galbraith, *The New Industrial State* (Harmondsworth: Penguin, 1967), we find what might be regarded as an account of the 'ecology' of corporations, and of the mutual adaptation between them and what Galbraith calls the 'technostructure'.

community within which value can be located. Our awareness of the complex passage of energy through such a system, or of its gradual maturity
through its seral phases, is likely to give further funding to the original
intuition that we and our fellow creatures are locked into one community
of value. We can call this variety of the deep position 'the community
theory'. It can itself take two forms. One kind of community theory denies
that systems—or processes within them—have any intrinsic value accruing
to them in their own right. Any value they have derives from the values of
their components, but since human beings are just one among many such
components, we can give value to the dormouse, the bacteria, and even
the nitrogen and carbon which find themselves locked with me into the
terrestrial ecosystem. We recognize that an 'ecosystem' and processes
within it are necessary for the existence and flourishing of things of value;
but this is recognition of a merely instrumental value.

A stronger version of the community view maintains that processes
within ecosystems, and perhaps the systems themselves, have a value in
their own right. One possible support for this kind of view would be the
recognition, along with Leopold, that natural systems and biotic communities have beauty and integrity. Now we generally agree that beauty and
integrity are intrinsically valuable so that—other things being equal—we
should strive to protect them.[32] Analogies with other communities may
also help here. Within my family I play various roles, am instrumental in
helping other members of the family achieve their goals, share their joys
and sorrows. These activities in which I engage as a member of the family
not only have a value in themselves, but have a value that enriches my own
life. Informed by the results of ecological study, the strong community
view suggests that the processes occurring within ecosystems are themselves valuable and life-enhancing. The community of value thus comes to
be recognized as a valuable community in its own right.

An alternative view uses the same results from ecology to support the
intuition that the community or ecosystem is a unitary *individual*. We can
call this variety of the deep position 'the super-individual theory'. As an
individual the ecosystem grows to maturity and, in its stable maturity, it in
some sense reproduces and regulates itself. As I will argue in a moment,
there is reason to doubt that ecological studies really support such a grand
view. But such a view does give us items which, although large, diversified,
and scattered, seem to be good candidates for the having of value in their
own right, in addition to any value that accrues to them on the weaker
conception. Why is this? The idea is, I think, that by purely descriptive

---

[32] See Rolston, 'Is There an Ecological Ethic'.

means we identify certain scattered entities as *individuals*. The super-individual theorist can thus avoid some of the complications of arguing that biotic communities are places of value, or that a community can have a value that transcends the value of the individuals within it. For suppose that the super-individuals do have some features like those of a living organism—homoeostatic feedback processes, resistance to analogues of disease, and so forth. Then, since some organisms are clear examples of items that have intrinsic value, it is not implausible that ecosystemic individuals are themselves items of intrinsic value. Put thus baldly, the gaps in the argument are fairly evident; but it has a certain strength as well. As we shall see shortly, current research in ecology does little to support the claim that any natural systems are individuals in the required sense.

One thing that the deep ecologist attracted to the second line of thought has to consider is why ecosystems, conceived as super-individuals, have a value that requires respect and protection, while other apparent super-individuals, like corporations and cities, seem to lack such value and—according to the deep ecologist—need to be kept strictly under control. Maybe one important difference is that cities and corporations are artefacts, while natural systems are not. But we would need to be convinced that this is itself a morally significant difference between the cases.[33]

Alternatively, it may be that all these systems are things of intrinsic value, and our problem is to protect and cherish the values of each when they come into competition or conflict. Such a view hardly fits the deep ecologist's person–planetary conception. Consider Roszak's denunciation of the city:

... the problem posed by the city as an imperialistic cultural force that carries the disease of colossalism in its most virulent form ... At the same time, the city is a compendium of our society's ecological bad habits. It is the most incorrigible of wasters and polluters; its economic style is the major burden weighing upon the planetary environment. Of all the hypertrophic institutions our society has inflicted upon both the person and the planet, the industrial city is the most oppressive.[34]

There is little recognition here of the city as an object to be valued, cherished, or respected.

Apart from this point, there is a further irritating difficulty which is common to the super-individual theory and to the stronger version of the community theory. The super-individual or global ecosystem may contain valuable communities within it. But if we are to take seriously the claim

---

[33] I think there are some grounds for regarding natural objects as having significantly different moral status from artefacts. See my discussion of this in connection with works of art in A. A. Brennan, 'The Moral Standing of Natural Objects', *Environmental Ethics*, 6 (1984), 35–56.

[34] T. Roszak, *Person/Planet* (London: Gollancz, 1979), 253–4.

that moral value involves in part being in, or being capable of entering into, certain relations with other things, then there is a real question over whether Gaia herself can have moral value. For there may be no larger community within which she has possibilities of enrichment, flourishing, or suffering. It is possible that there are no other planets in the universe with terrestrial ecosystems; ours may just be a one-off phenomenon. So again the deep position finds itself facing a difficulty when identifying communities as places of value. Maybe, as Stephen Clark has hinted, we can develop in the end holistic systems of thought which accommodate both the demands of communities and of individuals.[35] What I want to show now, however, is that there are serious problems of a quite different sort facing the perspective under consideration. For although the deep ethic may seem entirely natural given the ecological background so far set out, its foundations turn out to be less than secure.

Problems for Theoretical Ecology

The connection between fact and value, indeed the very distinction between these two notions, is dark and complicated. Both the community and super-individual theories try to draw some strength for their moral claims from the science of ecology as a source of theoretical and factual material. The community theory uses succession theory and tropho-dynamics to delineate the structure and complexities of the community of value into which we, our fellow creatures, plants, bacteria, minerals, and elements are locked. If we can recognize value in nature at all, this recognition is bound to be enhanced—and likely to be extended—by the study of ecology. Some version of this view will, I think, survive the problems to be raised.

The super-individual theory, however, finds itself in greater difficulties. On this account, the ecosystem is an ever-changing individual within which the conditions for the flourishing of humans and all else are set. Our value can then be seen, in Midgley's words, as that of a 'tiny part' in 'a vast, irreplaceable and fragile whole'.[36] If this whole is to have the status of super-individual, then current results in ecology hardly support such a conception; in fact, they tend—if anything—to undermine it.

Some biologists are themselves sceptical about how much of tropho-dynamics in the form I have presented it here deserves the title of science. Peters, for example, has argued that there is no sensible, non-trivial account to be given of the concept of trophic level, no clear definition of what it is for an item to be a ruminant, a detritivore, or any other sort of feeder, and no operationally useful definition of an ecosystem.[37] To some extent, these complaints are not new. Nearly forty years earlier Haskell tried to give mathematically precise definitions of the terms organism, habitat, and environment.[38] There is plenty of scope here for investigation by philosophers of science.[39] Rather than pursue this technical issue now, I will instead concentrate on the theory of succession, and some recent conclusions arrived at by Horn through applying stochastic methods to the area.[40]

Convergence and Markov Processes

Some biologists, Simberloff for one, take Horn's results as toppling succession from its central place in ecology. As Simberloff puts it: 'Horn's attempt ... not only reduces successional phenomena to the level of populations, but explicitly introduces stochasticity as a fundamental successional property, the antithesis of deterministic succession leading to a superorganismic climax.'[41] The suggestion, then, is that, if analyses such as Horn's are correct, we need only—like Gleason—take the community as a fortuitous aggregation of populations, and as an entity it need have no interesting biological properties *in propria persona*.

Let us look at Horn's work to see if it supports Simberloff's assertion. The outcome of Horn's study is that convergent succession can occur rapidly where there is a well-established competitive hierarchy. This is, ironically, rather different from the case described by Clements, where the existence of later species is dependent on the pioneering work of earlier ones. Moreover, the phenomena described by Horn are the realization of a Markov process. Crudely, such a process occurs in systems without memory. Suppose, for example, we are given the current state of a system. If the system is Markovian then we can assign a transition probability to what the next state of the system will be without taking into account any

---

[37] See R. H. Peters, 'The Unpredictable Problems of Tropho-Dynamics', *Environmental Biology of Fishes*, 2 (1977), 97–101.

[38] Haskell, 'Mathematical Systemization of "Environment", "Organism", and "Habitat"'.

[39] Peters's own complaints reveal little sensitivity to the problem of how to deal with any theoretical terms in the sciences, coupled with an almost positivistic contempt for anything that smacks of theory not directly linked to experience and observation.

[40] H. S. Horn, 'Markovian Properties of Forest Succession', in M. L. Cody and J. M. Diamond, eds., *Ecology and Evolution of Communities* (Cambridge, Mass.: Harvard University Press, 1975).

[41] D. Simberloff, 'A Succession of Paradigms in Ecology', *Synthese*, 43 (1980), 3–39.

states prior to the current one.[42] Now let us suppose that we can establish two things: first, the survival rate for individuals in a species present over a certain time in a locality; and secondly the ratio of replacement of those individuals who die over the time in question. The ratio of replacement will tell us how many of the individuals that die over the period in question are replaced by individuals of the same species and how many will be replaced by individuals from different species.

The information on survival and replacement allows us to draw up a *life table* for the populations that we are studying. This table will have the Markovian property that the sum of each row is 100 per cent. In such a table we record facts, let us imagine, about the species in a New Jersey wood over a period of fifty years. Of the grey birches alive at the start of the period, it may turn out that only 5 per cent will be alive after the fifty years have expired while 36 per cent have been replaced by blackgum, 50 per cent by red maple, and 9 per cent by beech. The hardy beech, by contrast, has 61 per cent of its representatives alive at the end of the period, 35 per cent replaced by more beech trees, 3 per cent by red maple, and only 1 per cent by grey birch.[43] Already, we may suspect that these replacement and survival figures are good news for the beech and bad news for the grey birch (see Fig. 2).

So indeed it turns out to be. Using a table of this sort for all the species in a wood, Horn shows how information about the composition of the wood at any one time predicts, in conjunction with the table, an eventual outcome in which beech predominates, grey birch becomes extinct and other species are represented in fairly small, but predictable, numbers. Studies of old, undisturbed patches of forest confirm the predictions. Given the life-span and replacement information, the rest is just a matter of calculation. Put another way, Horn's results may seem to show that the *convergence* in this kind of succession is more a statistical than a biological matter (see Table 2).

Of course, it is open to the critic of Horn's results to argue that why one species rather than another flourishes in a certain situation will itself be a matter of sophisticated individual–environment interactions. More recent work, for example by Tilman, suggests that microeconomic models may in

---

[42] Markov processes are a special set of processes involving time series (stochastic processes). Crudely, given a time series (with each element equally spaced), say $X_0, X_1, X_2, \ldots, X_n, X_{n+1}, \ldots$, we can say that if the conditional probability of X_{n+1} given $X_0, \ldots, X_n$ is equal to the probability of X_{n+1} given only X_n, then X is a Markov process. For precise definitions see D. Freedman, *Markov Chains* (San Francisco: Holden Day, 1971) and J. G. Kemeny, J. Laurie Snell, and A. Knapp, *Denumerable Markov Chains* (Princeton: van Nostrand, 1966).

[43] Figures notional, after Horn, 'Markovian Properties of Forest Succession', 190.

50 years hence Now	Grey Birch	Blackgum	Red Maple	Beech
Grey Birch	5 + 0	36	50	9
Blackgum	1	37 + 20	25	17
Red Maple	0	14	37 + 18	31
Beech	0	1	3	61 + 35

FIG. 2. Horn's Markov matrix.

Note: Diagonal is percentage of trees still standing plus percentage that have been replaced in 50 years by another of their own kind. Off diagonal terms are percentage of trees replaced by another species in 50 years. The percentage of trees still standing was estimated by assuming that trees die at a constant rate such that 5% are left standing after 50 years for grey birch, 150 years for blackgum and red maple, and 300 years for beech.

Source: H. S. Horn, 'Succession'.

fact be helpful when studying interspecific competition for resources.[44] What Horn's result seems to show is that the final, relatively stable state in the example given reflects the superior ability of beech to outcompete other species—an ability already implicit in the fifty year figures. In the presence of various disturbing factors, for example in a woodland regularly cleared, or subject to forest fire, the life-span and leaf arrangement of some other species of tree may favour its ultimate predominance, or we may find that diversity prevails.

In such cases, Horn's suggestion is that we should not always jump to the conclusion that succession must be a biological phenomenon; it may simply be the result of the working out of an essentially probabilistic process. As he puts it, 'several properties of succession are direct statistical consequences of a species by species replacement process and have no uniquely biological basis.'[45] This opposition, which Horn is not alone in suggesting, is something over which we have to take care. Why should it not be a piece of biologically interesting information that certain forms of succession have Markovian characteristics? Moreover, we could, if we wished, argue that virtually any causal transition is Markovian. A lot depends here on what we build into the characterization of a given state. Consider, for example, the study of animal foraging strategies. If we count into the

---

[44] See D. Tilman, 'Resources: A Graphical-Mechanistic Approach to Competition and Predation', *American Naturalist*, 116 (1980), 392–3.

[45] Horn, 'Succession', 196.

TABLE 2. *Convergence over time*

Age of Forest (years)	0	50	100	150	200	... 00	Very Old Forest
Grey Birch	100	5	1	0	0	0	0
Blackgum	0	36	29	23	18	5	3
Red Maple	0	50	39	30	24	9	4
Beech	0	9	31	47	58	86	93

Source: Horn, 'Succession'.

animal's current state memories and skills acquired from past experience, then we can give a transition probability to the next state that is purely Markovian. The opposition made between the statistical and the biological is, then, I suspect, a false one.

Marjorie Grene has objected to Simberloff's description of stochasticity as a fundamental successional property on the grounds that, in general, statistical relationships can indicate the existence of underlying causal mechanisims. We can think here of the statistical correlation between smoking and cancer of the lung.[46] Let us suppose, then, that interspecific competition is governed by mechanistic principles of the sort suggested by Tilman.[47] What Horn's study then shows is that, even under this assumption, the final stable state of the ancient forest is simply the outcome of competition for resources at the level of individual trees, or of populations of trees. The forest itself has no biologically significant role to play in the story. This is the real problem Horn's analysis poses for any theorist who would see the forest as itself a unitary individual behaving in biologically significant ways. At any stage in its history the kind of forest studied by Horn will be an adventitious collection of individuals or populations; its transition to some subsequent phase will be a biological phenomenon, but not one that makes reference to any biological properties of the forest as a whole.

There is, then, a modest moral that the super-individual theorist and the rest of us need to take to heart in this case. In using the results of a science to justify claims about the nature of any phenomena, we must use these results critically. Those who would use succession as evidence of the existence of transcendent principles of order should take more than a passing interest in these debates about probability and biological explanation. Further, in the case just described, succession did not lead to stable

[46] See M. Grene, 'A Note on Simberloff', *Synthese*, 43 (1980), 41–5.
[47] See Tilman, 'Resources: A Graphical-Mechanistic Approach to Competition and Predation'.

diversity, but rather to exclusion of some species and predominance of others. The deep ecologist thus also needs to consider the fact that the variety manifested by certain communities is often the result of what Horn calls 'a regular pattern of natural devastation'.[48] Some management, even in the form of human-engineered devastation, may thus prove necessary to maintain what we regard as a pleasant diversity of species in certain places.

That stochastic methods may be helpful in regimenting other forms of succession is something about which I do not have information. The possibility remains that when we encounter an apparently stable ecosystem manifesting diversity of species and apparent self-regulation, we thus may be confronted with an item that just happens to be the way it is.[49] Moreover, changes in a system, or even its collapse, will need to be seen in terms of changes in other systems around it. And the entire global ecosystem itself is subject to long-term influences (like the coming and going of ice ages), the effects of which are massive. In the face of all this, one kind of deep ecologist has to try to maintain a view of the ecosystem as a self-regulating, relatively isolated complex, as something that is, in Stephen Clark's words 'more like an organism than like a muddle'. Horn's results do seem to suggest that such a conception of the super-individual is going to be very hard to sustain. The defender of this variety of the deep position thus faces a difficulty worthy of some serious consideration.

Of course, there are *ad hoc* moves that may still enable us to keep alive the idea of the terrestrial ecosystem as a kind of super-individual even after noting Horn's results. It is hard to see how this kind of competition for resources in one specific location could be generalized to all the species that inhabit all locations. Thus, given the massive diversity of terrestrial habitats and resources, those species, like the grey birch, made extinct in one place are likely to thrive in some other. Even if parts of Gaia tend to uniformity over time, she may still herself show continuing sustained diversity including, perhaps, the ability to survive the next ice age. This response, though, still fails to take on board the problem of the local ecological community. If diversity is a good thing for ecosystems in general, we may only be able to ensure this in a particular forest, say, by

[48] Horn, 'Succession', 203.

[49] Given that such systems are likely to be far from thermodynamic equilibrium, an interesting question arises as to why such systems persist at all. Some illumination on this question may come from the work of Prigogine on dissipative structures, though I do not have enough competence in this area to make a confident judgement (see I. Prigogine, *From Being to Becoming* (San Francisco: Freemann, 1980)). Capra thinks that the theory of dissipative structures is ecologically significant (F. Capra, *The Turning Point* (London: Fontana, 1982)), and Prigogine suggests applications for the theory to non-microscopic phenomena (like the development of urban communities). Interestingly, Markov processes play an important part in the theory (see Prigogine, *From Being to Becoming*, for details).

regular interference of the sort that is familiar to good foresters. But this is to admit that local diversity, at any rate, may not be self-sustaining. If non-intervention, on the other hand, is a good policy, then we may have to live with a local environment which is becoming increasingly uniform through time. If we assume that self-sustaining diversity is the order of the day for ecosystems in general, then we obviously risk ignoring a practical problem of some urgency. Horn's results ought thus to be a topic for genuine concern among at least some deep ecologists. Of course, this is not to deny that the community theorist can still maintain a conception of the eco-system as a *place* of value; but it is hard to see that an essentially chance collection of items, or of populations, should be regarded as a unitary individual with its own intrinsic value. This is not to deny that chance arrangements of objects can have value. Some purely random aggregations may have, for example, an aesthetic value (and it is not easy to distinguish the aesthetic from the moral in any case). So some deep ecologists may be unmoved by the notion that the ever-changing pattern of terrestrial eco-systems reflects the unco-ordinated dance of millions. But those, like Clark, who find something of moral significance in the claim that eco-systems are unitary need to engage in urgent stock-taking.

Conclusion

I have not dwelt in this paper upon more than a few areas of ecological study and research. In passing, I hope to have shown philosophers new to ecology that there are conceptual issues of some interest waiting to be explored. At the same time, I have been silent on some of the main conceptual problems exercising ecologists and philosophers of ecology at the moment. The suggestions due to Strong that null hypotheses are of great significance in ecological theory deserve detailed treatment in their own right. Yet in this paper I have not so far mentioned them, nor the problems of island ecology that gave rise to their suggestion.[50] Nor have I looked at the complications of niche-theory, another area where the relation of theoretical terms to predictions and observations is hotly debated. What is perhaps surprising is that philosophers of science should have largely neglected an area that offers such a fascinating blend of technical problems and conceptual issues.

[50] See D. R. Strong, 'Null Hypotheses in Ecology', *Synthese*, 43 (1980), 271–85. Strong makes reference to the work of Williams which uses probability theory to reveal a biological puzzle about species representation in island communities (see C. B. Williams, 'Intra-Generic Competition as Illustrated by Moreau's Records of East African Birds', *Journal of Animal Ecology*, 20 (1951), 246–53 and O. Järvinen, 'Species-to-Genus Ratios in Biogeography: A Historical Note', *Journal of Biogeography*, 9 (1982), 363–70).

I have taken care, incidentally, to keep some distance from two issues which often loom large in this area. One concerns *reductionism*, while the other is concerned with *explanation*. What I have done is make the modest assumption that ecology—conceived as the study of organisms in their environment—does have a distinctive subject-matter. On the matter of reductionism, I have been studiedly neutral. Consequently, there has been no discussion of the views of ecological psychologists like J. J. Gibson, or of ecological physicists like Fritjof Capra.[51] As for explanation, I have been happy to take ecological explanation to be a variety of scientific explanation as standardly understood.[52] Sometimes, those who defend the deep position are drawn to espouse holism, which is taken to involve not just an anti-reductionist stance but also a new approach to the topic of explanation itself.[53] The deep position seems, however, to be able to make an interesting appeal to work in ecology without these added elaborations. Of course, this is not to dismiss these extra topics; rather, their study is best left to another occasion.

A hundred odd years of ecology have not been without effect, however, on general thinking on environmental issues. Almost every day, so it seems, we become aware of new environmental crises, and several philosophers and scientists have already urged that the issue of our relationship to nature is a matter of some moral urgency. In this paper, one of my modest aims will have been fulfilled if I have shown that there are good reasons for these philosophers to take a serious interest in the conceptual foundations of ecology. It has also been my intention to draw attention to the fact that the deep ecology movement is hospitable to a variety of positions, as illustrated by the differences between community and super-individual theorists. My own opinion is that some variety of the community theory will most plausibly capture the moral insights urged by deep ecol-

[51] See J. J. Gibson, *The Ecological Approach to Visual Perception* (Boston: Houghton Mifflin, 1979) and Capra, *The Turning Point*. For material on reductionism itself, there is a classic discussion in E. Nagel, *The Structure of Science* (London: Routledge and Kegan Paul, 1961), and some interesting distinctions are made by G. P. Hellman and F. W. Thompson, 'Physicalism: Ontology, Determination, and Reduction', *Journal of Philosophy*, 72 (1975), 551–64. In W. S. Wimsatt ('Reductionist Research Strategies and their Biases in the Units of Selection Controversy', in E. Saarinen, ed., *Conceptual Issues in Ecology* (Dordrecht: D. Reidel, 1982)) some very cold water is poured on the usefulness of the idea of reducibility in principle.

[52] So select your account (for example that of C. G. Hempel, *Aspects of Scientific Explanation* (New York: Free Press, 1965) and add to it any details about subject-matter and methods that are distinctive of ecology (for example, use of terms making essential reference to the history of populations and communities, use of dynamic models, study of systems relationships, and so on).

[53] This certainly looks like the position of Capra, *The Turning Point*. A hint of such a position may be read into Gibson's theory of affordances in Gibson, *The Ecological Approach to Visual Perception*.

ogists. With any luck, my arguments in this paper may have sown the seeds of some pioneer ideas from which, more mature conceptions may develop.[54]

[54] In writing this paper, I have drawn considerably from the material collected in Saarinen, ed., *Conceptual Issues in Ecology*. Particularly helpful was the historical survey in R. T. McIntosh, 'The Background and Some Current Problems of Theoretical Ecology'. The original version of this paper was given as the opening address to a conference on ecological thinking organized by the British Society for the Philosophy of Science and held in Bristol, Nov. 1984. I am grateful to the conference organizers for inviting my participation. Versions of the paper have also been read and discussed in Durham and at a Scots Philosophical Club conference in Stirling. In all cases, audiences have helped with stimulating discussion of the issues surrounding the deep ecologist's position. For individual comments that have shaped the present version, I am indebted to Stephen Clark, Murray MacBeath, Hugh Mellor, Alan Millar, and Holmes Rolston III.

XII

STASIS: THE UNNATURAL VALUE

COLLEEN D. CLEMENTS

I

In the last few years, a new myth has been created in Western civilization, the myth of a benign and balanced ecosystem. Thanks to popular interest in the science of ecology, an implicit model has been generated which both has major policy implications and seriously distorts the available empirical data. (I am talking about a popular model, about popularizers and some serious scientists in ecology, and not the majority of ecologists carefully working in the field. Certainly there are valid ecological models, specifically the computer models of entire ecosystems, simulations of specific environmental situations; and mathematical models designed to help discover general laws and form the basis of present theoretical ecology.) It is implied that, once a delicate balance has been achieved, once a system has successfully achieved homoeostatis, what we will have is a harmonious, benign bit of complex machinery recalling that awesome construction, the Clockwork Universe, in which everything has its appointed place and from which, for all practical purposes, change has been eliminated. Both the Clockwork Universe and the popular ecological model could probably be traced by a sociologist of knowledge to a common cultural base in modern thought; but the contrast between these two models and what I propose as a more accurate one goes even further back to the perennial tension between those who wish to characterize reality by permanence or by contingency. It is not my aim here to trace the new popular ecological model to its historical sources but, rather, to identify it, demonstrate that it is not supported by available observations, and trace out the implications of this error for the recent growth–no-growth debate.

The fairy tale ideal of an ecosystem of achieved and unchanging harmony goes aground on a number of biological and astronomical observations, and even, finally, on basic physical examples.

Reprinted by permission of The University of Chicago Press, from *Ethics*, 86, 136–43.

First, let us consider the interesting developments in Florida's red mangrove stands, as discussed by Rhem and Humm in a 1973 *Science* article.[1] A wood-boring isopod, *Sphaeroma terebrans* Bate, has been boring into the prop roots of the red mangrove, causing the eventual destruction of trees along shorelines. The authors describe this as an 'eco-catastrophe of serious magnitude', implying, I think, the faulty model I am attempting to elucidate. It is nowhere written in biology that mangrove stands are sacred or eternal or that the delicate balance between the stands and the shoreline and marine systems, once achieved, must always operate with the same mechanisms and subsystems: Nor is it an objective description or a necessarily defensible value judgement to say that a change in this interface ecosystem is an ecocatastrophe. It is simply an ordinary feature of subsystems that stasis is not indefinitely maintained and that, therefore, major and highly significant change occurs in biotic systems leading to both value and disvalue from a human point of view. However, change itself, I contend, is both inevitable in most systems and on the whole desirable.

In 1974, letters from two biologists to *Science* also picked up the defective model implied in viewing this change as an ecocatastrophe or, more generally, in viewing an ecosystem as always harmonious and benign.[2] Snedaker pointed out that what might devastate a component in a system may actually be necessary to perpetuate the system itself over a long period of time. *Sphaeroma* may be causing a necessary oscillation back to old salinity and tidal flushing patterns. He advised using long-term contexts when analysing ecosystems. However, even this will not automatically eliminate the model error unless relevant long-term data are stressed. Enright, an oceanographer, was inclined from his perspective to applaud the return to the marine ecosystem of the shore areas, which he felt had been encroached upon by the terrestrial mangrove system.[3] But he caught the larger error quite nicely. While the authors of the article had described the mangrove system as the 'normal' one, Enright viewed the 'catastrophe' as a normal and completely natural ecological event and saw no justification for fixing any one stage in the adaptive process (any one oscillation) as the preferred, normal one. He advocated ecological non-alignment. In this paper, I will try to draw out some general philosophic implications of these specific examples. For now, let me say that there are some biologists

[1] A. Rhem and H. J. Humm, '*Sphaeroma terebrans*: A Threat to the Mangroves of Southwestern Florida,' *Science*, 182 (1973): 173–4.
[2] Samuel C. Snedaker, 'Mangroves, Isopods, and the Ecosystem', *Science*, 183 (1974): 1036–8.
[3] J. T. Enright, 'Letters', *Science*, 183 (1974): 1038.

who are aware of the model error although they have not described the erroneous model in any but specific terms.

As another observational example, we have the cycle and balanced system holding between the wolf, the moose, and the parasite of both, *Echinococcus granulosus*. The wolf population seems beautifully balanced in terms of the moose population, as one could say of numerous predator-prey relationships. In turn, the parasite also seems to enjoy a balanced harmony with the other components of the system. Any increase in prey population (which could threaten their food supplies) is eventually brought into check by an increase in the predator population, resulting in a decrease in the prey population and in turn a decrease in the predator population. On Isle Royale, in fact, a stasis balance has been maintained for a number of years, perhaps because of its comparative isolation. While at first glance this seems an example of the smoothly working benign balance, a closer analysis illustrates the opposite. The first component ignored in the benign model is oscillation and its costs. When prey increase in number, there is a time-lag before predator control, during which period considerable damage can be done to the system (overgrazing and weakening of moose by undernourishment). Once the predators increase, this balance is restored, but at considerable cost to the predators, who must go through a starvation and culling process as the prey numbers swing back toward the original low figures. At any point in these oscillations, one or the other species has the opportunity for an evolutionary jump or adaptation which could seriously disrupt the stasis. One or both species could become extinct, a possibility that palaeontology demonstrates is a high probability. The predator could expand the system by evolving to a more general predator with many-species prey. The prey could develop sufficient defences to break the system and necessitate new food supplies and territories. The lowly parasite might become deadly enough to wipe out both wolf and moose, or these species might succeed in becoming so resistant that the parasite failed. And somewhere along this escalation, evolution indicates that most systems collapse under the strain.

The forest ecosystem is often used as the prime example for the benign and static model. But that 'stasis' is not static in the sense that we have very few empirical examples of systems in which stasis has not been ultimately (Snedaker's call for the long-range view) impossible to maintain. Palaeobotany indicates that floral succession has been a continuing process, with boreal forests once having existed where there is now grassland and oak forests giving way to boreal forests and eventually to tundra during recurring climatic swings. Nor do we have to reach so far into the past for examples. A look at any western US forest over a long period of time will give us the same results on a modern scale. A single lightning bolt can set into motion processes which destroy the balance in a particular forest ecosystem. Since trees need water, and rainstorms result in light-ning, the forest ecosystem is a subsystem in a much larger system in which lightning is not an unusual event. The resulting fires destroy stasis and bring into play whole successions of systems ranging from the thirty-year aspen grove to the centuries-old sequoia. There is no 'normal' level at which we can stop in this succession, no ecocatastrophe as one homo-eostatic system fails and is replaced by another. Not only does it seem very unlikely that we could successfully prevent stasis from breaking up, but so far there is no indication this would be a valuable goal.

We could point to the chemical warfare escalation between plant and insect systems, with lists of extinct species. Or we could point to the mathematical model results of ecology, specifically the theory of species equilibrium on islands.[4] This model indicates that species equilibrium is characterized by as many species becoming extinct as new species will arrive on an island. Equilibrium, or balance, or stasis is not, therefore, a well-meshed, smoothly-working, serene system but one representing many stasis breakdowns compensated for by new inputs which keep the oscillations within certain critical limits. For example, while the number of bird species on the Channel Islands off California remains about the same as before 1917, from 17 to 62 per cent of the species on a given island have been replaced by new ones. Stable equilibrium, in addition, is defined as equilibrium that can be perturbed but will return, after a period of time, to its former equilibrium.

But a more specific study of homoeostasis deserves an in-depth exam-ination. The formation of red blood cells in dogs (erythropoiesis) demonstrates periodicity, the oscillating nature of the 'steady state', very well. Morley and Stohlman, aware that the pituitary–adrenal axis and the pituitary–gonadal axis (in the female) are sustained oscillations and that on the cellular scale the activities of a number of biochemical intermedi-ates have been shown to oscillate constantly, investigated the canine ery-thropoiesis rhythm and found it also to be a steady state of sustained oscillation, this oscillation being inherent in the nature of the feedback circuit controlling erythropoiesis.[5] One of their conclusions is most relevant to our discussion of the faulty model. They state that, at least for the specific system they investigated, 'steady state' appears to be

[4] Gina Bari Kolata, 'Theoretical Ecology: Beginnings of a Predictive Science', *Science*, 183 (1974): 400–1, 450.

[5] Alec Morley and Frederick Stohlman, Jr., 'Erythropoiesis in the Dog: The Periodic Nature of the Steady State', *Science*, 165 (1969): 1025–7.

a misnomer and might be better replaced with a 'controlled-state' characterization of stasis, but an oscillating one, with possibilities for radical change in the system if these oscillations for some reason became uncontrolled.

To extend this discussion to its most general reaches, we could consider the evolution of non-biotic systems, such as star systems, to possibilities such as white dwarfs or neutron stars, or ultimately to black holes. Or to the destruction of subatomic systems if positive- and negative-matter theory holds. What we finally discover we are discussing, in fact, is entropy. Can systems maintain stasis indefinitely? Is the universe a finely balanced and eternal mechanism? Or must all systems eventually fail at stasis, from social, biological, or physical perspectives? And what value can we place on sustained stasis (no growth) or disorganization and change (growth)?

II

The general implications I wish to draw from the preceding sketchy analysis are the following:

1. Stasis is a process situation or controlled state, not a steady state with implications of immutability and eternality, and the current popular model is a descriptive error.

2. Stasis is maintained through continuous adjustments and re-evaluation in macro and micro interactions, and while abstractly the concept of adjustment does not bring to mind pain or crisis, on a concrete level that is frequently the result.

3. Stasis does not appear to be, for any component of the universe, a very permanent phenomenon.

4. The breakdown of stasis sets processes of change into action by which new (and, from a human perspective, either valuable or non-valuable) stasis systems emerge.

5. It is neither possible nor desirable to attempt to maintain stasis systems at any particular level of development. To achieve this would require maintenance of the universe at that common stasis level to preclude external input which would disrupt the system, a task we are hardly equipped to accomplish and which might involve contradictions. Further, if we were to grant this dubious capability, it would preclude any new development and negate the evolutionary process.

I hope the specific examples I have discussed, ranging from the biological to the physical sciences, will illustrate the error in the popular model of a balanced, steady-state system. It is important that we understand the character of stasis as it exists, and not as our classic philosophic heritage conditions us to expect it. The oscillations in a controlled state are not characterized by harmonious balance or smoothly interlocking structure. Rather, these oscillations are swings (sometimes wild swings) requiring negative feedback to bring them back into control. And this feedback often causes a swing in the opposite direction, again requiring feedback to regain control. The oscillations occur because of the time-lag inherent in a negative-feedback circuit, and since most complex systems contain such circuits, we need to examine just what a balanced, no-growth system could possibly mean for human society. It is not, as I have contended, the perfectly working harmony we would like to think. It is, rather, control of swings or changes for as long as the system can maintain itself. These oscillations can result in significant unpleasantness for us humans, and we must not conclude that in opting for stasis we are achieving any utopian dream. Furthermore, negative feedback must initiate compensatory processes which must succeed in thwarting (or balancing) the direction of a change. When the change is viewed as a social disvalue, this seems not an unsatisfactory trade-off. But what is our judgement when the change seems a social value? And what is our judgement concerning the parameters of this periodicity?

The adjustments I have been discussing translate into the social terms of crisis, dislocation, individual pain and stress, population segment suffering, institutional disorientation, and other associated social traumas. Even in a no-growth, homoeostatic situation, we are not, therefore, in paradise. The only basic difference, in fact, between no-growth stasis and growth situations is that the oscillations are controlled for long periods of time so that no extreme breakout from parameters occurs. The oscillations still involve typical human crises, but no crisis radical enough to result in the disintegration of the system or the rise of new (and perhaps better) ones.

Even so, it is my contention that the long-range view demonstrates that stasis is hardly a permanent state for any subsystem in the universe that we know. While negative entropy can be maintained for some time by open systems, their very openness makes them susceptible to contingencies that result in their eventual disintegration. The open systems are dependent on closed systems in which positive entropy eventually holds, and none of these systems maintain themselves indefinitely. So we are also not buying our salvation when we opt for a no-growth stasis, since even a no-growth stasis will probably not be capable of maintaining itself over the long run. We must be very clear that, on the basis of performance, there is no evidence that homoeostatic systems will operate indefinitely, maintain stasis under all contingencies, and ultimately do not depend on systems which exhibit positive entropy.

It is also important to understand the state of non-stasis before we attempt a value judgement. Under the press of sufficient new or old external factors, homoeostasis fails, but this needs a more concrete statement to help us evaluate the situation. Too often we have in mind the model of a complex, elegant system needlessly disintegrating under external brute force. Instead, let us imagine a homoeostatic system, that of the hominid *Ramapithecus*, functioning in the Siwalik area (pending confirmation of the recent Ethiopian jawbone, *Australopithecus* can no longer be regarded as a *Homo sapiens* ancestor). A no-growth stasis concept would necessitate maintaining this system, which was dealing with input more or less successfully. I say more or less because *Ramapithecus* was not an ideal system as judged by his population levels. Nor, in the light of what we now know about the potential of the human species, was he the complex pinnacle of the evolving hominids. Any major climatic change posed a threat to him, as did any major gain in predator effectiveness. The range of feedback mechanisms, natural and artificial, was limited in comparison to those affecting modern man. From the perspective of *Ramapithecus*, of course, an attempt to maintain stasis was most desirable. But if stasis had been maintained, there would have been to *Homo sapiens*. At many points in this history, steady-state stasis was not maintained and radical adjustments and changes forced new system organization. For some of our family tree, not even controlled-state stasis could be maintained and extinction occurred. The cost of our development has been the loss of many of our relatives. What has been gained is greater complexity and more options for adaptation. We must be very clear, however, concerning the necessity for change and stasis disruption in producing new structuring, new systems, new possibilities. The advantage of such new systems is that they are better able to handle new environmental systems, which brings me to my last contention.

In order to maintain stasis at any point, we have to ensure that no disruptive environmental inputs occur. This requires a twofold defence. We must prevent known environmental factors from occurring which would destroy stasis. But we must also attempt to anticipate new and unique events or new configurations of events which could occur, and we must be able correctly to project their likely effects on our system.

It would be a relatively easy task, if the environment never underwent change. MacArthur and May, for instance, have shown that in an environment which never changes, a community can be at a stable equilibrium.[6] There has been a long philosophic tradition of attempting to characterize change as only an apparent aspect of the universe, the appearance as opposed to the reality of enduring form. While I cannot become involved in that problem here, let me simply state that if change is appearance, what we are discussing here is also in the realm of appearance, which seems to be the only one relevant to the problem. Change is an essential component of our universe and must be dealt with if stasis is to be indefinitely maintained. But as we can see, this would amount to preventing change from occurring in the entire universal system, in order that we might prevent external input from destroying our local stasis system. The task before us would be to maintain the faulty steady-state model (without oscillation or positive entropy) for the entire universe. This is clearly not only beyond our abilities (we would have to master all contingencies), but is an erroneous concept, since it contradicts what we know of the way stasis functions.

Even if we were to grant, for the sake of argument, that the impossible and meaningless is possible, we must also be able to anticipate and prevent new configurations of events. We would have to be so adept at systems management and futurology that we could successfully predict and prevent any new future arrangements which would threaten stasis—an impossible task which even our dubious concept of omniscience could not make meaningful.

I hope to have highlighted some of the implicit conceptual problems behind the growth–no-growth formulation of the situation, because I think these model fallacies and characterization errors have important consequences for the more practical analysis of our modern predicament. It is very important that we make an actual appraisal of the situation not distorted by cultural or social conditioning factors which are not descriptive of the data we must deal with.

III

I would like to make a few brief practical observations based on the preceding philosophic analysis. The first position I would maintain is that growth–no-growth, because it is conceptually and empirically faulty, is not an adequate structuring of our problem. In this, I am in agreement with the conclusion of Ridker's article 'To Grow or Not to Grow: That's Not the

[6] Gina Bari Kolata, 'Theoretical Ecology: Beginnings of a Predictive Science', *Science*, 183 (1974): 400–1, 450.

Relevant Question', and for some of the same reasons.[7] Ridker correctly concludes that not only is growth a situation that must ultimately stop because of the second law of thermodynamics, the positive entropy I mentioned, but that this law also makes it certain that the no-growth, steady-state model also cannot be maintained forever. He does assume that a very low level of activity in balance with the flow of solar energy could go on indefinitely, but given the evolution of stars and the general positive entropy of the universe, we think that too is incorrect. Both growth and no-growth systems will eventually break down. The difference between the two as to *when* is not so easy to determine, and all the variables are not available for a simulation. While growth alternatives do use up energy and material inputs faster than no-growth ones, socioeconomic systems do not disintegrate *only* from lack of resource inputs. In fact, a temporary stasis between resources and use is no guarantee of social stability and long-term survival. Ridker makes a rather good case that both growth and no-growth alternatives could achieve controlled-state stasis between resources and use over a long period of time. But he hints at a much broader problem than 'bread alone'. In general terms, he maintains that we are not only ignorant of the disasters which may result from permitting economic growth to continue, but also of potential technological and institutional breakthroughs which could occur and which could both save future generations from disaster and also make them considerably better off than previous generations. These new factors could not rise in a no-growth society, since it must by definition close off new possibilities.

Ridker is also concerned with the negative effects of growth aside from resource depletion and pollution, effects such as the hecticness of modern life and its superficiality of personal relationships. One could add the pace of change, cultural shock, and cultural lag. These, if Oswald Spengler was right, would be much more important in social disintegration than economic scarcities. However, the reverse side of this coin also needs examination. No growth also has its negative effects, perhaps more destructive. Consider the social stratification which would occur in a no-growth society. Consider the controls and force necessary to prevent or dampen inputs which would threaten the system. These range from Iron Curtains, economic sanctions, educational indoctrination, sanctification of tradition, to the horrors of Inquisitions. Consider the state of knowledge in such a stasis model, remembering that ideas are the most dangerous

---

[7] Ronald G. Ridker, 'To Grow or Not to Grow: That's Not the Relevant Question', *Science*, 182 (1973): 1315–18.

inputs of all. Finally, even granting and ignoring the personal and cultural suffering implied by such necessary controls and negative-feedback mechanisms, let us consider the viability of such a social stasis. Remembering that we cannot control external contingency, that we cannot avoid a changing external environment that impinges on our stasis system, what are the probabilities that such a society could institute new adjustments, create new mechanisms, so that it could maintain stasis in the face of a new perturbation? Lest this pass as a rhetorical question, again consider the history of evolution. The specialized species, dependent on maintaining stasis with a particular highly specific environment, are not the species which, overall, have had the best survival record. It is, rather, the unspecialized systems, capable of adjustments to a changing, generalized environment, that over the long-run have been most successful.

So there are considerable negative features internal to a no-growth society, generalized as a static level of development in all institutions and controls necessary to maintain that level, and a diminished ability to make necessary adjustments to probable new external factors and new inputs. Social systems fall for these reasons more often, perhaps, than they fall for economic reasons such as resource depletion, although this is a question where interpretation renders the data less than conclusive. Even if social stasis were maintained over centuries, its desirability would be seriously questioned from our perspective and, even in the face of indoctrination and careful conditioning, perhaps from the perspective of the members of that society.

IV

Are we led, then, to a neo–social Darwinism? Should we adopt a laissez-faire stance and allow uncontrolled growth regardless of future dislocations? Should we patiently await the decline of the West?

It would be helpful if every individual learned to realize that all stasis systems fail at some point. Then our expectations and conceptual models would not outstrip actuality. But granting that realization, a social system functions not only to attempt to prevent chaos and collapse for as long as possible, but to soften the blow both physically and philosophically. Adjustments to the oscillations of stasis must be made on a cost-benefit basis, seeking trade-offs between continued stability and the limits of the citizen's endurance of discomfort. Most members of a society are willing to sacrifice for the preservation of that society, provided its cultural goals are still viable. But there is a limit to what a society can and should ask of its members. We certainly cannot ask our citizens to return to the agrarian society of the 1700s and 1800s in order to preserve stasis. Our population levels make that an impracticable alternative, if nothing else. Nor can we expect significant segments of our society to become locked into the burden of poverty. Nor should we insist that greatly increased mortality from environmental poisoning is an acceptable adjustment. Some mechanisms of a relatively controlled stasis are obviously called for. We may find that economic institutions must be greatly modified to maintain stasis. We may need additional institutions to dampen the personal suffering of oscillations. But all of this must be done with a view to the entire homoeostatic system and to the overcompensatory nature of many feedback mechanisms. (It is, for example, disastrous to introduce modern medical techniques into a society operating on a high-birth–high-mortality system, unless one also introduces effective birth control.) But we must exercise extreme caution lest our controlled stasis prevent the rise of the very systems necessary to adjust to internal and external perturbations. And we must also develop institutions that could function as the monasteries did in preserving the accumulated experiences of classical civilization, some of which could prove fit for survival in new systems. This has never been consciously undertaken; but it would appear a logical move and would considerably soften any system's collapse, ensuring for one thing that the energy spent in maintaining stasis had not been in vain.

While this paper's emphasis on long-term and non-anthropocentric perspectives may seem extreme, I think it is a necessary manoeuvre to place the human experience in relation to the universal system, as a counterweight to faulty models. Philosophically, we can call for a realistic attitude toward the prospects of immortality for stasis systems. Change and development should be neither defined away as appearance nor relegated to an inferior status in terms of some goal of permanence. It is, I contend, better to develop a stoicism that can accept the fall of a civilization as another experiment in the process of the universe rather than go to the Fall like the average Roman citizen, unaware of the collapse of the Empire or of Alaric marching on the gate.

XIII

PHILOSOPHICAL PROBLEMS FOR ENVIRONMENTALISM

ELLIOTT SOBER

I. INTRODUCTION

A number of philosophers have recognized that the environmental movement, whatever its practical political effectiveness, faces considerable theoretical difficulties in justification.[1] It has been recognized that traditional moral theories do not provide natural underpinnings for policy objectives and this has led some to scepticism about the claims of environmentalists, and others to the view that a revolutionary reassessment of ethical norms is needed. In this chapter, I will try to summarize the difficulties that confront a philosophical defence of environmentalism. I also will suggest a way of making sense of some environmental concerns that does not require the wholesale jettisoning of certain familiar moral judgements.

Preserving an endangered species or ecosystem poses no special conceptual problem when the instrumental value of that species or ecosystem is known. When we have reason to think that some natural object represents a resource to us, we obviously ought to take that fact into account in deciding what to do. A variety of potential uses may be under discussion, including food supply, medical applications, recreational use, and so on. As with any complex decision, it may be difficult even to agree on how to compare the competing values that may be involved. Willingness to pay in dollars is a familiar least common denominator, although it poses a number of problems. But here we have nothing that is specifically a problem for environmentalism.

[1] Mark Sagoff, 'On Preserving the Natural Environment', *Yale Law Review*, 84 (1974): 205–67; J. Baird Callicott in Essay II of this volume; and Bryan Norton, 'Environmental Ethics and Nonhuman Rights', *Environmental Ethics*, 4 (1982): 17–36.

The problem for environmentalism stems from the idea that species and ecosystems ought to be preserved for reasons additional to their known value as resources for human use. The feeling is that even when we cannot say what nutritional, medicinal, or recreational benefit the preservation provides, there still is a value in preservation. It is the search for a rationale for this feeling that constitutes the main conceptual problem for environmentalism.

The problem is especially difficult in view of the holistic (as opposed to individualistic) character of the things being assigned value. Put simply, what is special about environmentalism is that it values the preservation of species, communities, or ecosystems, rather than the individual organisms of which they are composed. 'Animal liberationists' have urged that we should take the suffering of sentient animals into account in ethical deliberation.[2] Such beasts are not mere things to be used as cruelly as we like no matter how trivial the benefit we derive. But in 'widening the ethical circle', we are simply including in the community more individual organisms whose costs and benefits we compare. Animal liberationists are extending an old and familiar ethical doctrine—namely, utilitarianism—to take account of the welfare of other individuals. Although the practical consequences of this point of view may be revolutionary, the theoretical perspective is not at all novel. If suffering is bad, then it is bad for any individual who suffers.[3] Animal liberationists merely remind us of the consequences of familiar principles.[4]

But trees, mountains, and salt-marshes do not suffer. They do not experience pleasure and pain, because, evidently, they do not have experiences at all. The same is true of species. Granted, individual organisms may have mental states; but the species—taken to be a population of organisms connected by certain sorts of interactions (pre-eminently, that of exchanging genetic material in reproduction)—does not. Or put more carefully, we might say that the only sense in which species have experi-

---

[2] Peter Singer, *Animal Liberation* (New York: Random House, 1975), has elaborated a position of this sort.

[3] Occasionally, it has been argued that utilitarianism is not just *insufficient* to justify the principles of environmentalism, but is actually mistaken in holding that pain is intrinsically bad. Callicott writes: 'I herewith declare in all soberness that I see nothing wrong with pain. It is a marvellous method, honed by the evolutionary process, of conveying important organic information. I think it was the late Alan Watts who somewhere remarks that upon being asked if he did not think there was too much pain in the world replied, "No, I think there's just enough"' (Essay II). Setting to one side the remark attributed to Watts, I should point out that pain can be intrinsically bad and still have some good consequences. The point of calling pain intrinsically bad is to say that one essential aspect of experiencing it is negative.

[4] See Sagoff, 'Natural Environment'; Callicott, Essay II; and Norton, 'Ethics and Nonhuman Rights'.

ences is that their member organisms do: the attribution at the population level, if true, is true simply in virtue of its being true at the individual level. Here is a case where reductionism is correct.

So perhaps it is true in this reductive sense that some species experience pain. But the values that environmentalists attach to preserving species do not reduce to any value of preserving organisms. It is in this sense that environmentalists espouse a holistic value system. Environmentalists care about entities that by no stretch of the imagination have experiences (e.g. mountains). What is more, their position does not force them to care if individual organisms suffer pain, so long as the species is preserved. Steel traps may outrage an animal liberationist because of the suffering they inflict, but an environmentalist aiming just at the preservation of a balanced ecosystem might see here no cause for complaint. Similarly, environmentalists think that the distinction between wild and domesticated organisms is important, in that it is the preservation of 'natural' (i.e. not created by the 'artificial interference' of human beings) objects that matters, whereas animal liberationists see the main problem in terms of the suffering of any organism—domesticated or not.[5] And finally, environmentalists and animal liberationists diverge on what might be called the $n + m$ question. If two species—say blue and sperm whales—have roughly comparable capacities for experiencing pain, an animal liberationist might tend to think of the preservation of a sperm whale as wholly on an ethical par with the preservation of a blue whale. The fact that one organism is part of an endangered species while the other is not does not make the rare individual more intrinsically important. But for an environmentalist, this holistic property—membership in an endangered species—makes all the difference in the world: a world with n sperm and m blue whales is far better than a world with $n + m$ sperm and 0 blue whales. Here we have a stark contrast between an ethic in which it is the life situation of individuals that matters, and an ethic in which the stability and diversity of populations of individuals are what matter.[6]

---

[5] See Essay II.

[6] A parallel with a quite different moral problem will perhaps make it clearer how the environmentalist's holism conflicts with some fundamental ethical ideas. When we consider the rights of individuals to receive compensation for harm, we generally expect that the individuals compensated must be one and the same as the individuals harmed. This expectation runs counter to the way an affirmative action programme might be set up, if individuals were to receive compensation simply for being members of groups that have suffered certain kinds of discrimination, whether or not they themselves were victims of discrimination. I do not raise this example to suggest that a holistic conception according to which groups have entitlements is beyond consideration. Rather, my point is to exhibit a case in which a rather common ethical idea is individualistic rather than holistic.

Both animal liberationists and environmentalists wish to broaden our ethical horizons—to make us realize that it is not just human welfare that counts. But they do this in very different, often conflicting, ways. It is no accident that at the level of practical politics the two points of view increasingly find themselves at loggerheads.[7] This practical conflict is the expression of a deep theoretical divide.

II. THE IGNORANCE ARGUMENT

'Although we might not now know what use a particular endangered species might be to us, allowing it to go extinct forever closes off the possibility of discovering and exploiting a future use.' According to this point of view, our ignorance of value is turned into a reason for action. The scenario envisaged in this environmentalist argument is not without precedent; who could have guessed that penicillin would be good for something other than turning out cheese? But there is a fatal defect in such arguments, which we might summarize with the phrase *out of nothing, nothing comes*: rational decisions require assumptions about what is true and what is valuable (in decision-theoretic jargon, the inputs must be probabilities and utilities). If you are completely ignorant of values, then you are incapable of making a rational decision, either for or against preserving some species. The fact that you do not know the value of a species, by itself, cannot count as a reason for wanting one thing rather than another to happen to it.

And there are so many species. How many geese that lay golden eggs are there apt to be in that number? It is hard to assign probabilities and utilities precisely here, but an analogy will perhaps reveal the problem confronting this environmentalist argument. Most of us willingly fly on airplanes, when safer (but less convenient) alternative forms of transportation are available. Is this rational? Suppose it were argued that there is a small probability that the next flight you take will crash. This would be very bad for you. Is it not crazy for you to risk this, given that the only gain to you is that you can reduce your travel time by a few hours (by not going by train, say)? Those of us who not only fly, but congratulate ourselves for being rational in doing so, reject this argument. We are prepared to accept a small chance of a great disaster in return for the high probability of a rather modest benefit. If this is rational, no wonder that we might

[7] Peter Steinhart, 'The Advance of the Ethic', *Audubon*, 82 (Jan. 1980): 126–7.

consistently be willing to allow a species to go extinct in order to build a hydroelectric plant.

That the argument from ignorance is no argument at all can be seen from another angle. If we literally do not know what consequences the extinction of this or that species may bring, then we should take seriously the possibility that the extinction may be beneficial as well as the possibility that it may be deleterious. It may sound deep to insist that we preserve endangered species precisely because we do not know why they are valuable. But ignorance on a scale like this cannot provide the basis for any rational action.

Rather than invoke some unspecified future benefit, an environmentalist may argue that the species in question plays a crucial role in stabilizing the ecosystem of which it is a part. This will undoubtedly be true for carefully chosen species and ecosystems, but one should not generalize this argument into a global claim to the effect that *every* species is crucial to a balanced ecosystem. Although ecologists used to agree that the complexity of an ecosystem stabilizes it, this hypothesis has been subject to a number of criticisms and qualifications, both from a theoretical and an empirical perspective.[8] And for certain kinds of species (those which occupy a rather small area and whose normal population is small) we can argue that extinction would probably not disrupt the community. However fragile the biosphere may be, the extreme view that everything is crucial is almost certainly not true.

But, of course, environmentalists are often concerned by the fact that extinctions are occurring now at a rate much higher than in earlier times. It is mass extinction that threatens the biosphere, they say, and this claim avoids the spurious assertion that communities are so fragile that even one extinction will cause a crash. However, if the point is to avoid a mass extinction of species, how does this provide a rationale for preserving a species of the kind just described, of which we rationally believe that its passing will not destabilize the ecosystem? And, more generally, if mass extinction is known to be a danger to us, how does this translate into a value for preserving any particular species? Notice that we have now passed beyond the confines of the argument from ignorance; we are taking as a premiss the idea that mass extinction would be a catastrophe (since it would destroy the ecosystem on which we depend). But how should that premiss affect our valuing the California condor, the blue whale, or the snail darter?

---

[8] David Ehrenfeld, 'The Conservation of Non-Resources', *American Scientist*, 64 (1976): 648–56. For a theoretical discussion see Robert M. May, *Stability and Complexity in Model Ecosystems* (Princeton: Princeton University Press, 1973).

III. THE SLIPPERY SLOPE ARGUMENT

Environmentalists sometimes find themselves asked to explain why each species matters so much to them, when there are, after all, so many. We may know of special reasons for valuing particular species, but how can we justify thinking that each and every species is important? 'Each extinction impoverishes the biosphere' is often the answer given, but it really fails to resolve the issue. Granted, each extinction impoverishes, but it only impoverishes a little bit. So if it is the *wholesale* impoverishment of the biosphere that matters, one would apparently have to concede that each extinction matters a little, but only a little. But environmentalists may be loathe to concede this, for if they concede that each species matters only a little, they seem to be inviting the wholesale impoverishment that would be an unambiguous disaster.[9] So they dig in their heels and insist that each species matters a lot. But to take this line, one must find some other rationale than the idea that mass extinction would be a great harm. Some of these alternative rationales we will examine later. For now, let us take a closer look at the train of thought involved here.

Slippery slopes are curious things: if you take even one step on to them, you inevitably slide all the way to the bottom. So if you want to avoid finding yourself at the bottom, you must avoid stepping on to them at all. To mix metaphors, stepping on to a slippery slope is to invite being nickelled and dimed to death.

Slippery slope arguments have played a powerful role in a number of recent ethical debates. One often hears people defend the legitimacy of abortions by arguing that since it is permissible to abort a single-celled fertilized egg, it must be permissible to abort a foetus of any age, since there is no place to draw the line from 0 to 9 months. Anti-abortionists, on the other hand, sometimes argue in the other direction: since infanticide of newborns is not permissible, abortion at any earlier time is also not allowed, since there is no place to draw the line. Although these two arguments reach opposite conclusions about the permissibility of abortions, they agree on the following idea: since there is no principled place to draw the line on the continuum from newly fertilized egg to foetus gone to term, one must treat all these cases in the same way. Either abortion is always permitted or it never is, since there is no place to draw the line. Both sides run their favourite slippery slope arguments, but try to precipitate slides in opposite directions.

[9] See Thomas E. Lovejoy, 'Species Leave the Ark One by One', in B. Norton, ed., *The Preservation of Species* (Princeton: Princeton University Press, 1986), 13–27.

Starting with 10 million extant species, and valuing overall diversity, the environmentalist does not want to grant that each species matters only a little. For having granted this, commercial expansion and other causes will reduce the tally to 9,999,999. And then the argument is repeated, with each species valued only a little, and diversity declines another notch. And so we are well on our way to a considerably impoverished biosphere, a little at a time. Better to reject the starting premiss—namely, that each species matters only a little—so that the slippery slope can be avoided.

Slippery slopes should hold no terror for environmentalists, because it is often a mistake to demand that a line be drawn. Let me illustrate by an example. What is the difference between being bald and not? Presumably, the difference concerns the number of hairs you have on your head. But what is the precise number of hairs marking the boundary between baldness and not being bald? There is no such number. Yet, it would be a fallacy to conclude that there is no difference between baldness and hairiness. The fact that you cannot draw a line does not force you to say that the two alleged categories collapse into one. In the abortion case, this means that even if there is no precise point in foetal development that involves some discontinuous, qualitative change, one is still not obliged to think of newly fertilized eggs and foetuses gone to term as morally on a par. Since the biological differences are ones of degree, not kind, one may want to adopt the position that the moral differences are likewise matters of degree. This may lead to the view that a woman should have a better reason for having an abortion, the more developed her foetus is. Of course, this position does not logically follow from the idea that there is no place to draw the line; my point is just that differences in degree do not demolish the possibility of there being real moral differences.

In the environmental case, if one places a value on diversity, then each species becomes more valuable as the overall diversity declines. If we begin with 10 million species, each may matter little, but as extinctions continue, the remaining ones matter more and more. According to this outlook, a better and better reason would be demanded for allowing yet another species to go extinct. Perhaps certain sorts of economic development would justify the extinction of a species at one time. But granting this does not oblige one to conclude that the same sort of decision would have to be made further down the road. This means that one can value diversity without being obliged to take the somewhat exaggerated position that each species, no matter how many there are, is terribly precious in virtue of its contribution to that diversity.

Yet, one can understand that environmentalists might be reluctant to concede this point. They may fear that if one now allows that most species contribute only a little to overall diversity, one will set in motion a political process that cannot correct itself later. The worry is that even when the overall diversity has been drastically reduced, our ecological sensitivities will have been so coarsened that we will no longer be in a position to realize (or to implement policies fostering) the preciousness of what is left. This fear may be quite justified, but it is important to realize that it does not conflict with what was argued above. The political utility of making an argument should not be confused with the argument's soundness.

The fact that you are on a slippery slope, by itself, does not tell you whether you are near the beginning, in the middle, or at the end. If species diversity is a matter of degree, where do we currently find ourselves—on the verge of catastrophe, well on our way in that direction, or at some distance from a global crash? Environmentalists often urge that we are fast approaching a precipice; if we are, then the reduction in diversity that every succeeding extinction engenders should be all we need to justify species preservation.[10]

Sometimes, however, environmentalists advance a kind of argument not predicated on the idea of fast approaching doom. The goal is to show that there is something wrong with allowing a species to go extinct (or with causing it to go extinct), even if overall diversity is not affected much. I now turn to one argument of this kind.

IV. APPEALS TO WHAT IS NATURAL

I noted earlier that environmentalists and animal liberationists disagree over the significance of the distinction between wild and domesticated animals. Since both types of organisms can experience pain, animal liberationists will think of each as meriting ethical consideration. But environmentalists will typically not put wild and domesticated organisms on a par.[11] Environmentalists typically are interested in preserving what is natural, be it a species living in the wild or a wilderness ecosystem. If a kind of domesticated chicken were threatened with extinction, I doubt that environmental groups would be up in arms. And if certain unique types of human environments—say urban slums in the United States—were 'endangered', it is similarly unlikely that environmentalists would view this process as a deplorable impoverishment of the biosphere.

---

[10] See Bryan G. Norton, 'On the Inherent Danger of Undervaluing Species', in Norton, *The Preservation of Species*, 110–37.

[11] See Essay II.

The environmentalist's lack of concern for humanly created organisms and environments may be practical rather than principled. It may be that, at the level of values, no such bifurcation is legitimate, but that, from the point of view of practical political action, it makes sense to put one's energies into saving items that exist in the wild. This subject has not been discussed much in the literature, so it is hard to tell. But I sense that the distinction between wild and domesticated has a certain theoretical importance to many environmentalists. They perhaps think that the difference is that we created domesticated organisms which would otherwise not exist, and so are entitled to use them solely for our own interests. But we did not create wild organisms and environments, so it is the height of presumption to expropriate them for our benefit. A more fitting posture would be one of 'stewardship': we have come on the scene and found a treasure not of our making. Given this, we ought to preserve this treasure in its natural state.

I do not wish to contest the appropriateness of 'stewardship'. It is the dichotomy between artificial (domesticated) and natural (wild) that strikes me as wrong-headed. I want to suggest that to the degree that 'natural' means anything biologically, it means very little ethically. And, conversely, to the degree that 'natural' is understood as a normative concept, it has very little to do with biology.

Environmentalists often express regret that we human beings find it so hard to remember that we are part of nature—one species among many others—rather than something standing outside of nature. I will not consider here whether this attitude is cause for complaint; the important point is that seeing us as part of nature rules out the environmentalist's use of the distinction between artificial–domesticated and natural–wild described above. *If we are part of nature, then everything we do is part of nature, and is natural in that primary sense.*[12] When we domesticate organisms and bring them into a state of dependence on us, this is simply an example of one species exerting a selection pressure on another. If one calls this 'unnatural', one might just as well say the same of parasitism or symbiosis (compare human domestication of animals and plants and 'slave-making' in the social insects).

The concept of naturalness is subject to the same abuses as the concept of normalcy. *Normal* can mean *usual* or it can mean *desirable*. Although

[12] Elliott Sober, 'Evolution, Population Thinking, and Essentialism', *Philosophy of Science*, 47 (1980): 350–83; and John McCloskey, 'Ecological Ethics and Its Justification: A Critical Appraisal', in D. S. Mannison, M. A. McRobbie, and R. Routley, eds., *Environmental Philosophy*, Monograph Series 2 (Philosophy Department, Australian National University, 1980), 65–87.

only the total pessimist will think that the two concepts are mutually exclusive, it is generally recognized that the mere fact that something is common does not by itself count as a reason for thinking that it is desirable. This distinction is quite familiar now in popular discussions of mental health, for example. Yet, when it comes to environmental issues, the concept of naturalness continues to live a double life. The destruction of wilderness areas by increased industrialization is bad because it is unnatural. And it is unnatural because it involves transforming a natural into an artificial habitat. Or one might hear that although extinction is a natural process, the kind of mass extinction currently being precipitated by our species is unprecedented, and so is unnatural. Environmentalists should look elsewhere for a defence of their policies, lest conservation simply become a variant of uncritical conservatism in which the axiom 'Whatever is, is right' is modified to read 'Whatever is (before human beings come on the scene), is right.'

This conflation of the biological with the normative sense of 'natural' sometimes comes to the fore when environmentalists attack animal liberationists for naïve do-goodism. Callicott writes:

... the value commitments of the humane movement seem at bottom to betray a world-denying or rather a life-loathing philosophy. The natural world as actually constituted is one in which one being lives at the expense of others. Each organism, in Darwin's metaphor, struggles to maintain its own organic integrity. ... To live *is* to be anxious about life, to feel pain and pleasure in a fitting mixture, and sooner or later to die. That is the way the system works. *If nature as a whole is good, then pain and death are also good.* Environmental ethics in general require people to play fair in the natural system. The neo-Benthamites have in a sense taken the uncourageous approach. People have attempted to exempt themselves from the life/death reciprocities of natural processes and from ecological limitations in the name of a prophylactic ethic of maximizing rewards (pleasure) and minimizing unwelcome information (pain). To be fair, the humane moralists seem to suggest that we should attempt to project the same values into the non-human animal world and to widen the charmed circle—no matter that it would be biologically unrealistic to do so or biologically ruinous if, per impossible, such an environmental ethic were implemented.

There is another approach. Rather than imposing our alienation from nature and natural processes and cycles of life on other animals, we human beings could reaffirm our participation in nature by accepting life as it is given without a sugar coating.[13]

In n. 45 Callicott quotes with approval Shepard's remark that 'the humanitarian's projection onto nature of illegal murder and the rights of civilized people to safety not only misses the point but is exactly contrary

[13] See Essay II (my emphasis).

to fundamental ecological reality: the structure of nature is a sequence of killings.'[14]

Thinking that what is found in nature is beyond ethical defect has not always been popular. Darwin wrote:

... That there is much suffering in the world no one disputes. Some have attempted to explain this in reference to man by imagining that it serves for his moral improvement. But the number of men in the world is as nothing compared with that of all other sentient beings, and these often suffer greatly without any moral improvement. A being so powerful and so full of knowledge as a God who could create the universe, is to our finite minds omnipotent and omniscient, and it revolts our understanding to suppose that his benevolence is not unbounded, for what advantage can there be in the sufferings of millions of the lower animals throughout almost endless time? This very old argument from the existence of suffering against the existence of an intelligent first cause seems to me a strong one; whereas, as just remarked, the presence of much suffering agrees well with the view that all organic beings have been developed through variation and natural selection.[15]

Darwin apparently viewed the quantity of pain found in nature as a melancholy and sobering consequence of the struggle for existence. But once we adopt the Panglossian attitude that this is the best of all possible worlds ('there is just the right amount of pain,' etc.), a failure to identify what is natural with what is good can only seem 'world-denying', 'life-loathing', 'in a sense uncourageous', and 'contrary to fundamental ecological reality'.[16]

Earlier in his essay, Callicott expresses distress that animal liberationists fail to draw a sharp distinction 'between the very different plights (and rights) of wild and domestic animals'.[17] Domestic animals are creations of man, he says. 'They are living artefacts, but artefacts nevertheless ... There is thus something profoundly incoherent (and insensitive as well) in the complaint of some animal liberationists that the "natural behaviour" of chickens and bobby calves is cruelly frustrated on factory farms. It would make almost as much sense to speak of the natural behaviour of tables and chairs.'[18] Here again we see teleology playing a decisive role: wild organisms do not have the natural function of serving human ends, but

---

[14] Paul Shepard, 'Animal Rights and Human Rites', *North American Review* (Winter 1974): 35–41.

[15] Charles Darwin, *The Autobiography of Charles Darwin* (London: Collins, 1876, 1958), 90.

[16] The idea that the natural world is perfect, besides being suspect as an ethical principle, is also controversial as biology. In spite of Callicott's confidence that the amount of pain found in nature is biologically optimal (see n. 3), this adaptationist outlook is now much debated. See e.g. Richard Lewontin and Stephen Jay Gould, 'The Spandrels of San Marco and the Panglossian Paradigm: A Critique of the Adaptationist Programme', *Proceedings of the Royal Society of London*, 205 (1979): 581–98; and John Maynard Smith, 'Optimization Theory in Evolution', *Annual Review of Ecology and Systematics*, 9 (1978): 31–56. Both are reprinted in E. Sober, ed., *Conceptual Issues in Evolutionary Biology* (Cambridge, Mass.: MIT Press, 1984).

[17] See Essay II.   [18] Ibid.

domesticated animals do. Cheetahs in zoos are crimes against what is natural; veal calves in boxes are not.

The idea of 'natural tendency' played a decisive role in pre-Darwinian biological thinking. Aristotle's entire science—both his physics and his biology—is articulated in terms of specifying the natural tendencies of kinds of objects and the interfering forces that can prevent an object from achieving its intended state.[19] Heavy objects in the sublunar sphere have location at the centre of the earth as their natural state; each tends to go there, but is prevented from doing so.[20] Organisms likewise are conceptualized in terms of this natural state model: '[for] any living thing that has reached its normal development and which is unmutilated, and whose mode of generation is not spontaneous, the most natural act is the production of another like itself, an animal producing an animal, a plant a plant . . .'[21]

But many interfering forces are possible, and in fact the occurrence of 'monsters' is anything but uncommon. According to Aristotle, mules (sterile hybrids) count as deviations from the natural state. In fact, females are monsters as well, since the natural tendency of sexual reproduction is for the offspring to perfectly resemble the father, who, according to Aristotle, provides the 'genetic instructions' (to put the idea anachronistically) while the female provides only the matter.[22]

What has happened to the natural state model in modern science? In physics, the idea of describing what a class of objects will do in the absence of 'interference' lives on: Newton specified this 'zero-force state' as rest or uniform motion, and, in general relativity, this state is understood in terms of motion along geodesics. But one of the most profound achievements of Darwinian biology has been the jettisoning of this kind of model.[23] It isn't just that Aristotle was wrong in his detailed claims about mules and women; the whole structure of the natural state model has been discarded. Population biology is not conceptualized in terms of positing

[19] Sober, 'Evolution, Population Thinking, and Essentialism', 360–5.

[20] G. E. R. Lloyd, *Aristotle: The Growth and Structure of His Thought* (Cambridge: Cambridge University Press, 1968), 162.

[21] Aristotle, *De Anima*, 415ª26.

[22] See Sober, 'Evolution, Population Thinking, and Essentialism', 360–5. See also Elliott Sober, *The Nature of Selection* (Cambridge, Mass.: MIT Press, 1984) for further discussion.

[23] Ernst Mayr, 'Typological versus Population Thinking', in Ernst Mayr, ed., *Evolution and Diversity of Life* (Cambridge, Mass.: Harvard University Press, 1976), 26–9, reprinted in Sober, ed., *Conceptual Issues in Evolutionary Biology*; Richard Lewontin, 'Biological Determinism as a Social Weapon', in *Ann Arbor Science for the People Editorial Collection: Biology as a Social Weapon* (Minneapolis: Burgess Publishing Company, 1977), 6–20; Sober, 'Evolution, Population Thinking, and Essentialism', 372–9; and Elliott Sober, 'Darwin's Evolutionary Concepts: A Philosophical Perspective', in David Kohn, ed., *The Darwinian Heritage* (Princeton: Princeton University Press, 1986).

some characteristic that all members of a species would have in common, were interfering forces absent. Variation is not thought of as a deflection from the natural state of uniformity. Rather, variation is taken to be a fundamental property in its own right. Nor, at the level of individual biology, does the natural state model find an application. Developmental theory is not articulated by specifying a natural tendency and a set of interfering forces. The main conceptual tool for describing the various developmental pathways open to a genotype is the norm of reaction.[24] The norm of reaction of a genotype within a range of environments will describe what phenotype the genotype will produce in a given environment. Thus, the norm of reaction for a corn plant genotype might describe how its height is influenced by the amount of moisture in the soil. The norm of reaction is entirely silent on which phenotype is the 'natural' one. The idea that a corn plant might have some 'natural height', which can be augmented or diminished by 'interfering forces' is entirely alien to post-Darwinian biology.

The fact that the concepts of natural state and interfering force have lapsed from biological thought does not prevent environmentalists from inventing them anew. Perhaps these concepts can be provided with some sort of normative content; after all, the normative idea of 'human rights' may make sense even if it is not a theoretical underpinning of any empirical science. But environmentalists should not assume that they can rely on some previously articulated scientific conception of 'natural'.

V. APPEALS TO NEEDS AND INTERESTS

The version of utilitarianism considered earlier (according to which something merits ethical consideration if it can experience pleasure and/or pain) leaves the environmentalist in the lurch. But there is an alternative to Bentham's hedonistic utilitarianism that has been thought by some to be a foundation for environmentalism. Preference utilitarianism says that an object's having interests, needs, or preferences gives it ethical status. This doctrine is at the core of Stone's affirmative answer to the title question of his book *Should Trees Have Standing?*[25] 'Natural objects *can* communicate their wants (needs) to us, and in ways that are not terribly ambiguous ... The lawn tells me that it wants water by a certain dryness of the blades

---

[24] Lewontin, 'Biological Determinism', 10.
[25] Christopher Stone, *Should Trees Have Standing?* (Los Altos, Calif.: William Kaufmann, 1972), 24.

and soil—immediately obvious to the touch—the appearance of bald spots, yellowing, and a lack of springiness after being walked on.' And if plants can do this, presumably so can mountain ranges, and endangered species. Preference utilitarianism may thereby seem to grant intrinsic ethical importance to precisely the sorts of objects about which environmentalists have expressed concern.

The problems with this perspective have been detailed by Sagoff.[26] If one does not require of an object that it have a mind for it to have wants or needs, what *is* required for the possession of these ethically relevant properties? Suppose one says that an object needs something if the object will cease to exist if it does not get it. Then species, plants, and mountain ranges have needs, but only in the sense that automobiles, garbage dumps, and buildings do too. If everything has needs, the advice to take needs into account in ethical deliberation is empty, unless it is supplemented by some technique for weighting and comparing the needs of different objects. A corporation will go bankrupt unless a highway is built. But the swamp will cease to exist if the highway is built. Perhaps one should take into account all relevant needs, but the question is how to do this in the event that needs conflict.

Although the concept of need can be provided with a permissive, all-inclusive definition, it is less easy to see how to do this with the concept of want. Why think that a mountain range 'wants' to retain its unspoiled appearance, rather than house a new amusement park?[27] Needs are not at issue here, since in either case, the mountain continues to exist. One might be tempted to think that natural objects like mountains and species have 'natural tendencies', and that the concept of want should be liberalized so as to mean that natural objects 'want' to persist in their natural states. This Aristotelian view, as I argued in the previous section, simply makes no sense.[28] Granted, a commercially undeveloped mountain will persist in this state, unless it is commercially developed. But it is equally true that a commercially untouched hill will become commercially developed, unless something causes this not to happen. I see no hope for extending the concept of wants to the full range of objects valued by environmentalists.

The same problems emerge when we try to apply the concepts of needs and wants to species. A species may need various resources, in the sense that these are necessary for its continued existence. But what do species want? Do they want to remain stable in numbers, neither growing nor shrinking? Or since most species have gone extinct, perhaps what species

---

[26] Sagoff, 'Natural Environment', 220–4.   [27] The example is Sagoff's, ibid.
[28] I argue this view in more detail in 'Evolution, Population Thinking, and Essentialism', 360–79.

really want is to go extinct, and it is human meddlesomeness that frustrates this natural tendency? Preference utilitarianism is no more likely than hedonistic utilitarianism to secure autonomous ethical status for endangered species.

Ehrenfeld describes a related distortion that has been inflicted on the diversity–stability hypothesis in theoretical ecology.[29] If it were true that increasing the diversity of an ecosystem causes it to be more stable, this might encourage the Aristotelian idea that ecosystems have a natural tendency to increase their diversity. The full realization of this tendency— the natural state that is the goal of ecosystems—is the 'climax' or 'mature' community. Extinction diminishes diversity, so it frustrates ecosystems from attaining their goal. Since the hypothesis that diversity causes stability is now considered controversial (to say the least), this line of thinking will not be very tempting. But even if the diversity–stability hypothesis were true, it would not permit the environmentalist to conclude that ecosystems have an interest in retaining their diversity.

Darwinism has not banished the idea that parts of the natural world are goal-directed systems, but has furnished this idea with a natural mechanism. We properly conceive of organisms (or genes, sometimes) as being in the business of maximizing their chances of survival and reproduction. We describe characteristics as adaptations—as devices that exist for the furtherance of these ends. Natural selection makes this perspective intelligible. But Darwinism is a profoundly individualistic doctrine.[30] Darwinism rejects the idea that species, communities, and ecosystems have adaptations that exist for their own benefit. These higher-level entities are not conceptualized as goal-directed systems; what properties of organization they possess are viewed as artefacts of processes operating at lower levels of organization. An environmentalism based on the idea that the ecosystem is directed toward stability and diversity must find its foundation elsewhere.

VI. GRANTING WHOLES AUTONOMOUS VALUE

A number of environmentalists have asserted that environmental values cannot be grounded in values based on regard for individual welfare. Aldo Leopold wrote in *A Sand County Almanac* that 'a thing is right when it

[29] Ehrenfeld, 'The Conservation of Non-Resources', 651–2.
[30] George C. Williams, *Adaptation and Natural Selection* (Princeton: Princeton University Press, 1966); and Sober, *The Nature of Selection*.

tends to preserve the integrity, stability, and beauty of the biotic community. It is wrong when it tends otherwise.'[31] Callicott develops this idea at some length, and ascribes to ethical environmentalism the view that 'the preciousness of individual deer, *as of any other specimen*, is inversely proportional to the population of the species.'[32] In his *Desert Solitaire*, Edward Abbey notes that he would sooner shoot a man than a snake.[33] And Garrett Hardin asserts that human beings injured in wilderness areas ought not to be rescued: making great and spectacular efforts to save the life of an individual 'makes sense only when there is a shortage of people. I have not lately heard that there is a shortage of people.'[34] The point of view suggested by these quotations is quite clear. It isn't that preserving the integrity of ecosystems has autonomous value, to be taken into account just as the quite distinct value of individual human welfare is. Rather, the idea is that the only value is the holistic one of maintaining ecological balance and diversity. Here we have a view that is just as monolithic as the most single-minded individualism; the difference is that the unit of value is thought to exist at a higher level of organization.

It is hard to know what to say to someone who would save a mosquito, just because it is rare, rather than a human being, if there were a choice. In ethics, as in any other subject, rationally persuading another person requires the existence of shared assumptions. If this monolithic environmentalist view is based on the notion that ecosystems have needs and interests, and that these take total precedence over the rights and interests of individual human beings, then the discussion of the previous sections is relevant. And even supposing that these higher-level entities have needs and wants, what reason is there to suppose that these matter and that the wants and needs of individuals matter not at all? But if this source of defence is jettisoned, and it is merely asserted that only ecosystems have value, with no substantive defence being offered, one must begin by requesting an argument: *why* is ecosystem stability and diversity the only value?

Some environmentalists have seen the individualist bias of utilitarianism as being harmful in ways additional to its impact on our perception of ecological values. Thus, Callicott writes:

On the level of social organization, the interests of society may not always coincide with the sum of the interests of its parts. Discipline, sacrifice, and individual restraint

---

[31] Aldo Leopold, *A Sand County Almanac* (New York: Oxford University Press, 1949), 224–5.

[32] Essay II (emphasis mine).

[33] Edward Abbey, *Desert Solitaire* (New York: Ballantine Books, 1968), 20.

[34] Garrett Hardin, 'The Economics of Wilderness', *Natural History*, 78 (1969): 176.

are often necessary in the social sphere to maintain social integrity as within the bodily organism. A society, indeed, is particularly vulnerable to disintegration when its members become preoccupied totally with their own particular interest, and ignore those distinct and independent interests of the community as a whole. One example, unfortunately our own society, is altogether too close at hand to be examined with strict academic detachment. The United States seems to pursue uncritically a social policy of reductive utilitarianism, aimed at promoting the happiness of all its members severally. Each special interest accordingly clamours more loudly to be satisfied while the community as a whole becomes noticeably more and more infirm economically, environmentally, and politically.[35]

Callicott apparently sees the emergence of individualism and alienation from nature as two aspects of the same process. He values 'the symbiotic relationship of Stone Age man to the natural environment' and regrets that 'civilization has insulated and alienated us from the rigours and challenges of the natural environment. The hidden agenda of the humane ethic', he says, 'is the imposition of the anti-natural prophylactic ethos of comfort and soft pleasure on an ever wider scale. The land ethic, on the other hand, requires a shrinkage, if at all possible, of the domestic sphere; it rejoices in a recrudescence of the wilderness and a renaissance of tribal cultural experience.'[36]

Callicott is right that 'strict academic detachment' is difficult here. The reader will have to decide whether the United States currently suffers from too much or too little regard 'for the happiness of all its members severally' and whether we should feel nostalgia or pity in contemplating what the Stone Age experience of nature was like.

VII. THE DEMARCATION PROBLEM

Perhaps the most fundamental theoretical problem confronting an environmentalist who wishes to claim that species and ecosystems have autonomous value is what I will call the *problem of demarcation*. Every ethical theory must provide principles that describe which objects matter for their own sakes and which do not. Besides marking the boundary between these two classes by enumerating a set of ethically relevant properties, an ethical theory must say why the properties named, rather than others, are the ones that count. Thus, for example, hedonistic utilitarianism cites the capacity to experience pleasure and/or pain as the decisive criterion; preference utilitarianism cites the having of preferences (or wants, or interests) as the decisive property. And a Kantian ethical

---

[35] Essay II.   [36] Ibid.

theory will include an individual in the ethical community only if it is capable of rational reflection and autonomy.[37] Not that justifying these various proposed solutions to the demarcation problem is easy; indeed, since this issue is so fundamental, it will be very difficult to justify one proposal as opposed to another. Still, a substantive ethical theory is obliged to try.

Environmentalists, wishing to avoid the allegedly distorting perspective of individualism, frequently want to claim autonomous value for wholes. This may take the form of a monolithic doctrine according to which the only thing that matters is the stability of the ecosystem. Or it may embody a pluralistic outlook according to which ecosystem stability and species preservation have an importance additional to the welfare of individual organisms. But an environmentalist theory shares with all ethical theories an interest in not saying that everything has autonomous value. The reason this position is proscribed is that it makes the adjudication of ethical conflict very difficult indeed. (In addition, it is radically implausible, but we can set that objection to one side.)

Environmentalists, as we have seen, may think of natural objects, like mountains, species, and ecosystems, as mattering for their own sake, but of artificial objects, like highway systems and domesticated animals, as having only instrumental value. If a mountain and a highway are both made of rock, it seems unlikely that the difference between them arises from the fact that mountains have wants, interests, and preferences, but highway systems do not. But perhaps the place to look for the relevant difference is not in their present physical composition, but in the historical fact of how each came into existence. Mountains were created by natural processes, whereas highways are humanly constructed. But once we realize that organisms construct their environments in nature, this contrast begins to cloud.[38] Organisms do not passively reside in an environment whose properties are independently determined. Organisms transform their environments by physically interacting with them. An ant-hill is an artefact just as a highway is. Granted, a difference obtains at the level of whether conscious deliberation played a role, but can one take seriously the view that artefacts produced by conscious planning are thereby *less* valuable than ones that arise without the intervention of mentality?[39] As we have noted before, although environmentalists often accuse their critics of

[37] John Rawls, *A Theory of Justice* (Cambridge, Mass.: Harvard University Press, 1971).

[38] Richard Levins and Richard Lewontin, 'Dialectic and Reductionism in Ecology', *Synthèse*, 43 (1980): 47–78.

[39] Here we would have an inversion, not just a rejection, of a familiar Marxian doctrine—the labour theory of value.

failing to think in a biologically realistic way, their use of the distinction between 'natural' and 'artificial' is just the sort of idea that stands in need of a more realistic biological perspective.

My suspicion is that the distinction between natural and artificial is not the crucial one. On the contrary, certain features of environmental concerns imply that natural objects are exactly on a par with certain artificial ones. Here the intended comparison is not between mountains and highways, but between mountains and works of art. My goal in what follows is not to sketch a substantive conception of what determines the value of objects in these two domains, but to motivate an analogy.

For both natural objects and works of art, our values extend beyond the concerns we have for experiencing pleasure. Most of us value seeing an original painting more than we value seeing a copy, even when we could not tell the difference. When we experience works of art, often what we value is not just the kinds of experiences we have, but, in addition, the connections we usually have with certain real objects. Routley and Routley have made an analogous point about valuing the wilderness experience: a 'wilderness experience machine' that caused certain sorts of hallucinations would be no substitute for actually going into the wild.[40] Nor is this fact about our valuation limited to such aesthetic and environmentalist contexts. We love various people in our lives. If a molecule-for-molecule replica of a beloved person were created, you would not love that individual, but would continue to love the individual to whom you actually were historically related.[41] Here again, our attachments are to objects and people as they really are, and not just to the experiences that they facilitate.

Another parallel between environmentalist concerns and aesthetic values concerns the issue of context. Although environmentalists often stress the importance of preserving endangered species, they would not be completely satisfied if an endangered species were preserved by putting a number of specimens in a zoo or in a humanly constructed preserve. What is taken to be important is preserving the species in its natural habitat. This leads to the more holistic position that preserving ecosystems, and not simply preserving certain member species, is of primary importance. Aesthetic concerns often lead in the same direction. It was not merely saving a fresco or an altarpiece that motivated art historians after the most recent flood in Florence. Rather, they wanted to save these works of art

[40] Essay VI.
[41] Mark Sagoff, 'On Restoring and Reproducing Art', *Journal of Philosophy*, 75 (1978): 453–70.

in their original ('natural') settings. Not just the painting, but the church that housed it; not just the church, but the city itself. The idea of objects residing in a 'fitting' environment plays a powerful role in both domains.

Environmentalism and aesthetics both see value in rarity. Of two whales, why should one be more worthy of aid than another, just because one belongs to an endangered species? Here we have the $n + m$ question mentioned in Section I. As an ethical concern, rarity is difficult to understand. Perhaps this is because our ethical ideas concerning justice and equity (note the word) are saturated with individualism. But in the context of aesthetics, the concept of rarity is far from alien. A work of art may have enhanced value simply because there are very few other works by the same artist, or from the same historical period, or in the same style. It isn't that the price of the item may go up with rarity; I am talking about aesthetic value, not monetary worth. Viewed as valuable aesthetic objects, rare organisms may be valuable because they are rare.

A disanalogy may suggest itself. It may be objected that works of art are of instrumental value only, but that species and ecosystems have intrinsic value. Perhaps it is true, as claimed before, that our attachment to works of art, to nature, and to our loved ones extends beyond the experiences they allow us to have. But it may be argued that what is valuable in the aesthetic case is always the relation of a valuer to a valued object.[42] When we experience a work of art, the value is not simply in the experience, but in the composite fact that we and the work of art are related in certain ways. This immediately suggests that if there were no valuers in the world, nothing would have value, since such relational facts could no longer obtain. So, to adapt Routley and Routley's 'last man argument', it would seem that if an ecological crisis precipitated a collapse of the world system, the last human being (whom we may assume for the purposes of this example to be the last valuer) could set about destroying all works of art, and there would be nothing wrong in this.[43] That is, if aesthetic objects are valuable only in so far as valuers can stand in certain relations to them, then when valuers disappear, so does the possibility of aesthetic value. This would deny, in one sense, that aesthetic objects are intrinsically valuable: it isn't they, in themselves, but rather the relational facts that they are part of, that are valuable.

In contrast, it has been claimed that the 'last man' would be wrong to destroy natural objects such as mountains, salt-marshes, and species.[44] (So

---

[42] Donald H. Regan, 'Duties of Preservation', in Norton, *The Preservation of Species*, 195–222.

[43] Essay VI.   [44] Ibid.

as to avoid confusing the issue by bringing in the welfare of individual organisms, Routley and Routley imagine that destruction and mass extinctions can be caused painlessly, so that there would be nothing wrong about this undertaking from the point of view of the non-human organisms involved.) If the last man ought to preserve these natural objects, then these objects appear to have a kind of autonomous value; their value would extend beyond their possible relations to valuers. If all this were true, we would have here a contrast between aesthetic and natural objects, one that implies that natural objects are more valuable than works of art.

Routley and Routley advance the last man argument as if it were decisive in showing that environmental objects such as mountains and saltmarshes have autonomous value. I find the example more puzzling than decisive. But, in the present context, we do not have to decide whether Routley and Routley are right. We only have to decide whether this imagined situation brings out any relevant difference between aesthetic and environmental values. Were the last man to look up on a certain hillside, he would see a striking rock formation next to the ruins of a Greek temple. Long ago the temple was built from some of the very rocks that still stud the slope. Both promontory and temple have a history, and both have been transformed by the biotic and the abiotic environments. I myself find it impossible to advise the last man that the peak matters more than the temple. I do not see a relevant difference. Environmentalists, if they hold that the solution to the problem of demarcation is to be found in the distinction between natural and artificial, will have to find such a distinction. But if environmental values are aesthetic, no difference need be discovered.

Environmentalists may be reluctant to classify their concern as aesthetic. Perhaps they will feel that aesthetic concerns are frivolous. Perhaps they will feel that the aesthetic regard for artefacts that has been made possible by culture is antithetical to a proper regard for wilderness. But such contrasts are illusory. Concern for environmental values does not require a stripping away of the perspective afforded by civilization; to value the wild, one does not have to 'become wild' oneself (whatever that may mean). Rather, it is the material comforts of civilization that make possible a serious concern for both aesthetic and environmental values. These are concerns that can become pressing in developed nations in part because the populations of those countries now enjoy a certain substantial level of prosperity. It would be the height of condescension to expect a nation experiencing hunger and chronic disease to be inordinately concerned with the autonomous value of ecosystems or with creating and preserving works of art. Such values are not frivolous, but they can become important to us only after certain fundamental human needs are satisfied. Instead of radically jettisoning individualist ethics, environmentalists may find a more hospitable home for their values in a category of value that has existed all along.[45]

[45] I am grateful to Donald Crawford, Jon Moline, Bryan Norton, Robert Stauffer, and Daniel Wikler for useful discussion. I also wish to thank the National Science Foundation and the Graduate School of the University of Wisconsin-Madison for financial support.

NOTES ON THE CONTRIBUTORS

Andrew Brennan is Professor of Philosophy, University of Western Australia. He is the author of *Conditions of Identity* (1988) and *Thinking About Nature* (1988).

J. Baird Callicott is Professor of Philosophy, University of Wisconsin at Stevens Point. He is the author of *In Defence of the Land Ethic* (1989).

Colleen D. Clements is Professor of Psychiatry at the University of Rochester. She has published a number of papers on the ethics of suicide as well as on environmental philosophy.

Robert Elliot is Senior Lecturer in Philosophy, University of New England. He has published a number of papers in environmental philosophy.

Freya Mathews is Lecturer in Philosophy, La Trobe University. She is the author of *The Ecological Self* (1991).

Mary Midgley was formerly Senior Lecturer in Philosophy, University of Newcastle upon Tyne. Her books include *Beast and Man* (1978), *Why Animals Matter* (1983), and *Wickedness* (1984).

John Passmore is Emeritus Professor of Philosophy and Visiting Fellow in Historical Studies, Research School of Social Sciences, Australian National University. His books include *Man's Responsibility for Nature* (1974), *Philosophical Reasoning* (1970), and *One Hundred Years of Philosophy* (1966).

Val Plumwood is a Lecturer in Philosophy, University of Tasmania, Launceston. She is the author of *Feminism and the Mastery of Nature* (1993).

Holmes Rolston III is University Distinguished Professor of Philosophy, Colorado State University, Fort Collins. His books include *Philosophy Gone Wild* (1986), *Environmental Ethics* (1988), and *Conserving Natural Value* (1994).

Richard Routley (now Sylvan) is a Director of the Eco-Logical Organization and Senior Fellow, Division of Philosophy and Law, Research School of Social Sciences, Australian National University. His books include *Exploring Meinong's Jungle* (1980) and *Deep Pluralism* (1994).

Val Routley (now Plumwood) see above.

Mark Sagoff is Director of the Institute for Philosophy and Public Policy at the School of Public Affairs, University of Maryland, College Park. He is the author of *The Economy of the Earth* (1988).

Elliott Sober is Professor of Philosophy, University of Wisconsin, Madison. His books include *The Nature of Selection* (1984), *Reconstructing the Past* (1991), and *From a Biological Point of View* (1994).

Mary B. Williams is Associate Professor of Philosophy, and of Life and Health Sciences, Center for Science and Culture, University of Delaware. She has published a number of papers in philosophy of biology and is a co-editor of *Computers, Ethics and Society* (1990).

FURTHER READING

I. General

Attfield, Robin, *The Ethics of Environmental Concern* (Athens: University of Georgia Press, 2nd edn., 1991).

Blackstone, William T. (ed.), *Philosophy and Environmental Crisis* (Athens: University of Georgia Press, 1974).

Callicott, J. Baird, *In Defense of the Land Ethic: Essays In Environmental Philosophy* (Albany: State University of New York Press, 1989).

Elliot, Robert and Gare, Arran (eds.), *Environmental Philosophy: A Collection of Readings* (St Lucia: University of Queensland Press, 1983).

Environmental Ethics

Environmental Values

Goodpaster, K. E. and Sayre, K. M. (eds.), *Ethics and Problems of the 21st Century* (Notre Dame and London: Notre Dame University Press, 1979).

Hargrove, Eugene C., *Foundations of Environmental Ethics* (Englewood Cliffs: Prentice-Hall, 1989).

Jamieson, Dale and Gruen, Lori (eds.), *Thinking of Nature: Readings in Environmental Philosophy* (New York: Oxford University Press, 1994).

Mannison, D.; McRobbie, M.; and Routley, R. (eds.), *Environmental Philosophy* (Canberra: Research School of Social Sciences, Australian National University, 1980).

Naess, Arne, 'The Shallow and the Deep, Long-Range Ecology Movements: A Summary', *Inquiry*, 16 (1973), 95–100.

Norton, Bryan G., *Toward Unity Among Environmentalists* (New York: Oxford University Press, 1991).

Passmore, John, *Man's Responsibility for Nature* (London: Duckworth, 1974, 2nd edn., 1980).

Regan, Tom (ed.), *Earthbound: New Introductory Essays in Environmental Ethics* (Philadelphia: Temple University Press, 1984).

Scherer, Donald (ed.), *Upstream/Downstream: Issues in Environmental Ethics* (Englewood Cliffs, NJ: Prentice-Hall, 1990).

Scherer, Donald and Attig, Thomas (eds.), *Ethics and the Environment* (Englewood Cliffs, NJ: Prentice-Hall, 1983).

VanDeVeer, Donald and Pierce, Christine (eds.), *The Environmental Ethics and Policy Book: Philosophy, Ecology, Economics* (Belmont, Calif.: Wadsworth, 1994).

Zimmerman, Michael; Callicott, J. Baird; Sessions, George; Warren, Karen J., and Clark, John P. (eds.), *Environmental Philosophy: From Animal Rights to Radical Ecology* (Englewood Cliffs, NJ: Prentice-Hall, 1993).

II. Obligations to Future People

Barry, Brian and Sikora, R. I. (eds.), *Obligations to Future Generations* (Philadelphia: Temple University Press, 1978).

Elliot, Robert, 'The Rights of Future People', *Journal of Applied Philosophy*, 6 (1989), 159–70.

Gunn, Alastair S., 'Why Should We Care About Rare Species?', *Environmental Ethics*, 2 (1980), 17–37.

—— 'The Restoration of Species and Natural Environments', *Environmental Ethics*, 15 (1993), 291–310.

Laslett, Peter and Fishkin, James (eds.), *Philosophy, Politics and Society* (New Haven: Yale University Press, 1979).

McMahan, Jefferson, 'Problems of Population Theory', *Ethics*, 92 (1981–2), 96–127.

Partridge, Ernest (ed.), *Responsibilities to Future Generations* (New York: Prometheus Books, 1981).

Routley, Richard and Routley, Val, 'Nuclear Energy and Obligations to the Future', *Inquiry*, 21 (1978), 133-79.

Sylvan, Richard, *Universal Purpose, Terrestrial Greenhouse and Biological Evolution* (Canberra, Division of Philosophy and Law, Research School of Social Sciences, Australian National University, 1990).

III. *The Value of Nature*

Brennan, Andrew, 'The Moral Standing of Natural Objects', *Environmental Ethics*, 6 (1984), 35–56.

—— *Thinking About Nature: An Investigation of Nature, Value and Ecology* (London: Routledge, 1988).

Callicott, J. Baird (ed.), *Companion to a Sand County Almanac: Interpretive and Critical Essays* (Madison: University of Wisconsin Press, 1987).

Carlson, Allen, 'Nature and Positive Aesthetics', *Environmental Ethics*, 6 (1984), 5–34.

Clark, Stephen R. L., 'The Rights of Wild Things', *Inquiry*, 22 (1979), 171–87.

Elliot, Robert, 'Intrinsic Value, Environmental Obligation and Naturalness', *Monist*, 75 (1992), 138–60.

Elliot, Robert, 'Environmental Degradation, Vandalism and the Aesthetic Object Argument', *Australasian Journal of Philosophy*, 67 (1989), 191–204.

Hill, Thomas Jr., 'Ideals of Human Excellence and Preserving Natural Environments', *Environmental Ethics*, 5 (1983), 211-24.

Miller, Peter, 'Value as Richness', *Environmental Ethics*, 4 (1982), 100–14.

Norton, Bryan (ed.), *The Preservation of Species: The Value of Biological Diversity* (Princeton: Princeton University Press, 1986).

Regan, Tom, 'The Nature and Possibility of an Environmental Ethic', *Environmental Ethics*, 3 (1981), 19–34.

Rolston, Holmes III, *Philosophy Gone Wild: Essays in Environmental Ethics* (Buffalo: Prometheus Books, 1986).

—— *Environmental Ethics: Duties to and Values in the Natural World* (Philadelphia: Temple University Press, 1988).

Sagoff, Mark, 'On Preserving the Natural Environment', *Yale Law Journal*, 84 (1974), 205–67.

Sprigge, T. L. S., 'Some Recent Positions in Environmental Ethics Examined', *Inquiry*, 34 (1991), 107–28.

——, 'Non-Human Rights: An Idealist Perspective', *Inquiry*, 27 (1984), 439–61.

Sylvan, Richard, 'A Critique of Deep Ecology', Parts I, II, *Radical Philosophy*, 40 (Summer 1985), 2–12, (Autumn 1985), 10–22.

Taylor, Paul, *Respect for Nature: A Theory of Environmental Ethics* (Princeton: Princeton University Press, 1986).

Thompson, Janna L., 'A Refutation of Environmental Ethics', *Environmental Ethics*, 12 (1990), 147–60.

IV. *Politics and Environmental Ethics*

Attfield, Robin, 'Methods of Ecological Ethics', *Metaphilosophy*, 14 (1983), 195–208.

Elliot, Robert, 'Meta-Ethics and Environmental Ethics', *Metaphilosophy*, 16 (1985), 103–17.

Griffin, Susan, *Women and Nature: The Roaring Inside Her* (New York: Harper and Row, 1978).

Plumwood, Val, *Feminism and the Mastery of Nature* (London: Routledge, 1993).

Ruether, Rosemary Radford, *New Woman, New Earth* (New York: Seabury Press, 1975).

Warren, Karen, 'The Power and Promise of Ecological Feminism', *Environmental Ethics*, 12 (1990), 121–46.

V. *Ecofeminism*

Cooper, David E. and Palmer, Joy A. (eds.), *The Environment in Question* (London: Routledge, 1992).

Eckersley, Robyn, *Environmentalism and Political Theory: Toward an Ecocentric Approach* (Albany: State University of New York Press, 1992).

Goodpaster, Kenneth, 'On Being Morally Considerable', *Journal of Philosophy*, 78 (1978), 308–25.

Merchant, Carolyn, *The Death of Nature* (New York: Harper and Row, 1980).

Rodman, John, 'The Liberation of Nature', *Inquiry*, 20 (1977), 83–145.

Sagoff, Mark, *The Economy of the Earth* (Cambridge: Cambridge University Press, 1988).

Stone, Christopher F., *Earth and Other Ethics: The Case for Moral Pluralism* (New York: Harper and Row, 1987).

Wenz, Peter S., *Environmental Justice* (Albany: State University of New York Press, 1988).

INDEX OF NAMES